THE UNREGIMENTED GENERAL

A BIOGRAPHY OF

Nelson A. Miles

THE
UNREGIMENTED
GENERAL

A BIOGRAPHY OF

Nelson A. Miles

BY

VIRGINIA WEISEL JOHNSON

ILLUSTRATED WITH PHOTOGRAPHS
AND WITH MAPS PREPARED BY
BRIGADIER GENERAL W. M. JOHNSON

The Riverside Press Cambridge
HOUGHTON MIFFLIN COMPANY BOSTON
1962

First Printing

Copyright © 1962 by Virginia Weisel Johnson
All rights reserved including the right to
reproduce this book or parts thereof in any form
Library of Congress Catalog Card Number: 62–8138

The Riverside Press

CAMBRIDGE • MASSACHUSETTS

PRINTED IN THE U.S.A.

To

My husband, Johnny,
and Our Two Girls,
Tex and Linda

ACKNOWLEDGMENTS

THIS BOOK could not have been written without the help of Major General Sherman Miles, U.S.A. Retired, who criticized as well as inspired. Brigadier General W. M. Johnson, U.S.A. Retired, helped in the same way as did Mr. George F. Weisel, Sr.

The author is also indebted to Mr. Samuel Reber for the loan of Mrs. Miles's scrapbooks and many of her letters; to Mr. Ross Toole, Director of the Museum of New Mexico; Miss Virginia Walton, formerly of the Montana Historical Society Library; Mrs. Malloy and Mrs. Dempsey of the Montana Historical Society Library; Mr. Michael Kennedy, Director of the Montana Historical Society; Miss Kathleen Campbell and Miss Lucile Speer of the Library of the University of Montana; Miss Evelyn Swant and staff of the Missoula Public Library; Mr. LeRoy Whitman of the Army-Navy-Air Force *Journal;* Mr. Steve Tillman, associate editor of the Army-Navy-Air Force *Register;* Mr. David C. Mearns, Chief of the Manuscript Division of the Library of Congress; Mr. Theodore Jacobs of the First National Bank, Missoula, Montana; Sergeant C. P. Reynolds, Leavenworth, Kansas; Sergeant Mike Gallagher, Fort Reno, Oklahoma, and Brigadier General George Powell and staff of Madigan General Hospital, Fort Lewis, Washington.

Boca Grande, Florida
February 22, 1958

Dear Mrs. Johnson;

Two years ago an old army chest was resurrected in Washington. It had been closed and forgotten for over fifty years. When opened it was found to contain my father's letters to my mother from their engagement in 1867 to the middle of the 1890's. Many were written from the field during his several Indian campaigns. They throw a strong light on those western days, commenting on and sometimes criticizing the crude ways through which the Indian lost his hunting ground and the settler, with the aid of the army, gained his homestead. They are frank in expressing very personal opinions on the conduct of the campaigns and the personnel involved. They were never expected to see the light of the printed page, and so far they have not seen it.

I am very glad to give these letters to you, for whatever use you care to make of them in the book on my father you are now writing.

Sincerely yours
SHERMAN MILES
Major General, U. S. Army
Retired

CONTENTS

LIST OF ILLUSTRATIONS

MAPS

PART ONE

The Civil War

CHAPTER I

THE TEACHER looked at the boy standing before his desk. He was a sturdy, handsome youngster with curly brown hair and blue-gray eyes, determined, aggressive, touchy and stubborn. His lower lip was thrust forward as though to say Hit-me-if-you-dare.

This was not the first time the boy had merited punishment. He had been birched; he had been made to stand in the corner. Each time he had grown more rebellious. He was not a student. He hated being indoors when he might have been hunting or fishing in the woods or playing soldier.

An idea occurred to the teacher. "Nelson," he said sternly, "you have disobeyed the command of your superior officer and are a prisoner of war."[1]

The command was more effective than a threat.

Psychology was not a requisite for teachers in New England rural schools of the mid-1800's, but the teacher had an advantage; he was Nelson's brother, the elder by twelve years, and he knew the boy's ambition to be a soldier.

In addition to Daniel and Nelson, there were two girls in the Miles family. Nelson, the youngest, seems to have been the favorite. Daniel Miles, the father, was an austere man with a high-bridged nose and a thin mouth. Mary, his wife, was a plump woman with small features, motherly, affectionate and deeply religious. The Mileses were Baptists. Their political beliefs were republican in the old, not the party, sense of the word. Daniel Miles believed that every man owed a duty to his country and that if he felt something was wrong, he had a right to stand up in the town meeting and speak against it. Young Nelson was greatly influenced by his father. On winter evenings he sat by the hearth listening to Daniel Miles's stories of the Welsh clergyman ancestor, the Reverend John Myles, who put aside the Bible in King Philip's War of 1675 to fight the Indians and of Daniel and Joab Miles who had starved with Washington at Valley Forge. Soldiers were heroes in those days and glory was to be won on a battlefield. Nelson's ambition was stirred by these tales of military exploits. Little opportunity existed for him on the farm where he had been born August 8, 1839. The farm with its woodlot and fields and white frame house would go to Daniel, the older brother, while the lumber business in nearby Westminster which eked out the family income was not profitable enough to attract a boy who wanted to make a name for himself. Nelson was ambitious and that, too, was laudable, for it was the time of Manifest Destiny. America was stirring to the future. Great merchant fleets were sailing from New York and Boston for European and eastern ports. There was talk of a transcontinental railroad. Irish and German immigrants were pouring into the country to ease the labor shortage in the textile mills. America had fought a war with Mexico and won vast territories in the Southwest. Across the Missouri the plains and mountains that had been the domain of the trapper and the Indian were being invaded by emigrants drawn west by gold and hopes of a better future than could be found in a factory. The early 1850's were a period of unprecedented prosperity. In 1857 occurred an economic recession. During this time the voices of dissension grew louder. Bitterness was increasing between the industrial North and the agricultural South. The fanatic John Brown declared personal war on slavery, seized the Arsenal at

Harper's Ferry and was hanged for it. With the election of 1860, a sad, awkward man entered the White House. His name was Abraham Lincoln.

When Lincoln was elected, Nelson Miles was in Boston working as a clerk in Collomare's Crockery Store. He had come to the city four years before and gotten the job through the influence of his mother's brother, a well-to-do merchant. In Boston Miles saw, for the first time, what a handicap the lack of a higher education would be in making his fortune. He had gone to grammar school and Mr. Galt's Academy in Westminster for two years but the young men he hoped to emulate were attending classes at Harvard or West Point while he waited on customers. Miles felt the discrepancy keenly. He was to feel it all his life. But he did not allow it to discourage him. He did what he could to remedy the schooling. He attended night school at Comer's Commercial College and lectures at Faneuil Hall where he heard the leading orators of the day. He read everything he could find, newspapers, periodicals and books. He went without sleep in order to study; he scrimped on his meals to buy the texts prescribed by Comer's. He had little social life. He was not popular, anyhow. In his late teens he was over six feet tall, with big hands and feet. At home with his family and with a few intimates, he was relaxed and friendly. With people he knew slightly, he was stiff and abrupt, inclined to be sensitive to slights and argumentative.

In 1860, Miles considered war inevitable. He felt strongly on the subject. The Union must not be allowed to fall apart. Slavery, which was based on greed, was secondary. Miles took his participation in a conflict as a matter of fact. When war broke out, he knew preference would be given to men with experience, so he intended to have that experience. Months before hostilities commenced, he was taking instruction in military drill and discipline from a French veteran. Not content with drill, Miles broadened his studies to include tactics and strategy and the study of Napoleon's campaigns.

Miles was still studying the French emperor's battles when, in April of 1861, he heard of the shelling of Fort Sumter. Keeping his head, he did not rush to get into action, although everywhere thousands of men were enlisting to the shout of "On to Richmond" — prematurely, as it turned out, for at the first battle of Bull Run those who shouted the loudest were the first to throw down their guns and flee back to Washington. In late summer, Congress, deciding the war was not going to be won in ninety days, authorized five hundred thousand additional men. Enlistees thronged the recruiting offices. The war was popular, as war always is in its first days. Bands played the "Star-Spangled Banner." Flags flew from every house. Miles felt, as he later declared, that the time was opportune to embark on his military career. Commissions in the army were being given, first, to veterans of the Mexican War, secondly, to West Pointers and lastly to volunteers. During the Mexican War, many of the volunteers had been unruly, complaining and cowardly, and prejudice still existed against them. However the only way Miles could win a commission was to enter the service as an officer of the volunteers. An individual could, if he had the funds, recruit a company with the view of being elected officer. Miles had managed to save a thousand dollars from his meager salary. He borrowed twenty-five hundred more from his uncle and with this sum recruited a company of a hundred volunteers in the town of Roxbury, a suburb of Boston, to form a part of Colonel Henry Wilson's 22nd Massachusetts Regiment. Twenty-five hundred dollars was a big debt for an impecunious clerk but Miles was willing to risk his future to obtain a captaincy. He was chosen to that rank by the men and the commission was approved by the Governor. Shortly before the regiment was to leave, Miles was informed the commission had been voided; political pressure had been brought to bear on the Governor and the captaincy given to another man. The excuse was that Miles was too young to command a company.

Furious, his hopes blasted, his money wasted, Miles struck back at the Governor. It is possible friends advised tact. Miles did not know the meaning of the word. He had been wronged. He would — figuratively — stand up in the town meeting and declare his grievances. The protest did not regain the captaincy; it did earn Miles the hostility of the Governor, which was unfortunate because the State Executive approved the promotions of volunteers in the Massachusetts Militia.

Miles never forgot the incident. It did not teach him tact; he was never to learn that, but it made him feel that, if he were to get anyplace, ability and hard work were not enough. He would need influential friends.

As a lieutenant, Miles was sworn to duty with the 22nd Massachusetts Volunteers, September, 1861. Shortly thereafter, the regiment entrained for Washington. The Capital was in a state of war. Artillery caissons and transport wagons struggled through the mud of unpaved streets. Battalions of cavalry splattered past the unfinished Capital building. There were soldiers everywhere. Troops bivouacked at the base of the partially completed Washington Monument. It was Miles's first sight of Washington. Emotion choked his throat. The 22nd marched in review past the President, and the lieutenant's sword, still untarnished, flashed a salute to the gaunt man on the steps of the White House.

After passing in review, the regiment wheeled and marched to the Long Bridge across the Potomac which led to Virginia and the valley of the Shenandoah. Daniel, who had accompanied his brother from Massachusetts, walked beside the column as far as the bridge. Daniel was to stay at home and take care of the old people, but the family had felt it necessary he come to Washington to bid goodbye to the youngest and the favorite son. Now came the moment of parting as the sentry barred Daniel's progress with a bayonet. A quick handclasp and Nelson turned away, not wanting Daniel to see he was suddenly doubtful and afraid. Once he had crossed the bridge, he would be lost among the multitude.

On the distant shore, a detail of cavalry galloped along the road, guidons fluttering in the breeze. A long line of white-topped commissary wagons lumbered across the bridge, the drivers exchanging taunts with the blue-clad infantrymen marching beside the rail, rifles aslant their shoulders. Somewhere sounded the best of drums, the high, shrill notes of a bugle. These were the sights and sounds of an army. Miles's pulses quickened. His shoulders straightened. He fell in with the troops responding to an exultation deep within him. He'd have no staff job. He'd win promotion on the battlefield. Someday he would help to shape the course of the nation.

If he confided his ambition to his fellow officers, they must have smiled. What chance did a lanky farm boy have to become a senior commander? Few volunteers were interested in a military career. All they wanted was to get the war over with in a few months and go home. Young Miles was too serious. He spent hours walking about the camps inspecting sanitation and the methods of supply, watching the drills and talking to the men. Much of what he saw dismayed and angered him. The Union army was bogged in a morass of waste and confusion.

Advancement, Miles saw, was not going to be easy. Rank

was held by regulars or recently graduated West Pointers. The regulars, remembering their experiences with volunteers in the Mexican War, distrusted civilian officers. Miles was touchy about the attitude of the professional military. At this time, he was unsure of himself, quick to resentment, a thin-faced, sober lieutenant with his hair parted on the side.

He had gotten off to a bad start. Not wanting to remain in the company commanded by the Governor's friend, he succeeded in being transferred to the command of General Silas Casey who instructed and organized incoming regiments, but there was little chance of promotion in the rear areas and, within a matter of weeks, Miles became aide-de-camp to General Oliver Otis Howard. Howard, a West Pointer, was a devout Christian and abolitionist, a humorless but conscientious officer. This assignment was marked by fate, for Howard was one of the men with whom Miles would be closely involved in the future. At the time the young aide and the General — Howard was born nine years before Miles but looked older because of his biblical beard — appear to have gotten along fairly well. During the autumn of 1861 Miles remained at Bladensburg, Maryland, with Howard while the Army of the Potomac was organized and trained.

The aged veteran, Winfield Scott, swollen with gout, had resigned as commanding general of the Union Army and the dashing George B. McClellan had been appointed in his place. By making a younger man Commander-in-Chief, Lincoln hoped to still the clamor of public and Congress of "On to Richmond." But when McClellan continued to drill the army instead of fighting, Lincoln and his new Secretary of War, Stanton, grew uneasy. At last, an order came from Washington telling McClellan to take the field by February 22nd. In the west, General U. S. Grant had won a victory at Fort Donelson, giving encouragement to the Union. Now it was the turn of the Army of the Potomac to produce a victory. McClellan determined to embark his troops on a flotilla to Fortress Monroe and approach Richmond from the southeast. Howard's brigade was attached to the First Division which was a part of Sumner's Second Corps. Under McClellan, the army advanced up the Peninsula to less than ten miles from Richmond where it halted before the strongly entrenched Confederates. The weather, which had been fine, changed and it began to rain. Chickahominy creek flooded. Mud mired troops and wagons. The country was densely wooded, swampy and tangled with vines. McClellan waited in vain for McDowell to reinforce him. Officials in Washington ordered the First Corps commander to the valley of the Shenandoah in pursuit of the elusive Jackson.

On the thirty-first of May, the Confederates attacked McClellan's left wing south of the Chickahominy. The resulting battle of Seven Pines was Miles's first experience of combat. The Federals on the left of the line fell back in great confusion before the rebel charge. Recruits threw down their guns and ran, blind with panic, through the swamp while officers cursed to rally them. Those who held their places in the second line of defense, earthworks and abatis, felt a sickening feeling and cold perspiration to see the gray-clad troops coming through the woods and to hear the high, shrill rebel yell born of the Texas plains. Miles experienced no fear, only an intense excitement. As aide-de-camp, his duty was to carry dispatches for General Howard. He spurred his horse through swamps where cannon shot crashed among the trees. Volleys of musketry cracked about his head. Bullets ricocheted through the dense tangle of underbrush. The battle raged for two days and at Fair Oaks Station on the morning of the second day, Miles saw his opportunity. The colonel of a regiment was killed and the troops fell back in disorder. Howard sent Miles to round up the fleeing men. The aide had begged the General to let him get into the fighting. He was a persistent young man and Howard finally acquiesced to his pleas in the emergency. Miles rallied a good part of the regiment and drove the men forward. In the fierce hand-to-hand fighting, Miles was slightly wounded and his horse lamed by a bullet but he beat back the Confederates. He was in combat only a few short hours. In that brief time he gained a confidence that was never to leave him. He learned his capabilities. His mind grew clear. He had an uncanny grasp of terrain and the movement of troops. He thought in terms of advance, always advance.

Miles's courage and quick thinking might have resulted in a promotion. Unfortunately Howard was wounded and he was sent to a hospital where his arm was amputated. Miles lost his job as aide-de-camp. For several weeks he acted as adjutant general of the brigade but that meant serving on a staff and Miles wanted a field command. Howard had been the only senior officer he knew. He had no political influence. His chance for promotion was nonexistent. The young lieutenant must have had his moments of discouragement but he held on, watching for a chance to bring himself to the attention of his superiors. This chance came while the army still tarried before Richmond.

General Edwin V. Sumner, Second Corps commander, called "Bull" Sumner because of his great, roaring voice, called for a volunteer to ascend a tree that stood on the line of battle to observe defenses of the Southern capital. Quickly Miles volunteered although the tree was within artillery range of the Confederate batteries and anyone who climbed it, a tempting target. A sailor, aided by a strap about his waist, had driven spikes into the trunk which helped Miles mount hand over hand to the top, swaying precariously in the breeze. Clinging to the trunk with one arm, Miles looked toward the Confederate lines while below, the white-bearded General and his staff waited for his report. From the treetop Miles could see the defenses of Richmond manned by a handful of Confederates marching and countermarching to the music of regimental bands, giving the effect of a large number of troops — Magruder's bluff that had fooled McClellan.

Miles could also see enemy brigades crossing the Chickahominy to attack the right wing of the Union Army, a bold stroke decided on by Lee. Climbing down the tree, Miles came to attention and reported what he had seen with a salute that pleased the old Regular Army general. There was little enough military courtesy in the army these days. What was the young chap's name? Nelson A. Miles. The General remembered him, now. He had told Howard, when young Miles was still Howard's aide, "That officer will get promoted or get killed."[2]

When the army was increased in size, Sumner recommended Miles for promotion to the Governor of Massachusetts: the same governor whom Miles had accused of political chicanery. Not surprisingly, the promotion was refused. Miles seemed destined to go no further.

CHAPTER II

A S ADJUTANT GENERAL of the brigade, Miles took part in the battles of Mechanicsville, Gaines Mill and Allen's Farm. In the latter battle he saved two batteries of artillery by organizing parties of pioneers to cut a road through the forest. He was also at Savage Station, White Oak Swamp, Glendale and Malvern Hill. A veteran now, he insisted Malvern Hill was the best example he had seen of an open field battle as, indeed, it was, for the Confederates advanced in a solid line as though on parade to the long rolling beat of drums straight into the artillery and musket fire of the Federals. Miles seized every opportunity to get into the fighting. He interfered; he gave advice. The soldiers were glad to see him; he had a way of getting things done. But many of the officers thought him too eager in his ambition and too outspoken. One officer, however, was impressed by his earnestness: Francis Barlow, Colonel of the 61st New York Volunteers.

What McClellan might have gained by his strategy, he lost by withdrawing to Harrison's Landing. His patience at an end, Lincoln gave the larger part of the army to General John Pope, the blustering, energetic comamnder from the West, allowing McClellan to keep only a small part of the troops. A new campaign was in the offing, and Miles wanted to participate in it. Realizing he would get nowhere in a Massachusetts division, he went to see the Colonel of the 61st New York Volunteers. At Fair Oaks, Miles had come to the aid of the 61st and Barlow had not forgotten it. Miles explained the situation to Barlow and Barlow wrote the Governor of New York to give Miles the commission of the executive officer who had been killed in action. Barlow was a pale, clean-shaven young man who looked like an intellectual rather than a soldier. Throughout his lifetime, he was one of Miles's greatest friends and admirers. In a letter he wrote some months later recommending Miles for promotion, he said:

> He [Miles] possesses great energy and is indefatigable in the performance of all military duties, has an excellent knowledge of tactics, is a firm and thorough disciplinarian and has the gift of commanding men and enforcing their obedience. In the various battles in which I have seen him, he has shown unusual bravery and self-possession and in my opinion he possesses in a more than ordinary degree that power of taking advantage of circumstances and localities which renders a man an efficient commander in battle.[1]

Miles was then twenty-three years old.

Barlow saw what others were to see in the future — Miles's ability to evaluate the terrain of a battlefield at a glance, a gift given only to the greatest of field commanders.

Governors seldom granted commissions to citizens of other states, preferring to bestow them as political favors on their own constituents; but Barlow was persuasive and Governor Morgan more broad-minded than most executives. In 1862 Miles was made a Lieutenant Colonel of the 61st New York Volunteers. Jubilantly he gave up his job and prepared to take the field.

The promotion came just in time, for Lee, seizing the initiative from the Union commanders, advanced toward Washington. This time there was no rain but dust hazing amid the green foliage of Virginia. Jackson, the incomparable, outflanked the Union General Pope's army of fifty thousand men, destroyed Pope's supply base at Manassas Junction and joined Lee at Bull Run to inflict the second defeat of that name on the Federal forces. Once again troops streamed back to the capital. Almost all of Virginia was lost. Morale was at a low ebb. Miles felt the condition of the army was chaotic. Lincoln, having relieved McClellan of most of his troops, restored them to "Little Mac" and called on him to make a last, supreme effort. McClellan might not have been a fighter but he knew how to win the loyalty of an army. The men cheered themselves hoarse when he galloped down the road on his big charger trailed by his glittering staff. Weary backs straightened beneath knapsacks. The Irish in the ranks began to crack jokes again. Miraculously refreshed, the troops marched along the Virginia lanes, column after column of blue curving from the valley to the hills. September fifteenth, the Army of Northern Virginia and the Grand Army of the Potomac prepared for battle at Antietam.

In the Union forces that day was another officer Miles was to encounter in the future, a man who was perhaps the bitterest rival of his career, George Crook. Crook was an Ohio farm boy, ten years older than Miles and a West Point graduate. Pictures show him with sharp, strong features and a heavy beard. He was slow moving and slow talking but beneath the seeming reticence lay strong emotions. To his admirers, he could be kindly and modest. He could also be stubborn, unforgiving and prejudiced. Crook commanded a brigade as a brigadier general at Antietam and won a brevet colonelcy in the regular army for his actions on that day. He felt he should have received a greater reward.

All day the armies faced each other across the valley still green with summer while Jackson, having executed another of his lightning attacks by capturing Harper's Ferry, hurried to join Lee. The day was fair and warm. In the orchards, fruit was ripening on the trees and in the fields, the corn stood in rows. During a lull in an artillery duel, two young Union officers staged a steeplechase between the opposing lines, jumping ditches and fences to the cheering of Confederates and Federals alike. Miles watched with admiration not unmixed with envy. He would have liked to make such a gallant gesture himself but he lacked the poise.

At dawn of the seventeenth the battle began. Caldwell's first brigade of Richardson's division, to which the 61st was attached, turned the flank of the opposing Confederate corps, wheeled to the right and enfiladed a sunken road between cornfields and orchards where the dead piled so deep that it became known as "Bloody Lane." Inch by inch, the Confederates were driven back through the cornfield and orchards, the Federals advancing in line against the deadly fire of grape and canister from two brass pieces in the orchard and shell and spherical case shot from a battery on their right. General Richardson was mortally wounded. Sumner, disabled by a fall from his horse, had to retire from the field. Colonel Barlow, desperately wounded in the groin, was carried to the rear, and Miles, assuming command, gave his first order as a field officer — Advance!

Once again on the point of victory, McClellan hesitated. The sun went down blood-red behind the hills. Lee withdrew beyond the Potomac with the remnants of his tattered forces and McClellan had lost his last grasp on immortality.

Miles, remaining with the Union Army to bury the dead on the battlefield, was discouraged by McClellan's failure to pursue the victory and depressed by his surroundings. The stench was terrible. When they had dug graves for the soldiers, they piled fence rails and brush on the swollen carcasses of the horses and set them afire.

But Miles's depression did not last long. Colonel Barlow, while still convalescing, was promoted to brigadier general, and the New York Governor, who was proving himself a friend indeed to the young officer from Massachusetts, made Miles the Colonel of the 61st. He could hardly help it. Both Sumner and Barlow recommended Miles for promotion in the highest terms. Miles's aggressiveness that irritated so many people did not seem to have bothered Barlow. The New Yorker was a lawyer; he knew men. Perhaps he saw that the aggressiveness concealed a keenly felt lack of education. The bluntness was not intentional. Miles was sensitive to criticism but he brought it on himself. In his struggle to make something of himself, he would be his own worst enemy. The characteristics that made him a fighting soldier made him a poor politician.

On September 30, 1862, Miles formally assumed command of the regiment in his new rank, determined to make the 61st the best outfit in the Army of the Potomac.

He did not have long to wait before he led his men in battle again. Lincoln, despairing of McClellan, replaced him with Burnside. The choice was not fortunate. The general with the notable whiskers and broad-brimmed hat proved no more aggressive than "Little Mac," or at least not aggressive at the right moment. After waiting for days to bridge the Rappahannock, he finally forced a crossing in the face of concentrated artillery fire and attempted to drive the Confederates from their strongly entrenched positions above the town of Fredericksburg. It was December and very cold. A fog shrouded the town and the surrounding hills, lifting suddenly at ten o'clock in the morning to reveal the blue-uniformed troops in the valley, flags aflutter, sunlight gleaming on rifle barrels. From the woods, this gorgeous and well-equipped army was surveyed by Jackson's ragged infantry and Jeb Stewart's gaunt cavalry. To the blare of bugles and the roll of drums, the Federals advanced. Miles, leading the 61st New York, attached to Caldwell's brigade, was again engaged in the hottest part of the fighting. The troops charged the stone wall at Marye's Heights on the double-quick with loud cries of "Hi! Hi! Hi!" They carried their arms at right shoulder shift and their colors aslant the shoulders of the color sergeants. In columns of brigades, they advanced into a pitiless fire from the rebels behind the wall. Shells burst in their ranks and still on they came.

Miles was leading his regiment when a Minié ball pierced his throat. He refused to be carried from the field until he had seen General O. O. Howard reassigned to duty as Second Division commander. Seated on a stretcher and holding the lips of the wound together with his fingers, he had himself carried to Howard so that he could tell the one-armed general where he could put his troops into action to the best advantage. Miles had difficulty speaking. The blood pulsed over his fingers onto his uniform. He did not pause to think that a twenty-three-year-old colonel of volunteers, wounded or sound, did not tell a division commander how to deploy his troops in battle. Fortunately, Howard did not resent his advice. It was sound; Miles usually knew what he was talking about when it came to military matters, but members of Howard's staff felt Miles was brash and forward and dramatically calling attention to himself. Miles felt only that he was doing his duty.

Thanks to a remarkably strong constitution, Miles survived and within a few weeks was back in the field.

By this time Hooker had replaced Burnside, who had been allowed no more mistakes after Fredericksburg, and winter had stalled hostilities. Fredericksburg, like Bull Run, had been a blow to Union morale and the winter was spent by General Hooker, who had McClellan's talent in some respects, in reorganizing and equipping the army until, by spring, the troops were in fighting trim. The country was green again and the rains were flooding the streams when Hooker drew up the army near the junction of the Rappahannock and Rapidan rivers. From the pillared mansion of Chancellorsville he boasted, "I have got Lee just where I want him; he must fight me on my own ground."[2]

The General's words hid a faint heart. He made the fatal mistake of undertaking to "consummate offensive strategy with defensive tactics."[3] At the beginning of the battle, he withdrew his troops from their favorable positions to thickets of scrub oak, cedars and pines. The Second Corps was assigned to the left of the Federal line, and Miles's regiment held the front line of his division which was commanded by Hancock. Miles was fortunate in having Hancock as a commander, for Hancock was one of the few Regular Army men who showed no preference for regulars over volunteers. He was a big, bluff, hearty fellow and was to do much to forward the career of his handsome young colonel.

Scouting around in the woods about Chancellorsville, Miles found a wooded hillock fronted by a marsh, a position he strengthened during the ensuing day and night by digging rifle pits and constructing abatis of fallen timber. When the attack came, it was in force. The Confederates assaulted Miles's position *en masse* and in line of battle. A rebel colonel leapt his horse over the Union barricade as though it were a fence in the hunting field, to crash dead within the Federal defenses. They fought and died well, those Southern gentlemen. Miles had the greatest respect for them. All the next day, Miles held his line against attack by brigades and divisions. Hancock sent reinforcements but made sure the regimental commanders were junior to Miles, leaving him in command. Hancock showed his confidence in his young regimental commander.

He knew Miles was touchy about his new rank, and wanted the credit as well as the responsibility.

While the Confederates were feinting at the front of Hooker's line, Stonewall Jackson marched the length of the Union forces and, turning west, struck at Hooker's exposed right flank. Howard's Eleventh Corps fled in pandemonium while their commander, clutching the colors beneath the stub of his arm, strove to rally them with tears streaming down his bearded cheeks.

If night had not fallen and if Jackson had not been fatally wounded, the panic might have extended to the entire Union army. Miles was still holding his position on the front of the line when he was hit by a sharpshooter's bullet. The bullet, striking his belt buckle, penetrated the abdomen. The sword dropped from his nerveless fingers; he clutched the pommel of his saddle, feeling deathly ill and paralyzed below the waist. His horse stopped, turned around and walked back until it reached a group of soldiers who lifted the wounded colonel from his saddle and, putting him in a blanket, carried him to Chancellor House, where, pushing a dead man off a sofa, they made Miles as comfortable as possible. There was no surgeon or anyone to care for him. Within a short time a shell hit the house, setting it on fire. Miles, who was suffering terribly by this time, was carried out of the house and for five miles through the woods on a stretcher. That night he lay on the ground covered by a blanket, biting his lips against the pain unrelieved by sedatives. The next day he was hoisted into a horse-drawn ambulance and jolted twelve miles over a corduroy road to a field hospital where his wound was bandaged. From the hospital, he was sent to Washington. Daniel, grave and concerned, met him there and took him back to Massachusetts.

By all rights, Miles should have died. Abdominal wounds

were usually fatal, even when given prompt care. The Massachusetts surgeon, finding the ball had crushed through Miles's hip and lodged in the muscles of his left leg, operated to remove the bullet and splintered bones. The doctor was skillful, but Miles's recovery was due, as it had been at Fredericksburg, to his perfect health. His incomparable physique saved him from infection.

As soon as he was out of bed, he wanted to get back into action. His family urged him to stay a while longer amid the peaceful hills of New England. The lilacs were blooming and there were blossoms on the apple trees. But Miles, too restless to remain at home, went on crutches to rejoin his regiment, and when he was told he was physically unable to assume command, he made his way, still on crutches, to Pennsylvania where he raised a brigade of volunteers to help defend the state from a threatened invasion by rebel forces.[4]

He was still convalescing when he heard of Gettysburg. One of the disappointments of his life was that he missed that decisive engagement. He could not be consoled even by the probability that he would be rewarded for his courage at Chancellorsville. He was later to receive the Medal of Honor for his conduct in the battle.

When he returned to duty, he found he was at last beginning to win recognition; he was assigned to command of a brigade. On May 12, 1864, the year after Chancellorsville, his commission as a brigadier general was signed by Abraham Lincoln.

Grant was commander of all the Union armies with his headquarters the Army of the Potomac. The first months after Grant took over, Miles was not sure about the cigar-chewing, rumpled general so different from Stonewall Jackson or Sumner. He thought Grant would have done better after the Battle of the Wilderness to turn to the right and force Lee into an open field of battle like Gettysburg than move to the left which brought him into heavily wooded country difficult for marching. But as he saw Grant's doggedly aggressive tactics bring results in battle after battle, uncertainty became respect. Here was a general who would bring victories, at last, to the Union armies.

The victories were not without sacrifice. The casualties under Grant earned the new commanding general the title "Bloody Butcher." Grant was to play a role in Miles's later career. Grant was a West Pointer as was his right-hand man, William T. Sherman. Sherman had red hair and a stubble of red beard on his jaw. He was a tough, hard man dedicated to the army. When Grant made him an army commander and ordered him to cut the Confederacy in half by marching through Georgia, Howard went with Sherman and made the best record as a corps commander he had ever made. His record with Sherman was to his advantage in later years. It was to Miles's disadvantage that he was not on that famous march to the sea, for a general is inclined to favor the officers who have served him well. It took Sherman some time to know Miles. But Miles's ill luck in one respect was made up for by his brief acquaintance with Phil Sheridan, "Fighting Phil," the black-haired, hard-riding little general whom Grant made commander of all the Union cavalry. Sheridan was a West Pointer too, a classmate of George Crook.

Miles commanded a brigade in the Wilderness and, later, at Spottsylvania where charge was met by countercharge until the trenches slopped with blood and the wounded suffocated beneath the weight of the dead. Following Spottsylvania came Cold Harbor. The casualty lists grew longer. Women mourned the death of sons and husbands. The wounded crowded the hospitals. Entire brigades and divisions ceased to exist. Before Cold

Harbor, three young colonels with whom Miles had served since they had been lieutenants talked together far into the night of the battle planned for the coming day. By sunset, all three were dead. Miles was depressed by such losses. The carnage of these years convinced him that battles should be planned with respect for life.

After Cold Harbor, Grant executed a flank movement to the James River where McClellan, two years before, had based the Army of the Potomac. Lee had withdrawn to Richmond with what was left of the Army of Northern Virginia. As the Federals advanced, the Confederates met them at Petersburg where Miles was wounded a fourth time but not seriously enough to keep him from duty. At Reams Station, following Petersburg, he commanded the First Division. Francis Barlow, exhausted by the hardships of the campaign, had had to retire temporarily from command. Miles was then twenty-four.

Reams Station was fought for control of the all-important Weldon railroad. Major General John Gibbon, whom Miles was also to meet in future years in the West, commanded the other division of Hancock's Second Corps. Some miles of the railroad tracks had been torn up and burned by Gibbon and Miles when Hancock sent word that an estimated ten thousand Confederates were moving in from the left. Preparations were immediately made for defense. Gibbon's division was drawn into the left breastworks, which were strengthened and extended to the rear, and Miles with the First Division was stationed on the right. Both flanks were exposed to reverse fire from the front. At two o'clock the Confederates attacked Miles; they were repulsed and again attacked more vigorously and were again repulsed, leaving their dead and wounded within a few yards of Miles's position. The situation was growing serious. Hancock asked for reinforcements and General Orlando Wilcox's division was ordered up. The troops, throwing off their blanket rolls, started for the front at the double-quick. The Confederates were also receiving reinforcements, and Miles could hear them chopping trees and hauling up artillery.

Hancock, until now, had thought only of keeping a road open by which reinforcements might reach him, or, if necessary, by which he could retreat. At four-fifteen he telegraphed army headquarters that heavy skirmishing was going on and an attack pending and he thought it was too late for reinforcements. Should he retire from his position? Hancock was worried about his troops, most of whom were recruits who "never had come to fight, but to run off the first chance, or get into the hospital and ho! for a pension afterward!"[5]

At five o'clock the Confederate comander, A. P. Hill, opened fire with his artillery. The first assault came, once again, on Miles. For a time the severity of Miles's fire and the defenses he had constructed from logs and slashings discouraged the Confederates, but at a crucial moment, the recruits gave way. Two regiments broke on the right. Miles ordered up what few reserves he had but the reserves — who were recruits, too — refused to move forward. Gibbon's men would not obey the order of their commander either, so the entire Federal front threatened to collapse. At this desperate climax of the battle, Miles rallied the men of his old regiment, the 61st New York, formed line at right angles, and swept down to recapture considerable of the ground lost. Not content with that, Miles counterattacked by throwing two hundred men across the railroad to threaten the enemy's rear. The attack surprised the Confederates by its unexpectedness and daring, but two hundred men were not enough to hold the position. Gibbon's men were ordered to reinforce them and, once again, refused to move. In the end, dismounted cavalry assisted in repulsing the Confederates.

As a result of Reams Station, Miles was mentioned for gallantry in action. In August of the same year he was brevetted a major general, and in February of the following year temporarily commanded the Second Army Corps in the absence of General Humphreys, who had succeeded Hancock. Miles had his picture taken in his high-collared, brass-buttoned blue uniform with the insignia of rank on his shoulders. His arms were folded formally on his chest. He wore a mustache, waxed on the ends, and an imperial. His hair, which was naturally curly, was parted on the side. His gaze was severe. The mustache and beard made him look older, which no doubt was his intention. The general in the United States uniform in the picture, confident, mature, bore no resemblance to the young Lieutenant of Volunteers who, four years previous, had posed self-consciously beside a table with his new sword.

The war had shaped the youth into a man, but the war was drawing to a close. The Confederate Jubal Early marched up the Shenandoah to Washington for a last despairing attempt to draw the Federals from Richmond. Close behind rode Phil Sheridan with two dashing brigadiers, George Armstrong Custer of the yellow hair and thirst for glory and the boy-faced Wesley Merritt. Custer was to become Miles's friend on the frontier. Miles was to know the quiet, scholarly Alfred Terry too, who commanded the Union forces at the capture of Fort Fisher in North Carolina. And he was to know Forsyth who served on Sheridan's staff as well as Ranald Mackenzie who commanded a cavalry detachment. Mackenzie was a lean, dedicated man, a fighter from his cadet days at West Point.

On the eighth of April, 1865, the Union leaders heard their guns on the rear of the Confederates and knew that Lee had been outflanked.

Phil Sheridan bought the table at which Lee signed the surrender terms and gave it to Custer to take to his wife. Hoisting the souvenir on his shoulder, the young cavalryman started off at a gallop for his camp. While the news of the surrender spread and men cheered and wept, Generals Sheridan and Williams invited their former enemies and West Point classmates for a visit. Longstreet came, and Gordon and Pickett.

And Miles? He thanked God the Union had been saved . . . "that the nation was reunited in the strongest bonds of brotherhood."[6]

CHAPTER III

IN THE ARMY Miles had found what his vital, aggressive nature demanded. Ambition fused with idealism. At the end of the war, he applied for a commission in the Regular Army. Having profited by his experience with the Governor of Massachusetts, he did not rest on his record alone; he made contact with prominent men to give him recommendations. As a young and remarkably handsome major general, doors were open to him that would have been closed to a clerk in a crockery store. Miles was acquainted with a number of the highest-ranking officers in the Union Army, with influential government officials and with Senator Charles Sumner of Massachusetts and John Sherman, brother of the General and one of the outstanding men in the Senate. Miles got in touch with Sheridan, Grant, Meade, Humphreys, Howard and Secretary of War Stanton, all of whom wrote letters favoring his commission.

Officers applying for regular army had to accept a reduction in rank. Miles hoped for a brigadier-generalcy but was told he would be lucky to become a field grade officer. He lacked a university education. He was not a West Pointer. Competition would be severe in the post war army. When Lee signed the surrender terms, there were one million five hundred and sixteen names on the Union muster rolls. The regular army was to be established at fifty-four thousand six hundred and forty one men, an optimistic figure which Grant and Sherman — to whom fell the task of reorganizing the army — did not doubt would be reduced. Within five years, the figure was cut to thirty thousand. In the new peacetime organization, there would be one general (Grant), one lieutenant general (Sherman), five major generals (Halleck, Meade, Sheridan, Thomas and Hancock), ten brigadiers (McDowell, Cooke, Pope, Hooker, Schofield, Howard, Terry, Ord, Canby and Rousseau); ten regiments of cavalry, five of artillery and forty-five of infantry. Of necessity, this limited the number of commissions that could be granted.

While Miles waited for his application to be acted upon, he served as commander of Fortress Monroe in Virginia. The assignment, which at first looked promising, nearly cost Miles his career.

By early summer the enthusiasm that had greeted the victorious army of the Potomac marching past the Capitol with their battle flags wreathed in flowers, had faded and the reaction was setting in. Vindictiveness and hate animated reactionary groups in the North and in the defeated South. The country between Washington and Richmond, fought over for four years, was in ruins. Homes, barns, entire towns stood as blackened shells. Railroads were torn up. Rolling stock was destroyed. Roads were pitted with mudholes. Bridges were down. Weeds choked the fields. Cattle had been stolen or slaughtered. The Confederate currency was worthless. The tired, hungry soldiers of Lee's army trudged home to find their families starving. In the North, Thomas Nast, cartoonist for Harper's Weekly, depicted the duplicity of the South. Thaddeus Stevens argued against compromise with the "rebels." Clergymen preached that the Southerners should be punished by God. The politicians were taking over. The generals were stepping back. The professional soldiers, on the whole, felt little animosity toward their former enemies. Miles wrote that at the end of the war the victorious troops gladly shared their rations with the destitute and starving Confederates. Miles himself had the greatest respect for the Southern leaders and the men who had fought so long and honorably, a respect civilians found hard to understand and politicians inconvenient.

A $100,000 reward was offered for Jefferson Davis, believed to have been implicated in the assassination of Lincoln. When the ex-President of the Confederacy was captured in the pine woods of southern Georgia, he was taken north and imprisoned at Fortress Monroe.

Davis was not one of the Southerners whom Miles respected. Miles thought Davis was a neurotic weakling. In turn, Davis called Miles a "miserable ass." But the personal animosity between the two men did not cause the crisis that arose. Miles had too high an ideal of his profession as a career soldier to mistreat a prisoner. As a matter of fact he leaned over backward to be considerate. When Davis complained he could not sleep because of the sentry's walking his post at night, Miles had the hall outside Davis's door covered with matting to deaden the sound of the sentry's tread. The restrictions that Miles imposed on Davis were at the order of the Assistant Secretary of War, Charles A. Dana, who, acting for the Secretary of War, went to Monroe to see that precautions were taken to prevent Davis's escape. On May 22, 1865, Dana authorized Brevet Major General Miles to "place manacles and fetters upon the hands and feet of Jefferson Davis." He (Davis) was allowed no visitors and no books except the Bible. For five days while grated doors were being fitted to Davis's room and workmen were going in and out, Davis was ironed. After the grates were installed, the irons were removed. Davis was put in one of the casemates which was adjacent to the moat, and damp, because there were no other facilities for prominent prisoners at Monroe.

If Davis had been any ordinary captive, his plight would have been ignored, but in the bitterness that followed the peace, he became a symbol of the Suffering South and Miles, as his jailer, became a symbol of the Northern oppressor. Southern sympathizers described Davis's room as a dark and foul casemate; clanking chains had been riveted about his poor emaciated limbs. When the post surgeon, who had a Southern wife, published sympathetic accounts of Davis's sufferings, indignation rose to new heights. Conservative people in the North were disturbed. Some still wanted to hang Davis, others to free him, but they did not like to be accused of cruelty to a helpless prisoner. The picture did not fit their conception of righteous victors. Prominent lawyers volunteered their services in Davis's defense. Mrs. Davis wept before President Johnson who, suddenly, assumed no responsibility for Davis's incarceration. Miles, the cruel jailer, was responsible for Davis's plight.

Stung by the accusations in the press, Miles reacted vigorously. He wrote Secretary of War Stanton protesting that the reports on Davis were harming his career. This was true. His Regular Army commission had not been granted. The furore stirred up by Davis's imprisonment could mean the commission would be refused. The accusations, Miles felt, were unjust. He was acting under orders. Miles's protest burned with resentment. A year ago he had been a hero, now he was a scoundrel. It was no consolation that Sherman and Grant were experiencing somewhat the same metamorphosis.

Miles went to see Sherman. The Lieutenant General and Grant were having their own difficulties with the administration of President Johnson and his Secretary of War, but at Miles's request, Sherman sent the Surgeon General of the

Army to Monroe to examine Davis. The health of the ex-
President, the Surgeon General announced, had not been
injured by his confinement. This statement[1] did not quiet the
storm. Miles asked that newspaper reporters be allowed to visit
the Fortress so that they could see how fairly Davis was being
treated, but Sherman thought it was unnecessary; newspaper
correspondents were "gossip mongers." This was Sherman's
first experience with Miles's aggressiveness. Overburdened
with army problems, he could well have felt that Miles was un-
necessarily belligerent in the attempt to vindicate himself.

The feeling mounted; a newspaper demanded Miles's dismissal from the service. The Administration, finding it con-
venient to have a scapegoat, announced that Miles would be
relieved from the command of Fortress Monroe. Believing this
to be a reflection on his conduct — which it was — Miles wrote
Stanton again, objecting to this treatment. The objection was
overruled. In September Miles was replaced as commander at
Monroe, and within a matter of weeks mustered out of the
volunteers as a major general. The public was satisfied. Justice
had been done.

Miles was furious. He did not have to worry about his
Regular Army commission; it had been granted; but the principle involved in the Davis matter rankled. It was to rankle for
a long time. Unfortunately it did not teach him tact in dealing
with the press and his superiors in the army and in the government, any more than had the Roxbury incident.

In October 1866, Miles was sworn into the Regular Army as
a colonel and ordered to the Freedman's Bureau in North
Carolina under his old commander, Major General, now Brigadier General O. O. Howard. Miles was disappointed that he
had not been given a higher rank. Alfred Terry, a volunteer,
had been made a brigadier and Miles felt he had participated

in many more engagements than Terry. Actually Miles was fortunate to be a colonel. George Armstrong Custer, who had been a major general, was a lieutenant colonel. John Gibbon, senior to Miles, was a colonel. Many brigadier generals had been made major. Officers with fine war records were destined to waste their lives at isolated army posts. Miles determined that the obscurity of a small command would not be for him. He would start over again to win his way to the top.

An administrative job, such as establishing civil control in the war-ravaged South, was new to Miles. He tackled it with his customary vigor. The experience was to help him in the future, but the assignment was not the sort that led to promotion. Raleigh, North Carolina, was farther from Washington than Fortress Monroe but Miles managed to visit the capital occasionally to keep in touch with what was going on at the War Department.

On a visit in 1867 to the house of Senator John Sherman, he met the Senator's niece, Mary Hoyt Sherman, daughter of Judge Charles Sherman of the Ohio branch of the family, the new commissioner of the Union Pacific Railroad. Mary Sherman was auburn haired, vivacious and friendly. Miles was six feet tall, broad shouldered with icy blue eyes and a sweeping mustache. (He had shaved off the imperial.) The hearts of Washington belles fluttered when he walked into a room. The young colonel was not a man about town, skilled at whispering sweet nothings into a lady's ear. He was a man more at ease in the saddle than in the drawing room. If anyone told Mary that the handsome officer was of a controversial nature, she did not heed the warning.

Miles had met few unattached young ladies socially. His poverty as a clerk in a china store and, later, the war, had seen to that. He fell deeply in love with Mary Sherman and she with him. It was inevitable that he would be accused of seeking Mary Sherman because she was the niece of the General. Undoubtedly Miles was impressed by the relationship in the beginning, but after a few meetings, he would not have cared if Mary's name had been Davis instead of Sherman.

When Mary told her parents of the attachment, they immediately sought to know more about the young officer whom their daughter found so interesting. The Judge wrote Senator Charles Sumner of Massachusetts, and the Senator wrote back:

> I answer your inquiry at once. General Miles was in the habit of visiting my house last winter, and I always found him intelligent, pleasant and of agreeable manners. He seemed to be a favorite with the ladies. Only a few days ago he called at my house in Boston, being there on furlough for a few days. He was staying with a friend in the neighborhood, and was about to leave for Vermont. So far as I know, he is self-made, as this term is usually understood, though to my mind, every man is more or less self made; but he has not the advantage of a liberal or University education. I think he was in business — left business for the war and was successful. . .[2]

The Senator felt that his wife might be able to give the Judge more information if he would care to write her, but the Judge must have been satisfied, for Miles was sufficiently encouraged to write in September from Raleigh to the Honorable Charles T. Sherman in Cleveland, Ohio. The letter was not penned in Miles's usual scrawl but in careful script.[3]

> Dear Sir;
> The subject of this communication will I think be deemed a sufficient apology for my writing. I confess I have felt less trepidation in meeting our enemy than I do in addressing you on the subject when your answer involves my life interest and future happiness. You are aware of my interest in your

daughter Mary. An acquaintance formed some months hence, and a strong attachment is the result. I believe it to be mutual. And now my dear Sir, my duty to her Parents prompts me to seek their consent to the final consumation of a life union.

I assure you Sir, that it will be my study to care for and make her happy, and as far as in my power to cause her life to glide peacefully to that promised rest on high.

I have the honor to remain with great respect
Your obt. Svt, NELSON A. MILES U. S. A.

The Judge perused the letter carefully. The army was an acceptable career for a son-in-law. Inquiries in regard to Nelson Miles had been favorable. Most important, Mary was very much in love.

Miles asked the scholarly Alfred Terry to be his groomsman. Terry accepted but was unable to come at the last moment because he had been appointed to a commission to meet with the Sioux at Laramie. It was duty and duty alone, he assured Miles, that kept him from being present. ". . . As a soldier you know too well what duty means . . ."[4]

Mary and Nelson Miles were married in Trinity Church, Cleveland, Ohio, on Tuesday evening, June 30, 1868. The night was hot and still, the wedding a large, formal affair followed by a reception at the Sherman home on Prospect Street. The list of invited guests included the Chief Justice of the Supreme Court, Generals Grant, Sherman, Sheridan, Meade, Hancock, Howard, Barlow and other prominent military men and civilians. Nor did Miles forget his family and the proprietor of the crockery store in Boston.

In March of 1869, eight months later, Mary and Miles were en route to Miles's new assignment on the frontier.

PART TWO

*The Kiowa-Comanche
Campaign*

CHAPTER IV

IMPATIENCE was a vice with Miles as well as a virtue. He wrote Sherman that perhaps he should transfer to the cavalry since that seemed to be the favored branch of the army and promotion might be quicker.[1] By this time, Grant was President and Sherman was General of the Army. Miles could write Sherman personally as his uncle-in-law. But Sherman would show no favoritism. Let the impetuous young officer who had married his niece serve a tour of duty on the frontier. A skirmish with the Indians, now and then, would keep him occupied.

Miles, who had led a brigade against the Confederates, felt there was little interest in a skirmish with savages. He would have preferred a post near Washington to the command of the Fifth Infantry in Kansas. But, as he journeyed west via St. Louis, he could not help being impressed by the raw, violent land he glimpsed from the train. He was the first to get off at the frequent stops, the last to get on. Mary could not keep up with him. She did not try. She was to have a child in the autumn and had to guard her health. Despite the cinders and primitive washing facilities, she managed to keep her gown fresh and her auburn hair combed in poufs. What were her thoughts as she observed her husband's growing enthusiasm for the vast, strange country? She had been raised in a sheltered home. Duty on the frontier, to an army wife, meant isolation, fear and discomfort. It meant weeks alone while her husband was on a scout from which he might never return. It was natural Mary should be afraid, yet she hid her fears well. She had known before she married that the army was her husband's first love and that she, as his wife, would have to accept whatever the Service demanded.

After the train left Kansas City, settlements became smaller and farther between. On the wind-blown platform of a shanty town stood a dirty, blanketed figure.

Indian country!

On the Great Plains, the Indians were fighting a savage battle for survival. The end of the Civil War had released thousands of emigrants to westward migration. The railroads advanced mile by mile into the hunting grounds of the red men. White hunters were killing off the buffalo — the Indians had many other grievances. In the North, the tide of immigration lapped about the Sioux country; in the South, settlers grew more numerous daily — the Cheyennes and Arapahoes raided north to Kansas; the Kiowas raided down to Texas.

The southern Cheyennes were a strong, intelligent people, proud and quick tempered. Among warriors, they were noted as warriors. Like the Cheyennes, the Arapahoes were of Algonquin stock but were more amenable. A small tribe, they had a remarkable artistic sense and imagination. The Kiowas were a dark, stocky people. The Medicine Lodge Treaty of 1867 guaranteed the Indians reservations south of the Arkansas, roughly, Oklahoma. When settlers continued to trespass on lands reserved for the Indians and annuities promised the tribes failed to arrive, the Kiowas and Comanches began raiding the settlements. The Cheyennes soon followed the example of their allies. Wagon trains were attacked. Isolated ranches were burned. Women and children were scalped and tortured. As tales of Indian cruelties were spread by survivors, hatred blazed on the frontier. Men went armed and grim lipped in their determination to wipe out the murdering savages. Pressure of public opinion forced the Indian Bureau, who normally controlled the tribes, to turn them over to the War Department for punishment. Sherman, tired of governmental policies that did nothing to settle the Indian question, wrote to Sheridan who commanded the Division of the Missouri to hit the southern tribes and hit them hard. In November of 1868, Sheridan ordered the Seventh Cavalry reinforced by the 19th Kansas Volunteers to take the field. The Seventh was commanded by George Armstrong Custer.

When the Mileses began their westward journey, the troops had not yet returned from their winter campaign to their camp near Fort Hays, which was headquarters for Miles's Fifth Infantry.

The post was located on the prairie a quarter of a mile from Big Creek, a tributary of the Smoky Hill Fork of the Kansas River. In summer, sun and wind scorched the land. In winter the wind blew unceasingly and wolves howled across the snow. The barracks and officers' quarters were heated by wood fireplaces and stoves which were inadequate in winter to keep out the cold. Water was brought from the stream in wagons and dumped into barrels at the kitchen door. There were no bathrooms.

Miles was in command of the Fifth Infantry less than a month when he was informed that the Seventh Cavalry, led by Custer, was returning to Fort Hays. As the Seventh rode across the prairie, Miles galloped out to greet Custer, accompanied by his officers and the band playing "Garry Owen," the famous tune of the Seventh Cavalry. Elizabeth Custer, impressed by the welcome Miles gave her beloved husband, wrote, ". . . the manner in which he [Miles] welcomed our regiment . . . from their long campaign, won all hearts."[2]

Miles was greatly stirred by the sight of the gaunt, hard-bitten troopers led by Custer sitting his spirited mount with ease, yellow hair flowing over his collar, white teeth flashing in an exultant grin. Custer had routed Black Kettle's band of Cheyennes on the Washita, killed the chief and burned the village. In the column rode a number of squaws and prominent warriors as hostages for the Indians' future good behavior.

Miles, Elizabeth Custer remarked, "did not hesitate to say he envied the success of the regiment and should emulate their successful mode of Indian fighting as soon as he had an opportunity."[3]

Miles considered Custer one of the most ". . . . fearless cavalry leaders the Civil War produced . . . ambitious and enterprising."[4] The two men were approximately the same age, rivals for promotion. In the spring of 1869, Custer had the advantage. Prominent sportsmen and senior officers visited the camp of the Seventh in the ensuing months.[5] Newspaper reporters traveled west to interview the famous Indian fighter. Settlers acclaimed the victor of the Washita. Custer, once again, tasted the heady wine of fame. And Miles, observing, felt opportunity might exist, after all, on the frontier.

Frequently, Custer and Miles met dignitaries at the station platform in Hays City which was one of the wildest towns in a notoriously wild area. On one occasion, as Custer and Miles paced the platform, bullets from a street fight began to sing about their ears, forcing them to take refuge in the telegraph office until the combatants had settled their differences; probably the only time those two experienced professionals ever retreated from a battle.

During this time, the Indian hostages, confined in a stockade at the Fort, waited uneasily for word from their relatives that they had obeyed Custer's ultimatum to surrender. Custer visited the three chiefs frequently and even took his wife into the fifteen-foot-high stockade.[6] The squaws, who had seen few white women, thronged about Mrs. Custer, feeling the material of her riding habit, her kid gloves and the stuffed bird on her hat. Custer laughed but Elizabeth was frightened, fearing knives beneath the blankets of the wrinkled old crones.

Mrs. Custer's fears were not unjustified. Indians were sighted in the vicinity of the post, and it was feared an attempt would be made to liberate the hostages. A sergeant and guard were detailed to move the three chiefs from the stockade to the security of the guardhouse. It is not clear whether Miles issued the order, but as troop commander he must have known about it. The soldiers did not speak Cheyenne or understand the sign language and the Indians did not understand English, which meant that the sergeant could not explain the purpose of his visit. The squaws, seeing the soldiers fully armed, thought the white men had come to hang the chiefs. Knives flashed from beneath blankets. An old woman sprang on the officer in charge. One of the chiefs gashed a soldier. When Custer, summoned hastily from camp, arrived, he found one chief dead, another mortally wounded and a third unconscious from a blow with a rifle butt. Custer was careful not to blame anyone, publicly, at least, and Miles said little about the incident in later years. The riot was the first of many lessons that led Miles to an understanding of the Indian.

The riot impeded the negotiations with the Cheyennes, who considered, not without reason, that their trust had been broken. It also made the troops at Hays apprehensive of Indian revenge. But it did not strain the relations between the Seventh Cavalry and the Fifth Infantry. The ladies from the post rode out frequently to the camp of the Seventh in an army ambulance escorted by their husbands on horseback. There were picnics, dinners, horseback rides, hunts. Elizabeth Custer and Mary Miles were invited on one of the buffalo hunts. The prairie shriveled in the sun. Along Big Creek the cottonwood leaves crackled like paper in the wind. Miles and Custer rode in the lead of the hunting party, alert for game or hostiles — Custer tawny haired, tawny mustache, talking in a high, excited voice. Custer was a beautiful horseman. Miles was nearly as expert. His blue-gray eyes glinted with the prospect of the hunt. Behind the two men, and the escort of soldiers, the ambulance jolted over the cracked earth with Elizabeth Custer and Mary Miles peeping from behind the curtains to see Indians hiding in every clump of cactus or sagebrush. When buffalo were sighted, the men spurred their horses across the prairie after the grazing animals. Miles and Custer cornered one great beast which, wounded, sought to charge first one and then the other of his tormentors. Elizabeth Custer watched terrified, yet fascinated, ". . . those lithe young men . . . bright eyes dancing with excitement."[7] Jerking their feet free of the stirrups, Miles and Custer rode with legs tight-clenched against their horses's sides. At last, the *coup de grâce* was administered and the great beast, blood pouring from his nostrils, sank to the ground.

The happy interlude at Fort Hays came to an end in the autumn. Custer received orders to another station and Mary left for Cleveland, Ohio, where the baby was born, a girl baptized Cecelia. Miles moved his headquarters from Hays to Fort Harker and then to Leavenworth. This post was headquarters for the Department of the Missouri commanded by General John Pope, the same Pope whom Lee defeated at Second Bull Run. Leavenworth, the largest military installation on the frontier, was the supply base for plains expeditions that rode out in every direction in the spring.

Leavenworth was more to Mary's liking than Fort Hays or

Harker. No hostile Indians threatened the post. The brick quarters were commodious and it was possible to have a nurse for the baby. "Little Cecelia," Miles called the child. He was an affectionate father. His marriage was a success. Mary, outgoing, loving and friendly, was an ideal wife for a man who could be aggressive in battle but who stiffened to formality in the drawing room. Miles loved hunting, dogs and horses — physical activity of any kind. He liked to drink with men and talk "shop" but he could not tolerate meaningless chitchat. At Leavenworth, he fretted against inaction. Mary wished he were not so determined in his ambition. She was happy to have her beloved husband at home. Miles saw himself wasting the best years of his life while other men made names for themselves. There was so much to be done. He did not want to sit on the sidelines. He wanted to play a part. He saw the "wave of civilization moving over the western horizon. Its onward march was irresistible." The Indians were the "most democratic people in the world, strong, intelligent and honest."[8] Any soldier would admire their courage. They had reason to fight, abused and starved as they were by the Indian Bureau. But they must not be allowed to check the westward expansion of the nation any more than the South had been allowed to shatter the ties that bound it to the Union.

Give him a command, he wrote Sherman, and let him prove his ability. His impatience grew when he heard that Ranald Mackenzie, who had the Fourth Cavalry in New Mexico, captured an important Comanche village on McClellan Creek in 1872 and in the spring of 1873 led his regiment against maurading Indians into Mexico. In the north, Custer took the headlines once more by his discovery of gold in the Black Hills. In 1871, George Crook was jumped from lieutenant colonel to brigadier general and given command of the Department of

New Mexico. This was hard news for Miles. Why, he demanded of Sherman, had he been passed over? As a colonel, he had seniority over Crook. He felt there had been undue favoritism and suspected Grant and Sherman had preferred Crook because he was a West Pointer. Since the end of the war, Miles had grown increasingly sensitive about West Pointers. Perhaps he overemphasized the Academy clique. Perhaps not. The "Benzine" Board weeded out the unfit but there was no board to recommend promotions in an army whose appropriations were annually cut by Congress. If an officer expected to get ahead, he had to do more than a good job. He had to establish a reputation. He had to make himself known to his superiors in Washington.

Undoubtedly, Sherman was tired of Miles's demands when, at last, in 1874, Miles was ordered to organize and lead an expedition against the Kiowas and Comanches. Now, the eager commander of the Fifth could prove whether or not he could fight Indians.

CHAPTER V

THE SITUATION had grown desperate on the southern plains and called for desperate action. The truce that followed Custer's expedition of 1868 and 1869 did not last. By 1872 the railroads had penetrated the buffalo country. Until that time, the Indians had been able to find all the buffalo they wanted. In 1871 Colonel Richard Irving Dodge estimated the buffalo moved north in an immense column from twenty to fifty miles in width and of an unknown depth from front to rear. A year later some enterprising Yankee discovered that buffalo hides could be used for belting for machinery in eastern factories. There were other uses for hides, too, which brought the price up to three dollars per hide on the market. The doom of the buffalo was sealed. Hunters swarmed into the country by foot, by horseback, by wagon train and by railroad. The hide hunting that existed previously was nothing compared to the wholesale slaughter that presently occurred on the Arkansas plains. Merchants in small towns like Dodge City, Kansas, along the railroads did a thriving business selling arms and supplies. Bars and hotels prospered. Hunters established camps on the prairie. They rode out from the towns. Along the South Platte, they lay in wait to kill the buffalo who came to water. There was no sport about the slaughter. It was a bloody, stinking business motivated by dollars. In the fall of 1873 where the great herds had once grazed along the Arkansas, the air was sickening with the stench of buffalo carcasses, the prairie was a "dead, solitary putrid desert."[1] From 1874 to

1879, Miles wrote than five million buffalo were killed.

The Indians on the reservations, no longer able to find the buffalo who had fed and clothed them from time immemorial, grew hungry. Indeed, in 1874 they were starving, the prey of unscrupulous agents and traders.

In the spring of 1871, the Kiowas and Comanches began raiding again. Actually, the predatory Kiowas were glad of an excuse to burn and pillage the settlements while the Comanches needed no urging to attack the Texas ranchers. Emboldened by the success of the raids against the whites, the Kiowas grew boastful, and the biggest braggart of the tribe was Satanta who had orated at Medicine Lodge in 1867. Satanta was a good-sized, muscular Indian with a tendency to obesity and to too much talk. Quanah Parker, the half-white chief of the Kwahadis, led the Comanches. Of all the tribes between Texas and Arkansas, the Comanches were one of the most feared. Even among the Indians the Comanches were noted for skill and stealth.

In 1874, the Kiowas, Comanches and southern Cheyennes saw a threat to what little freedom remained to them in the establishment of a camp set up at Adobe Walls in the Indian Territory country by a group of hide hunters. Dodge City merchants, anxious for a renewal of good times which had disappeared with the buffalo, had staked the hunters to food and ammunition. Who cared if the hunters invaded land reserved by treaty to the Indians when money could be made out of the project?

Led by Quanah Parker, the Comanches, Kiowas and Cheyennes swept down on Adobe Walls in the graying light of dawn. The hunters, who were all experienced plainsmen, beat them off but the country around Adobe Walls was no longer safe for buffalo hunters. The merchants of Dodge City were due to lose their investments. More peaceable settlers than the hide hunters were attacked by the aroused Indians. In September, a Cheyenne war party raided the Germaine family on the Smoky Hill River in Kansas, killing the parents and two children and carrying off four sisters.

From the settlers on the frontier arose a great outcry. Call out the army! What's the matter with the government! Why aren't we protected against these murdering savages! The most vociferous were the merchants of Dodge City. Sherman heard them in St. Louis and was disgusted. The General of the Army, battling with W. W. Belknap, Secretary of War, whom he accused of usurping military authority, had moved Army Headquarters to St. Louis in May of 1874 — an astonishingly independent thing to do, but Sherman was an independent man and saw no reason to play politics with Belknap. Sherman was, also, angry because the army had been cut to such an extent that its efficiency was impaired. A handful of troops had to keep peace in Montana and the Dakotas where the Sioux were causing trouble.

On July 31, 1874, the Department of the Interior granted authority to the War Department to proceed against the hostile tribes. This time, Sherman wrote, do not allow the Indians to take refuge in the agencies. The directions were to Sheridan's liking. The Indian problem was a military one and should be settled once and for all. The wiry little lieutenant general issued his orders.

Miles set out from Fort Dodge, Kansas, with two battalions of the Sixth Cavalry, one battalion of four companies of the Fifth Infantry, a detachment of artillery and a company of Delaware Indians, scouts and guides. Simultaneously, four troops of the Eighth Cavalry under Major W. R. Price were ordered from New Mexico to assist Miles while a third column, the Fourth Cavalry under Colonel Ranald Mackenzie, moved north from Texas into Indian Territory.

Miles had waited five years for this opportunity to lead a command against the hostiles and he was determined that neither Mackenzie nor anyone else would get ahead of him. On the 7th of August, he wrote Mary: "I have received today a report of Mackenzie's proposed movements and think we will be in the field quite as soon as the troops from that Department."[2]

Some time later, he wrote again.

> We are five days ahead of Price. He should really be under my orders. The idea of any one presuming to direct movements against Indians five hundred miles away and ten days away from telegraph communication! Still I intend to go ahead with what I have and do the best I can with it . . . We are in very good spirits, but it takes some time and a great deal of labor to get a good command working the way I want it. I find I have to be Captain and Sergeant and Wagon Master and a little of everything. But I think I will get matters straightened out so that the command will be more in hand.[3]

The reference to the absent staff directing operations was a criticism of Pope in Leavenworth. Miles had not respected Pope during the Civil War and he still did not respect him. Second Bull Run had been inexcusable to the aggressive Miles. He did not care that Pope was his senior and that he would do well to placate rather than antagonize him. He was ambitious but he would not win promotion by being a party to military ineptitude. It does not seem to have occurred to him that by asserting his independence he also asserted his responsibility for his success or failure.

From Cayote Creek on the Beaver, Miles sent Lieutenant Frank Baldwin, chief of scouts, swinging far to the right by way of Adobe Walls. Frank Baldwin was an ex-Volunteer officer who was to be closely associated with Miles in the future. He was a dark, stocky fellow, coolheaded and reliable. Baldwin's move was made to deceive the Indians into thinking Miles's force was stronger than it actually was and to confuse them about the direction of Miles's march. Billy Dixon, noted frontiersman who had been at Adobe Walls when the first attack took place, rode with him. So, too, did a young fellow

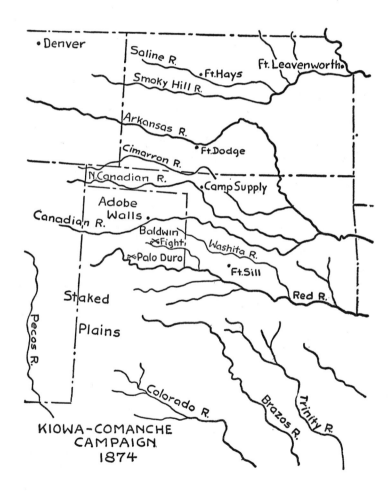

KIOWA–COMANCHE
CAMPAIGN
1874

named Bat Masterson.⁴ As the party approached the hide hunters' camp, a sickly-sweet odor greeted their nostrils. The hunters had cut off the heads of the dead Indians and stuck them on the stockade, leaving the bodies to decompose in the hot sun. Two of the hunters who had been afraid to leave the stockade until the troops arrived rode out on the prairie. Immediately, a party of warriors galloped from behind a ridge, killing one of the hunters and pursuing the other to within sight of the soldiers.

Miles, meanwhile, from a camp on Bluff Creek, wrote Mary.

> We had a very severe march today and the men suffered for want of water. We marched twenty two miles with no water except what was carried, and many men fell out from utter exhaustion. The Infantry complained that the Cavalry marched too fast for them, and the Cavalry complained that the Infantry kept them back. It is always the same when they march together. The heat was very oppressive and I do not think I ever wanted water more.
>
> It was so hot that many of the dogs died along the road. Poor old Jack [Miles's setter dog] was about played out, but his sagacity saved him. He went off to a canyon and found a little water. Coming back to the road some soldiers who had fallen by the way, nearly dead from thirst, saw that Jack was wet. They said, "Jack, show us that water." Whereupon Mr. Jack marched off to his little pool of very poor water, which to the soldiers was a great blessing. So you see the old gentleman is still doing good work and his beneficial acts will long be remembered.⁵

Dust hazed above the long column of men and horses and wagons. The scouts ranged two miles in the lead. The advance guard led the column with flankers to the right and left. At the head of the main body of troops, comprising 744 effective men, rode Miles, gray-blue eyes narrowed on the horizon, alert, tireless . . .

The pace was too slow for him. A few days later he wrote to Mary again.

Yesterday we marched to Buffalo Springs, about eighteen miles, going into camp about eleven o'clock in the morning. We started very early, about three or four o'clock, as the sun gets very hot. After dark last night I started from camp with an escort and rode through to Camp Supply making about 37 miles and arriving here about midnight. . . The command is in good spirits. I am confident we can overcome any body of Indians that we may meet, although they have been supplied with an abundance of rifles and ammunition under authority of the Interior Department.[6]

Miles signed these letters, "Thine ever loving, Nelson," or "Thine own, Nelson." Mary was his confidante. To her he could express himself as he could to no one else.

When Baldwin rejoined Miles on the Canadian River, he reported the boldness of the Indians who had pursued the hunters within sight of the troops at Adobe Walls. He also told Miles about the heads on the stockade, which angered Miles to exclaim that some white men on the frontier were worse savages than the Indians. Such retaliatory acts of brutality were uncalled for.

Miles's biggest problem proved to be to find the Indians. Warriors never fought a large force when they could flee from it, as Hancock had learned to his chagrin in 1867 when he had led an expedition against the hostiles. To help him find the elusive Indians, Miles had as scouts Ben Clark who had been with Custer on the Washita, Amos Chapman, who was married to a Cheyenne woman, and William F. Schmalsle. Ben Clark often rode with Miles at the head of the troops. Clark did not have to tell Miles that the Indians were watching them. That clump of sagebrush, that gully that eroded the semi-arid land provided excellent cover for a Kiowa or Comanche lying half naked and painted. Like wolves, the Indians stalked the column waiting to pounce on the unwary straggler or un-protected detail.

Chapman and Clark frequently talked with Indians turned spies and informers on their fellow tribesmen, for it was from such Indians they secured much of their information. A Ute might hate the white men but he hated his traditional enemy, the Kiowa, even more. Or a band that had not left the reservation might report on their warring relatives in order to gain favor with the agent or with the troops. A question Miles often asked was — are the Germaine girls, whose parents were killed on the Smoky Hill River, still alive and if so, where are they? He was told that two of the girls were in the camp of the Cheyenne chief, Grey Beard, and two in the camp of Stone Calf, the head chief of the same tribe. Miles determined to rescue them, although Ben Clark must have told him he would be lucky if he found the girls. The Indians could have killed them, or the girls could have killed themselves, as some white women did who fell into the hands of the Indians.

On the first day's march south of the Canadian, a large Indian camp was found abandoned. A trail made by travois poles and ponies led south toward the Red River and Llano Estacado. Miles reined in his horse, eyes squinting on the ocher-colored plain shimmering in the heat. Llano Estacado! A land so vast and empty that early day travelers drove stakes along the trail to mark their way. In the Staked Plains the Indians believed the buffalo sprang full grown every spring from endless caverns. For years the Kiowas, Cheyennes and Comanches had taken refuge in the canyons of the Red and Canadian Rivers that cut the Plain, knowing the troops did not dare follow them into such a desolate area. A commander could lose his entire force in that country. The men could die of thirst or be ambushed in the narrow defiles.

Miles did not hesitate. At his order, the troops continued southwest for a hundred miles to the bluffs where the Red River broke from the Staked Plains. There, Baldwin was caught by surprise. As the scouts approached the cliffs, mounted warriors poured down from the boulder-strewn heights, whooping and yelling. Immediately, the scouts dropped to the ground and began firing under Baldwin's direction. Dust puffed beneath the feet of racing ponies. Shots, the whooping of warriors and the neighing of horses echoed against the bluffs. Fall Leaf, the seventy-year-old chief of the Delaware scouts, galloped up and down the line, his gray hair flying about his shoulders, shouting encouragement to his warriors. Warned of the attack on the scouts, Miles sent the cavalry forward at a gallop.

"Right front into line!" The trumpets sang out. Major Compton's battalion of the Sixth went on the right, Major James Biddle's on the left. Lieutenant Pope of the artillery brought the Gatlings into action. Captain Chaffee shouted, "Forward! If any man is killed, I will make him a corporal!"[7] Major Compton, waving his hat, led the cavalry charge up the bluffs after the Indians, who, panicked by the attack, broke and fled.

Miles ordered immediate pursuit. He was no man to be content with victory in a skirmish, which had, too often, been the case with officers fighting Indians on the frontier. Across the rugged bluffs and down the steep and clifflike canyons of the Red River they pursued the fleeing hostiles. When the Indians stopped to fight, the troops attacked and scattered the warriors so that retreat became rout. The sky curved above the earth like a metallic bowl. The heat rose to 110°. With tongues swollen by thirst, the men fought to the bed of the Red River only to find it drifted dry with sand. In their extremity, a number of them opened the veins in their arms and drank their own blood.[8]

Llano Estacado became the enemy. Like children, the Indians had fled to their savage Mother Earth, and she stood ready to protect them. More experienced men than Miles had died in the attempt to penetrate her defenses. Miles did not consider retreat. Cursing troopers dismounted to drag their horses along the cliff. The infantrymen, sweating beneath their packs, stumbled among the rocks. The heat-paled sky crimsoned to sunset. The canyon gorge filled with violet shadow. At last Miles called a halt. In his bivouac on the Red River he wrote Mary, dating the letter September 6.

> I have just dismounted after a long and most fatiguing ride. I have been in the saddle for about 22 hours, making about fifty four miles. The Indians are still before us; at least we have not lost sight of their trail although they are thoroughly stampeded. This is a terrible country to operate in. I have had every obstacle but intense cold to contend with — heat, dust, sand, canyons, ravines, mountains, bluffs and a scarcity of water. Added to that, I find altogether too many incompetent and inefficient officers who have no interest in their duties.

During the night Lieutenant Pope dragged his Gatlings up the wall of the canyon. In the morning, the men climbed the bluffs of the Tule onto the Staked Plains, a high plateau of some four hundred miles north and south and in places nearly two hundred miles wide, covered with short buffalo grass and as level as a billiard table, without a tree or a shrub to be seen as far as eye could reach. Miles reported they marched over it sometimes for days, and it seemed like being in mid-ocean in a dead calm.

Tracks of unshod ponies and travois poles showed the direction in which the Indians were fleeing. But, finally, Miles was unable to pursue them further. Circumstances forced him to turn around and go back to the Washita. Angrily, he wrote to Mary, dating his letter the fourteenth of September on the Washita.

We have been compelled to march back one hundred and forty one miles to meet our supplies, through terrible storms, swimming rivers, and all for nothing, simply because this command is not furnished with sufficient transportation. Price, with four companies, is given forty wagons, and this command only sixty. Custer, who went no further from his base than we did, was given four hundred. It is discouraging and demoralizing to any command. We can not follow the Indians beyond a certain distance.

When I arrived here I found one of those cold blooded letters from Department Headquarters saying to the commanding officer of Camp Supply that I must get my supplies with my own wagons and that he was not to furnish me more. It was another case of one man thinking he knows more five hundred miles away than one who is on the ground. I felt enraged and sent my dispatch accordingly.

Pope's reaction to Miles's blunt criticism of this conduct of the campaign can be imagined! But so far, Miles had been successful in his pursuit of the Indians. If he blundered, he would be shown no mercy. He had made too many enemies and was rapidly making more.

He was having trouble with his officers. Miles told Mary about it in a letter.

Captain Baldwin is one of the good officers and is a valuable assistant to me, but some of the others are worse than useless. They had rather gamble and drink at a post than serve in the field. During good weather they do well, but in the first rain, they curl up like wet hens and do nothing but growl and whine[9]. . . I am obliged to do twice as much labor as I ought to, owing to the indifference or incapacity of many of the officers. I find that the officers of the old army can not compare for a moment with the volunteers [from the Civil War] either in experience, or capacity of interest. . . My campaign to the Red River would have been far more successful if my orders had been carried out and if it had not been for the incapacity of some of my subordinates. You will remember that I took the command with all the disadvantages against me, both above and below. I was very much enraged when I returned to this river and found Pope's letter and saw a dispatch of his in which he fairly robbed me of what little credit there was in it.

We are now losing valuable time here in not receiving our supplies and not being able to assume the offensive. . .

I have some very disagreeable officers that I shall try and get rid of, and the time we are here will be spent weeding out the worthless ones and reorganizing.[10]

Miles sent Major Biddle and one battalion of the Sixth Cavalry back to Camp Supply.

Mackenzie was having better luck than Miles. While Miles was held back by lack of supplies, Mackenzie found and destroyed a Kiowa, Comanche and southern Cheyenne village of one hundred lodges and captured fourteen hundred ponies, the most effective blow that had so far been dealt the southern tribes.

Miles continued to fume at the delay. He wrote Mary, and the letter was lost when hostiles attacked the couriers carrying dispatches from the Washita to Camp Supply. The country swarmed with Kiowas and Comanches. Captain Wyllis Lyman, who commanded the Fifth Infantry detail that guarded the all-important supply train, was attacked by two hundred and fifty warriors near the head of the Washita. Corralling the wagons, the troops held off the Indians until Major W. R. Price, on his way from New Mexico to join Miles, came up with his detachment of the Eighth Cavalry. The arrival of reinforcements discouraged the hostiles from further attack. Dividing into two bands, one group rode southwest to the Staked Plains and the other group rode east. The latter band was followed beyond Antelope Hills and made to surrender in early October at the Cheyenne Agency. Presumably, it was the other band that encountered the couriers — four enlisted men and scouts Billy Dixon and Amos Chapman. The couriers traveled mostly at night, holing up during the day, but despite these precautions, at dawn of the second day they ran into a party of Kiowas and Comanches who, sighting the six white men, immediately charged with the shrill and spine-chilling ki-yi-yi of the war whoop. Chapman and Dixon knew that if they tried to run, they would be picked off. Taking refuge in a buffalo wallow, they began firing at the Indians who were circling them. Private Smith, hit in the lungs during the wild dash for the wallow, lay on the ground some distance from his friends — presumably dead. Chapman was wounded in the leg. One of the soldiers in the temporary moment of panic, yelled, "No use, boys; no use; we might as well give up!"[11]

The scouts' reply could be imagined. What pleasure the Kiowa and Comanche squaws would take in the torture of two noted scouts and four soldiers! Sure of their prey, the Indians continued to circle the wallow yelling taunts and shooting. Occasionally a young buck dashed up with poised lance to spear one of the defenders, but when the white men's bullets brought down three or four of the reckless warriors they stopped these displays of bravado. It began to rain and then grew freezing cold. The wallow filled with water. Ammunition ran low. Private Rath, who volunteered to go out and get the revolver and ammunition from Smith's body, discovered the soldier was still alive. Rath and Dixon brought him back to the wallow and Dixon stuffed a handkerchief in the gaping hole in his back, but the soldier was suffering terribly and begged his comrade to shoot him. That night, the men lay in the wallow not daring to sleep. Every breath that Smith drew, blood and air bubbled from the wound in his lungs. Toward dawn he died. After some discussion, the men determined that one of their number must go for help. Dixon volunteered and, crawling out of the wallow, struck for the trail leading to Camp Supply. Employing his skill as a frontiersman, he eluded the Indians and had only gone a few miles in a northwesterly direction when he saw moving figures on the horizon — Major Price with four troops of the Eighth Cavalry escorting the commissary train. Stepping into the open, Dixon frantically waved his rifle. He could have cried with relief!

Price sent his surgeon to look at the wounds of the men in the buffalo wallow but, for some reason (it may have been he felt responsible for the supply train and did not want to tarry in hostile country) he refused to leave reinforcements or ammunition. The feeling of the men in the wallow, exhausted, suffering from wounds, exploded into blasphemy. Wait until the "General" heard the news! They were sure Miles would not desert them. All that day they waited with the body of Smith beside them and Chapman gritting his teeth on the pain of his fractured leg. Close to twelve o'clock, the notes of a bugle sounded in the darkness and the cavalry detail that Miles had ordered to the rescue rode out of the night.

Miles was furious. He was a disciplinarian, although he did not go as far as Mackenzie who allowed an officer to string an enlisted man up by the thumbs. He drilled his troops relentlessly. He marched them to exhaustion. He demanded instant obedience, but he never asked a man to do what he would not do himself and he was as quick to reward as he was to punish. An officer who abandoned men in time of need broke the code of honor. Price received a dressing down he was never to forget from the cold-eyed commander of the expedition.

Afterward, Miles wrote to Mary: "Yesterday I assumed command of Price's command and gave him orders. I do not know how General Pope will take it."[12]

Miles suspected Pope had no sympathy with his command and was trying to withdraw it. To say that Pope had "no sympathy with the command" was probably an understatement. The Department Commander was furious with his subordinate's independent behavior. And now Miles roused his ire even further.

When Miles could, still, not get supplies; when his wagons had to wait at Camp Supply or come back to the Washita half loaded; when Price, irked by the dressing down that Miles had given him, refused to co-operate, Miles wrote to Mary, October 1, from the Canadian River.

> I would like to know if Sheridan is going to take any interest in this Indian affair. I am satisfied that there must be gross mismanagement somewhere in our rear and would not be surprised if it was Vleit's fault! [Van Vleit, the quartermaster.] Still I must remain here, much as it is disagreeable for me, until I can obtain supplies and then go for them again, unless MacKenzie and Davidson[13] finish it up in the meantime.
>
> I have been able to get rid of some of my growlers and have sent two drunkards to Camp Supply, but still I am handicapped by disinterested and indifferent officers.
>
> There are certainly troops enough to finish this campaign in thirty days if they were moved in concert or under one head, but it is useless to have half a dozen different commands. It required a peculiar kind of genius to conduct an Indian campaign from West Point or Boston, although they know a great deal about Indians in that model city — at least they think they do, which is very important.

Miles wrote many of these letters to Mary in his tent at night by the light of a flickering candle. His shadow loomed large on the canvas. Getting up, he paced to the open tent flap. Outside, the cooking fires glowed dully. The men slept in their blankets, rifles stacked close by. A sentry's boot grated on the gravel. A horse stamped restlessly on the picket line. The nights were cool in this semi-arid land, the stars immense and glittering in the sky. Knuckling his jaw and mustache with a quick, impatient gesture, Miles returned to the ammunition box that served for a table. As the expedition's commander, he had no intimates, no one to whom he could blow off steam. His letters to Mary were his only release. Mary's letters, in turn, soothed and encouraged him. "This morning," he wrote, "the trains came in bringing me three sweet letters from you."[14]

He did not like the idea of driving the hostiles south into Mackenzie's arms so that cavalry commander could claim credit for the surrender. But he felt better when he heard Big Tree and several other chiefs had surrendered at the agency and that a band of 104 lodges had come into Fort Sill. The surrenders had been the result of encounters with Miles's forces. Perhaps the campaign had not been unsatisfactory, after all, and Sheridan and Sherman would be pleased by the results. Supplies finally arrived and the command moved out, this time without Jack, the setter, who was getting footsore. On October 13, from camp on the Washita, Miles wrote Mary that the setter dog was convalescing at Camp Supply.

Poor Jack is doing very well after his long journey back from near the battlefield on Red River. His feet got very sore in travelling over the rough grass in our rushing march after the Red fellows. One of the doctors drove him out of the ambulance — of course he had to make room for the soldiers. I expect Jack thought he had had enough of the war path. In his long march he fell in with another dog and a cat which had been lost by some Buffalo hunters from Adobe Walls. The three made a rather desolate family. I do not know who was chief, but presume Jack was for he would never accept any subordinate position in which his superior wisdom might not be appreciated. I presume Miss Puss was the commissary to catch what game there was, and as for a quartermaster department they did not have any, or like this expedition a very indifferent one. When found I believe they all went on the sick report except the Commander who always looks out for Number One. I believe they are now all of the opinion that even summer campaigning is not the thing, and that more conciliatory measures should be adopted. They are willing to accept appointments as Peace Commissioners, and think that the army ought to go into camp immediately. At last accounts Mr. Jack had made good use of his amiable qualities, had cultivated the good graces of the people at Supply and as usual had become a favorite. (I have given you quite an account of this as I thought it might interest little Baby.)

Miles moved fast. On the night of the twelfth of October, Baldwin and young Pope started out with sixty picked men and a Gatling gun. Young Pope seems to have been devoted to those guns. They marched cross-country by night and holed up in the timber during the day. Their objective was to find out if there were any Indians on the Sweetwater, North Fork, McClellan Creek or Elm Fork. The morning of the thirteenth, Captain Hartwell, Captain Chaffee and Lieutenant Whittier started for the head of the Salt Fork to scout for Indians, while Compton's command was ordered into the vicinity of Adobe Walls for the same purpose.

Price was still giving trouble. His outfit was, Miles said, "a useless affair and more of an embarrassment than assistance; but he, like some others, is a favorite. The officers seem to be a very fair set, but the organization seems better adapted to marching around all summer and making maps than fighting Indians."[15]

It was growing cold and Miles asked Mary to send him warm woolen stockings, buffalo overshoes, a small camp stove for his tent and a gallon of old rye whisky. Mary was not to worry about the whisky. It was only needed in case of emergency. When the rescue detail had brought Amos Chapman back after the buffalo wallow fight, there hadn't been a drop of spirits in the camp to ease the pain of his broken leg. Miles himself could have done with a drink the night he swam his horse across the river. His clothes and his blankets got wet and he nearly froze before morning.

Miles felt the campaign was nearly over. Winter was approaching and the Indians did not like to fight in cold weather. Besides, the constant pursuit had not given them time to hunt and they had lost many of their belongings when they'd had to abandon their camps. An old squaw seeking a scrap to eat from the soldiers told Miles her people had been living for five days on wild grapes.

Where, then, were the hostiles who refused to surrender? Major Compton reported that the main body of Indians had retreated onto the Staked Plains. One of these Indian bands was led by Stone Calf who held the two elder Germaine girls prisoner. The two younger girls were on McClellan Creek with Grey Beard's band. Lieutenant Baldwin discovered the village on the 8th of November and decided to attack.

CHAPTER VI

BALDWIN's detail, this time, was not a combat force but an escort for empty wagons returning to the Washita for supplies. Before Baldwin left camp, Miles told him, "I want you to take this detachment of cavalry, infantry and scouts, one mountain howitzer and a train of twenty-three six-mule teams with empty wagons, and proceed northward and eastward. Should you run across no Indians or trails which you deem advisable to attack or follow, you will convoy the train to the supply camp on the Washita River. Should you find any considerable body of Indians, you will communicate with me and attack or pursue, as you deem expedient."[1]

The orders left much to Baldwin's judgment, showing the confidence Miles had in his junior officer.

Baldwin struck across the prairie, taking advantage of gullies and river bottoms to screen him from the Indians. The third night, he camped on McClellan Creek. It was bitterly cold but Baldwin would only allow the men to build tiny fires to heat coffee. This caution was justified when the next morning at dawn, as the troops were preparing to move out, Scout W. F. Schmalsle came racing back to report a large Indian camp. "We're sure it's Grey Beard's band; his tepee is there!"[2]

Baldwin received the news with mixed emotions. He was encumbered by wagons. The safe move would be to avoid the Indians. But the two younger Germaine girls were with Grey Beard and Baldwin knew Miles's determination to rescue them. After only an instant's hesitation, he ordered Schmalsle to ride back to headquarters camp and notify the General he was going to attack the village.

From the top of a ridge a mile from the Indian camp, Baldwin looked down on a grove of cottonwoods. A few sere leaves still clung to the branches. The creek glinted cold and gray in tangled thickets. As far as Baldwin could see, the winding course of the stream was lined with wickiups and tepees. There must be, Baldwin estimated, more than a hundred lodges in the valley, which meant three hundred warriors. The young officer decided on a daring ruse. Putting the infantry in the wagons, he formed the train in a double column with the lead teams on a line with the most advanced troops. The blue-clad men shivered as much with excitement as with the cold. The horses fought their bits. The trumpeter moistened his lips, watching Baldwin for a signal.

"Charge!" The trumpet rang out in the gray dawn. Down the slopes the wagons rocketed, teamsters cursing, soldiers shooting and troopers yelling. Terrified Indians, half asleep and half clad, rushed from their tepees to flee in terror down the stream. Warriors caught by surprise put up a halfhearted defense to cover the retreat of their families. The valley echoed with the neighing of horses, the screams of the Indians, the shouts of the soldiers, the blasting report of guns. Tepees were knocked over, ponies stampeded. Through the village the attackers swept out and onto the grassy plain after the Indians running for their favorite refuge — the Staked Plains. For twelve miles the troops fought, charging, re-forming and charging again until, at the end of four hours, the Indians had scattered and disappeared.

In Grey Beard's tepee, a soldier of Company D of the Fifth Infantry found two terrified children, scared, bruised and in rags — Adelaide and Julia Germaine. The soldiers crowded around them, swearing beneath their breath when they saw the poor emaciated little bodies. The scouts thought they were lucky to be alive. The Indians usually killed their captives when troops attacked their camp.[3]

Miles, riding hard with a troop of cavalry, galloped to the scene of the fight on McClellan Creek to congratulate Baldwin; he told him he would recommend him for the Medal of Honor, which he did and which, in due course, Baldwin received. Miles wanted to see the Germaine children, and they were brought to him. Still dazed from the events of the last days, little Julia and Adelaide gazed at the lean, broad-shouldered officer in the high-collared uniform. The gray-blue eyes that had frozen many an erring soldier were smiling and friendly. The man who could not relax with his contemporaries found pleasure in children. The two girls were given into the care of the surgeon, Dr. Powell, and sent to Leavenworth. Miles assumed responsibility for their welfare.

Miles described the girls' hands as being like bird claws. They had been obliged to travel rapidly by night and by day with the Indians in their long journeys, with but insufficient and coarse food.

If you have an opportunity to do anything for those poor children to make them comfortable [Miles wrote Mary], please do so. Also show Dr. Powell all the attention you can, invite him to stop at the house as he is poor and would appreciate it. He is a rather rough specimen of a Virginian but has done his duty faithfully and well, and under all difficulties has been very cheerful, which is not the case with some of the officers . . .[4]

Miles was more determined than ever to find the two older girls.

I am quietly waiting here for supplies [the quartermaster had failed him again], and as soon as they are received I intend to make one more movement towards the head of Red River, with the hope of driving out the Indians that have taken refuge in that region or of making it uncomfortable for them, even if I can not capture them. And possibly we may be able to do something towards rescuing those poor white girls who are still in their hands. As much as I long to return to my darling little family, I am unwilling to turn eastward and leave them in captivity. Last night I could not sleep thinking about their sufferings. I judge from the story told by the younger ones that a scene is enacted in their camp every night that would chill the blood of the sternest soldier of my command. And when I think how much more we could have done had not Van Vleit [the quartermaster] neglected his duty and indulged a contractor in making a few thousand dollars of money, I get quite indignant. This command has been actually starved nearly to death, that is the horses and mules, by his bad management. I understand he was ordered to visit my camp, but got very sick at Camp Supply.[5]

Price, who had not ceased to resent Miles's assumption of command, had done as much as Van Vleit to hinder operations. Miles's pen scratched indignantly across the paper in his letter to Mary.

The plan that I made two or three weeks ago on Wolf Creek was successfully carried out and crowned with victory. The only part of it not successful was owing to failure of Major Price who had done everything to block my plans. I intend to place him in arrest, at least if the reports which I received are correct. He marched his command up within sound of the fight. His position was in the rear of the Indians and he should have captured them, but he turned and marched the other way.[6]

And, again, four days later:

I am satisfied that if Major Price had obeyed my orders or come up to the attack, instead of turning his back to the field, the campaign would have been ended. Or if he and his command had been in New Mexico instead of blocking the Indians' road to the Agency we would have driven them in before this. You will see by my order to him that I intended and expected the week before the fight to drive the Indians along his front or into his vicinity. I have placed the little gentleman in arrest, ordered him to Camp Supply and shall prefer charges against him . . .[7]

Miles did not waste time with an officer who refused to cooperate. Campaigning on the Staked Plains in winter demanded discipline or disaster. Miles himself did occasionally flout Pope's orders; he had the fighting man's distrust of staff and of diliatory command, but woe betide the officer who disobeyed Miles in the field! This was the sort of thing that sometimes infuriated Miles's superiors, and, it must be admitted, not without cause.

I would not have you think, [he told Mary], [that] Price's failure destroyed the movement on the Staked Plains. The general result was satisfactory. We drove them out after their retreat, chased them a very long distance, routed them out of their camps, whipped them in a good running fight and scattered them in every direction, besides capturing much of their property . . . The last reports I got from General Neil[8] is that the Cheyennes are coming in and are all anxious to get back to their agencies. This cold weather will assist us, even if it is hard to endure . . . The troops suffer very much and some have frozen feet, although I have heard of none seriously frozen yet.[9]

Miles told Mary he was sending his favorite mare, Virginia, back to Leavenworth; she was growing gaunt and footsore from months of hard riding. At the same time, he was sending a white pony captured from the Indians to Baby Cecelia. But en route to Camp Supply, the pony along with sixteen other horses perished in a blizzard.

By the custom of plains warfare, Miles should have given up the campaign. Custer's expedition of 1868 and 1869 had been one of the few to continue through the winter. An entire force could perish in the terrible northers that swept the plains in January and February. The mercury plummeted to below zero. Visibility disappeared in swirling snow and shrieking wind. The soldier plodding with bent head and limbs numbed by the cold could not see the man in front of him. The troopers had to dismount and lead their horses. The steel of rifle barrels and bridle bits froze on the soldier's hands.

Pope decided there was no need to risk the loss of a command in such merciless weather. Doubtless he was glad of an excuse to recall Miles, anyhow. He could say, justifiably, that the campaign had been a success and that there was no need to continue the pursuit of the Indians. Kiowas, Comanches, Arapahoes and Cheyennes had surrendered by the hundreds at their various agencies. The troops had, the Indians reported, made it impossible to "have a quiet night's sleep." They were, Pope reported, to Sheridan, "completely broken down, nearly starved to death, and in a deplorable condition in every respect."[10] The Fourth Cavalry had been ordered to Fort Sill and Ranald Mackenzie assigned command of that installation. Miles had the only force left on the Plains. In December of 1874, Miles received orders to construct a cantonment on a tributary of the North Fork and to withdraw what forces remained to him from the field. One or two scouts were authorized. Miles felt this was quitting before the job was finished. He had no intention of abiding by such orders. The middle of December, he wrote Mary.

> . . . The next day marched in a snow storm to Red Deer Creek or Elk Run, cleared away the snow, pitched our tents, and the next day marched to this point. I intend to go to the

head of Muster Creek and then may strike down the head of Red River, if I do not get information to take me elsewhere. I have with me only one company of cavalry but shall take other troops as circumstances require. My men are in good spirits and fairly provided for the winter climate. I have sent back all but three companies of cavalry and three companies of infantry of the original command, and shall start the 8th Cavalry to New Mexico as soon as the Keokuk contractors furnish grain. I am bound to make one more effort to drive in what Indians remain out and rescue if possible those little girls. I know the chief who has one or both of them. He offered to trade them to some Mexicans for squaws. I expect my command will be withdrawn even when it is in position to finish the affair, and against my earnest protest. Yet any man who gives the order to withdraw troops under these circumstances and leaves those innocent sufferers to their fate, dams his name to eternal infamy for all time. It does seem as if the General of the Army could afford to take a little time and interest in this important matter. There never was a campaign more grossly mismanaged.[11]

Miles reached Muster Creek in a blizzard, and on the 4th of January the command crossed the head of the Tule with a norther howling on their heels. Morale remained high.

. . . the troops did not seem to suffer or complain. They are as jolly as ever, and it was quite amusing to hear them sing "Marching Through Georgia" way out on these plains. They might as well have sung that as anything else, for they did not know where they were going, and it is doubtful if the foot of the white man had ever passed over much of this ground before.[12]

Miles froze his left ear and could not sleep at night for the cold, despite a buffalo robe and six blankets. But he, like his campaign-hardened men, did not get discouraged. Scouts found moccasin and pony tracks in the snow.

Huddling closer in the greatcoat, Miles blew on his stiffened fingers. His breath smoked on the icy air. The tent canvas creaked in the wind.

> I expect to move east to scout [Miles wrote Mary] . . . which is about all I am authorized to do. I dislike the word [scouting] very much for it means so little, and so little is accomplished by it. Still, I am in good spirits, as I hope that before this movement is over, I will be able to report that there are very few if any hostile Indians in the Department of the Missouri, even within the region north of the Red River.[13]

On the 11th of January, in camp on Elm Fork, Miles wrote:

> As I am only authorized to scout now, I intend to make that as effective as possible and shall be very glad if we can clear the Department of Indians even as far south as the Red River. This march has been quite a rapid one and has been accomplished in much less time than I anticipated. The weather has been extremely cold. The ice on some of the streams has been frozen so hard that it would bear a loaded army wagon. This has its advantages and disadvantages. The wagons can move rapidly over the frozen ground and the men make long marches. But the nights are awful. . . It is possible that in continuing this scout east you may next hear from us at Sill, Supply or Wachita. I have not heard from the Department of the Headquarters since the 10th of last month or received a telegram since the 16th of December, the date of your last letter. For some unaccountable reason they seem to be very indifferent about sending out our mails from Camp Supply.

Miles should have realized the difficulty a courier would have catching up with him. From the head of the Tule he marched east as far as Fort Sill on a faint Indian trail. The thermometer showed twenty-five degrees below zero. The ground was frozen as black and hard as basalt. The wind, that never ceased to whine and howl, swept the earth free of snow.

When Miles returned from this scout, he had covered seven hundred miles.

By this time, he was convinced the Indians were in such desperate circumstances that they would surrender if they had a chance. Therefore, he determined to send a party of friendly Indians to the camp of Stone Calf on the Pecos River in New Mexico with summons to surrender at the agency. Dr. Powell, who had returned from Leavenworth after escorting the two younger Germaine girls to that post, had brought back with him a picture of Julia and Adelaide which had been taken to show Miles how the children's appearance had improved with food and care. On the back of this picture Miles scrawled a note to the two older girls, Sophie and Catherine.[14]

> Headquarters Indian Territory Expedition
> In the field, January 20, 1875

> To the Missis Germaine; — Your little sisters are well and in the hands of friends. Do not be discouraged. Every effort is being made for your welfare.
> NELSON A. MILES
> Colonel and Brevet-Major General
> United States Army Commanding Expedition

This note, so typically formal — Miles could not express himself with ease on paper or, indeed, verbally — was given to an Indian to carry four hundred miles across the frozen reaches of the Staked Plains to Stone Calf on the Pecos. The surrender terms demanded the return of the Germaine sisters. Stone Calf immediately sent for Sophie and Catherine and putting them in a tepee adjoining his, treated them with a kindness he had not exhibited before. The eldest girl, who had received the picture from the messenger, cried with thankfulness and relief. Both she and her sister had been half starved and beaten. The next morning the Indians started back the cold, weary miles to the agency on foot. They had only a few gaunt ponies remaining of their once numerous herds. When they reached the agency, Stone Calf surrendered the Germaine girls, his entire band, horses, bows and arrows, thus ending the armed resistance of the southern tribes in any great numbers.

With the Germaine girls safe at Leavenworth, Miles was at last satisfied he had done his duty. The troops returned to their barracks for rest and recuperation. There is no record of Miles's meeting with Pope. The official reports of both Miles and the Department Commander were impersonal, as such reports usually were. But no one could deny that Miles had fought a successful campaign.

"All the bands of Indians in the Southwest," Pope reported to Phil Sheridan, "Cheyennes and Arapahoes, Kiowas and Comanches, are now at their respective agencies, brought there by military force after a campaign of eight months . . ."[15]

The plight of the Indians after the surrender made a lasting impression on Miles. To him the Indian was a respected foe, and he had one more cause for which to take up the cudgels when he saw what happened to the tribes after they were turned back to the jurisdiction of the Bureau of Indian Affairs. The chief, Satanta, who had pleaded for freedom at Medicine Lodge in 1867, threw himself from the second story of a prison hospital where he was confined. Grey Beard was shot by a guard en route to prison in Florida. Owing to the disappearance of the buffalo on the southern plains, the Indians confined to the agencies faced actual starvation. Slop barrels and dump piles were searched for scraps. The offal about the butcher shops was seized and fought over. Colonel Dodge reported the Indians cut up and ate the putrid flesh of a horse that had been dead for some days. It was not surprising, Miles felt, that the Indians preferred fighting to starving to death at an agency.

PART THREE

*The Sioux Campaign
of 1876-77*

CHAPTER VII

THE CAMPAIGN of 1874 was more successful in its final results than the winter campaign of 1869, but Miles did not win the acclaim that Custer did. Mackenzie was given publicity for his capture of the hostile village in Palo Duro canyon; Miles received little recognition for his fights on the Staked Plains. Miles felt he was being discriminated against, and was sure of it when his old rival, George Crook, was again given an assignment he would have liked very much. In the spring of 1875 Crook was ordered to command the Department of the Platte. The Platte was a plum for any officer, for it included Iowa and Nebraska, the Territories of Utah and Wyoming and Fort Hall in Idaho — much of it Sioux country where the tribes were preparing for a final stand against the whites. Crook, Sherman felt after Crook had subdued the Apaches in Arizona, was the most capable Indian fighter in the army. In military parlance, Crook was "on the way up." Not only was he highly regarded by his superiors, but he was popular with the press who liked writing about a general who went into the field in a canvas hunting suit and a disreputable hat, his luxuriant beard braided and thrown over his shoulders.

Miles was not encouraged by Sherman when he criticized Crook for being overrated. Crook's Apache campaigns, Miles felt, had been skirmishes and had resulted in no lasting peace. Miles would have done better to keep his opinion to himself.

Instead of going north to the Sioux country, as he would have liked, Miles was ordered south to Cimarron, New Mexico, in the fall of 1875 to deal with a threatened outbreak of Jicarilla Apaches and Muache Utes. New Mexico was within Pope's Department of the Missouri. Miles does not say what his relations were with Pope in the fall of 1875 but, undoubtedly, they were not of the warmest.

Miles had learned a great deal about Indians during the five years on the frontier and, especially, during his campaign of the previous winter. He remembered, too, what had happened to the tribes who had surrendered in the spring. Unlike Mackenzie, he was no Indian hater.

The Cimarron trip was a thankless one and Miles was not happy about it.

The Cimarron agent, John Pyle, wrote in his report that the trouble with the Apaches and the Utes was caused by white men selling whisky to the Indians and by cattlemen grazing their herds on tribal lands. Outlaw white men on the reservation were also a source of trouble as were the settlers who were cutting timber that belonged to the Indians. Miles did not entirely agree with this, possibly because he had no patience with a man who fled from his reservation — as the agent did — in the face of Indian threats.

Miles had a detachment of cavalry and could have immediately attacked the rebellious tribes. By winning a battle with the Indians, he could have gained prestige that would have given him an advantage when he again requested a field command in the Sioux country. But, characteristically, he sought to conciliate before admitting that he must fight.

The day after he arrived in Cimarron, November 6, he wrote his wife who was at Leavenworth.

> . . . Today I sent out for the principal chiefs and they came in and we had a long talk. They seem opposed to going to war and anxious to live at peace. As near as I can ascertain the

whole trouble arises from whisky, bad rations and a want of proper discretion in their management. The contracts are in the hands of a parcel of [moneygrabbers] and the Indians appear to have no friends. They promise to bring all their people in tomorrow or the next day, to be good Indians and give no trouble. I believe if they are not interferred with they will do it for they impressed me very favorably. Should they make good their promise I shall probably return the companies of the Fifth Cavalry to Fort Lyon in a day or two and a part of this force to Fort Union . . . I will only have time to write you this few lines before the mail closes but these lines I would write to convey my hearts devotion and constant love for my precious darlings.

Ever thine own,

NELSON

Five weeks later, Miles wrote to Mary again that he had made a trip into the mountains to visit the Apache camps on Ute creek and found everything peaceful. Baldwin, who was proving to be Miles's right-hand man, was sent on a scout up Vermigo Canyon with a detachment of cavalry to see if matters were satisfactory in that area. They were, and on the sixteenth of December, Miles wrote to Mary that he was returning to Leavenworth. The spelling in the letter, as in the other letters, was not exact. The punctuation could have been improved on. Miles had not had the time to study grammar as had Alfred Terry, a Yale graduate, but he managed to convey his feelings to Mary.

"I can scarcely realize that I am so soon to have the pleasure of embracing my precious ones again . . ."

In the next sentence, he revealed the uncertainty that underlay his seeming confidence. "I often wonder if you are as happy to receive me as I am to return."

He reassured himself. "Yet I judge by your dear letters that

I can feel assured of a cordial welcome and it is a satisfaction to know that I have found more real happiness in the last seven years of my life than I did in all that precluded them."

Miles planned to return via Lawrence, Kansas . . . "to see about letting those two little Germaine girls go over there." He took his duties as guardian seriously and wanted to be certain Julia and Adelaide were well looked after.

". . . I am pleased to learn that your dear father and mother have joined you," Miles continued, "and I hope it may seem a home to them and that they can enjoy it. Please give them my love . . . We may not always be able to entertain them so pleasantly and I would like to have them enjoy our beautiful home with us."[1]

Sooner or later, Miles was determined to go north to the Sioux country.

Miles watched events in the North closely. In that remote part of the country, the same situation faced the Sioux as had faced the southern Cheyennes, semi-starvation on the agencies or war with the army whose duty it was to protect the emigrants. The Sioux were a great nation, two thirds of whom belonged to the Teton or Prairie Sioux roaming the country from the Wind River Mountains in Wyoming to east of the Missouri; from the South Platte to the Musselshell in Montana. Settlers came later to the North then to the South. The Northern Pacific Railroad had penetrated only as far as Bismarck, Dakota Territory, in 1875. Solemn pledges had been made by Washington never to violate the Black Hills — sacred stronghold of the Sioux — but when rumors of gold began to circulate in the bars of Sioux City and Cheyenne following Custer's expedition into the Hills in 1874, the promises were forgotten. The army tried, unsuccessfully, to prevent the rush that followed. The

Indians, furious at the invasion, threatened war on the whites. In 1874, the Commissioner of Indian Affairs estimated there were seven thousand Sioux off the reservations. Of this number four thousand reported to Standing Rock Agency, which was located on the west bank of the Missouri seventy miles south of Bismarck, leaving, the Commissioner said, three thousand non-agency Indians under the leadership of Sitting Bull.[2] The Commissioner underestimated the number of hostiles. Perhaps "Fighting Phil" Sheridan, too, underestimated the Sioux, who had been called the "finest light cavalry the world has ever known." And their chiefs, Sitting Bull of the Hunkpapa and Crazy Horse of the Oglalas. A miner in the Black Hills reported that near the Belle Fourche River he crossed a trail leading west that looked as though thousands of Indians had passed over it. All over the plains that summer and fall of 1875, the tracks of moccasins and unshod ponies led toward the Powder River and the Big Horns where Sitting Bull and Crazy Horse had their camps.

Sitting Bull was to some a courageous and stubborn leader and to others a mountebank. He could hardly have been the latter, or he would not have exerted so much influence among the Sioux. A newspaper correspondent described him as a man an inch or two over medium height, broadly built, rather bow-legged and walking with a slight limp. He wore his hair parted in the middle. His face was broad, with a prominent hooked nose and wide jaws. His eyes were fierce, half blood-shot. His regard was a blend of curiosity and insolence.[3]

A chief of a different sort was Crazy Horse. Indian and white alike agreed the Oglala deserved a paramount position among the Sioux. Crazy Horse was a leader a nation produces once or twice in its history. Of more than average intelligence, he was devoted to his people, skilled in council and in war. As a tactician, he commanded the respect of the frontier army. He was lighter in color than most Indians, slight of build and quiet in manner. Disdaining the elaborate ornaments of a warrior, he preferred to wrap his long braids in fur and to dress simply. Sitting Bull's hatred of the whites bordered on frenzy. He seems to have thought he could drive the white man from the Powder River Country. Crazy Horse had no such illusions. He remained hostile because he would rather die than suffer the humiliation of living on an agency.

Indian attacks on isolated farms, wagon trains and mining parties became so frequent that Crook wrote to Sheridan, his division commander: "Unless some arrangement can be made by this winter by which the Indians will be satisfied to cede the mining regions, my impression is that serious trouble will ensue."[4]

Runners were sent out to the wild bands the latter part of December to notify Sitting Bull and Crazy Horse that if they did not report to the agencies by the thirty-first of January they would be considered hostiles. It was impossible for the Indians to make the long trek to the agencies in Dakota and Nebraska within the specified time — a fact Sheridan must have known. The Sioux, he felt, should be dealt with, once and for all, as had the southern tribes and the only way to do it was by military action. When the tribes did not come in Sheridan ordered Crook, waiting at Fort D. A. Russell in Cheyenne, to proceed against the hostiles. Sheridan had little doubt that Crook would make an end of Sitting Bull and Crazy Horse. In March Crook marched from Fort Fetterman for the Powder River and the Big Horns with ten full companies of the Second and Third Cavalry and two companies of the Fourth Infantry. Picturesque as always, Crook wore corduroy trousers badly burned at the ends, a felt hat with a hole in the crown and an old army overcoat lined with red flannel and collared by a wolf shot by him on one of his hunting trips. The result of the expedition was an abortive attack on a village mistaken for Crazy Horse's and the court-martial of the officer who left wounded men to die at the hands of the Sioux.[5] Crook, however, still held his superior's confidence, for when Sheridan prepared another expedition against the Sioux the following spring, Crook was again in command of a column of troops. This time Sheridan planned a three-pronged drive on the stubborn hostiles similar to the campaign against the southern tribes that had proved so successful. Colonel John Gibbon, the same Gibbon who had fought with Miles at Reams Station, marched from Fort Shaw, Montana, down the Yellowstone valley with four hundred and fifty men of the Seventh Infantry and the Second cavalry. Terry, commanding the Department of the Dakotas, with a detachment of infantry and cavalry from Fort Lincoln, came up the Yellowstone while Crook with forty-seven officers and a thousand men marched north up the Tongue. The hostiles, it was hoped, would be crushed in the pincers.

At the head of the Seventh Cavalry, which was under Terry, rode Custer. The tawny-haired hero had fallen from favor and was lucky to be with his regiment. Impetuous as always, he had dashed back to Washington on his own initiative to testify against Belknap, Secretary of War, who was being tried on charges of fraud, thereby angering President Grant who took Custer's action as criticism against his administration. Even Sheridan was annoyed with his protégé and would have relieved Custer of his duties, but Custer took the train west, anyhow, orders or no orders. The kindly Terry interceded and Custer rejoined his beloved regiment in time to march for the Yellowstone.

On a clear June morning, the Seventh staged a review for Terry and Gibbon on the banks of the Yellowstone. The steamer *Far West* that had brought supplies upriver for the troops was anchored to the shore. From the river, the hills rolled away to the horizon tufted with bunch grass and prickly pear. In the hollows grazed herds of buffalo. Guidons fluttered and sunlight winked on accouterments as the troopers passed in review. Custer paused for a last handshake with Terry and Gibbon and then, touching spurs to his horse, galloped after his troops winding down the long trail to the Little Big Horn.

"Now, up to this moment," Sherman reported later, "there was nothing official or private to justify an officer to expect that any detachment could encounter more than 500 or, at the maximum, 800 hostile warriors."[6]

Thus the field commanders, who should have known better, continued to underestimate the Indians. Communications were, also, extremely faulty. No one on the Yellowstone knew that on the 17th of June, the third prong of the attacking force under Crook had encountered Crazy Horse and been defeated. The attack was so sudden and in such force that Crook barely had time to deploy his troops. The Sioux were here, there and everywhere. They struck the command in the flanks, retreated before the cavalry charges and struck again in the rear. From the crest of the bluffs poured hundreds of naked, painted warriors led by Crazy Horse, black hair unbound, a calfskin cape whipping from his shoulders.

Crook refused to concede that he had been bested by the Sioux, but the friendly Indian scouts and the officers alike felt the Indians had won the battle. In the long run, Crazy Horse won more than a battle, for Crook, seeing he had underestimated the Indians, grew as cautious as he had been overconfident and decided not to continue his march to the Yellowstone until he received reinforcements. For the next few weeks, he remained in the Tongue River valley hunting and fishing. The creeks that splashed and foamed down from the Big Horns teemed with trout. Crook shot a cinnamon bear. No word came from Terry. The country swarmed with hostiles and couriers could not get through. A vague tale circulated in camp about smoke to the northwest on the Little Big Horn. Crook, beginning to worry, climbed the Big Horn mountains where he could survey the vast sweep of plain and rugged range with his field glasses. Bourke, his aide-de-camp, was with the six officers who acompanied him. There were also four newspaper correspondents.

Crook was on top of the mountains vainly searching for signs of a marching column of troops when, miles away, on the Big Horn River, Captain Grant Marsh of the steamboat *Far West* looked out his pilot house window to the water rushing between narrow banks and said weakly, "Boys, I can't do it. I'll smash her up."[7]

The responsibility of the boat's cargo overwhelmed him. On fresh-cut grass spread on the decks lay rows of wounded from the surviving companies of Custer's comand on the Little Big Horn. In the extreme end of the *Far West* in an improvised stall stood a claybank sorrel horse, stiff and bloodied — the mount that Captain Keogh of the Seventh Cavalry had ridden to his death.

After a moment, the Captain's courage returned. He pulled the bell cord and the *Far West* started on the 710-mile journey to Fort Abraham Lincoln. Under full steam, the Captain raced down the Big Horn to the Yellowstone, and thence to the Missouri, spinning the boat in and out between rocks, scraping over gravel bars and fighting the wheel in treacherous currents.

The 5th of July, the flag hanging at half mast, the boat touched the dock at Bismarck. The surgeon and the able-bodied troopers prepared to move the wounded ashore, while other men, choked with emotion, hurried to the darkened post above the town. Citizens roused from their beds as Grant Marsh, in company with the editor of the *Bismark Tribune,* raced to the telegraph office. With unsteady fingers, the operator tapped out this message. "Bismark, D. T., July 5, 1876. General Custer attacked the Indians June 25, and he, with every officer and man in five companies, were killed."[8]

The claybank sorrel horse, whose name was Comanche, had been the only living thing found on the battlefield.

At Leavenworth, Miles opened the paper. Large black type sprang from the page: "HORRIBLE!" Smaller type beneath told the story of the Custer Massacre.

An exclamation escaped Miles. There must be some mistake! Custer was one of the most able cavalry leaders in the army. He knew Indians. Agitated, Miles sought more information. The report was correct. Mary Miles, thinking of Elizabeth Custer, wiped tears from her eyes. Miles, pacing his office, came home to pace the living room. What terrible blunder had occasioned the death of his friend and so many of his men? The prestige of the army had suffered an irreparable blow! Less than a month before, he had written Sherman offering to go up into the Sioux country and keep after the hostiles until they surrendered or were worn out, as the Cheyennes and Kiowas had been, by constant pursuit.[9] Perhaps, now, Sherman would listen to his plea to be sent north.

Rumors flew about the post. Wesley Merritt was reinforcing Crook. Ranald Mackenzie was ordered north. Five companies of the Fifth Infantry were being sent to the Yellowstone. Miles

wired a request to command this detachment of his regiment —
a request that could hardly be denied. In a few days, the men
were equipped and ready to go. No need for volunteers. There
wasn't a man who did not want to avenge Custer's death. When
Mary bade her husband goodbye, she clung to him a moment
longer than usual. Would she see him again? She did not try
to hold him when the bugle called; she knew she could not.
He was eager to get started. Promising to write, he strode off,
erect in his blue uniform, booted and spurred and with his
pistol holstered at his hip.

His first letter was written to Mary from Yankton, Dakota
Territory, on the 16th of July. The tone showed his preoccupa-
tion with the task ahead of him; his anxiety to meet the Sioux
who promised to be even more skilled a foe than the Kiowas or
southern Cheyennes.

> This has been a very busy day as the steamer arrived at
> twelve noon and before dark the command was all on board
> and now we are waiting to set sail. I expect we will go up this
> river and the Yellowstone seventeen hundred miles before we
> take wagon transportation. The Captain thinks it will be fif-
> teen or sixteen days before we reach the head of the river
> transportation.
>
> Of course we receive all sorts of Indian reports and rumors,
> but they sound very much like those we heard when we started
> out before, after the fight at Adobe Walls. Many think before
> we get up there the Indians will be gone, either south or far
> north.

"Steamer" E. H. Durfee
Upper Missouri
July 20, 1876

As we passed Fort Sully the officers came down to the river
bank and signalled "Success," which was answered by some of

our officers. We passed the Cheyenne Agency and several large camps of Sioux — saw many women and children, but very few men, indicating that the families are being fed by the Government while the men are fighting the troops. Some of the soldiers who are stationed at the Cheyenne Agency informed the men of this command that there had appeared in their camps U. S. pistols of a recent mark. It may be possible that some of them were taken from Custer's Command.

Missouri River
Near Standing Rock Agency
July 22, 1876

Tomorrow morning we hope to reach Fort Lincoln. As we passed Standing Rock Agency we learned that seven warriors had come in the day before from Custer's fight, one of them wounded. They admit having suffered severely in that engagement and are now doing what they can to urge the others not to go out. The officer in command, Captain Bland of the Sixth Infantry, informed me that as near as he could learn the traders at that place had sold the Indians about one hundred thousand rounds of ammunition. Another establishment in which the Belknap creatures were interested.[10] He gave the name of one Indian who, when he went out took three thousand rounds. I will gather some facts, if not altogether agreeable, would be interesting.

I received a Bismark paper at the Standing Rock Agency, that said I was to garrison the new posts. I can hardly think so, or that they would exhaust the strength of the troops in such work, when a wild savage can place his followers between two Brigades, defy them both and out-general someone else. Still I will have two very good posts if I am to do that work. Possibly Sheridan is mad because the other four companies were ordered up and may have thought I had something to do with it.[11] I will disabuse his mind of it soon.

Fort Lincoln
July 23, 1876

I have time to write you but a few lines as I have been more than busy the few hours that we were detained here. We were inspected by General Baird and had to obtain supplies and recruits and are not crossing over to Bismark.

I sent a polite note up to Mrs. Custer and received an answer that I should see her. She seemed very glad to see me. You can have no idea of the gloom that over-hangs that post with twenty-seven widows. I never saw anything like it. Mrs. Custer is not strong and I would not be surprised if she did not improve. She seemed so depressed and in such despair. What makes it more unfortunate, she has scarcely any relatives of her own.

As the boat continued upriver, rumors continued to circulate. The Sioux had gone north to Fort Peck, had turned south to the Tongue River valley. They had scattered into small bands; thousands of warriors remained with Crazy Horse. Miles was confident his regiment was the equal of any number of Sioux warriors. Not only were his men expert marksmen, but they were trained athletes, fit, disciplined and eager. Experienced in Indian fighting, "they knew how to take care of themselves, were ever watchful, could not be surprised and were not afraid to meet the Indians under any circumstances or conditions . . ." "With such a command," Miles said, "I had no hesitation in going into any hostile country."[12]

Such confidence bordered on arrogance. The citizens who had seen the disaster wrought so recently by military conceit must have thought — here's another one.

The country grew wilder; the river narrower and faster. At one moment, it wound between high bluffs and, the next, flowed between flat, grassy meadows where herds of buffalo grazed. The buffalo grew more numerous, until the hills and valley were dark with them, moving slowly toward the river. A big bull plunged into the water, dust rising about him as the bank crumbled beneath his hoofs. Others followed him. The water, from shore to shore, was jammed with shaggy heads. Snorting and bellowing, the great beasts crashed against the sides of the boat and became entangled in the wheel. So numerous were the animals, the Captain had to signal "Stop" until the last buffalo had lumbered out on the opposite shore, water streaming from its flanks, to follow the herd across the prairie.

The country fascinated Miles. On the 29th of July, he wrote to Mary, datelining his letter:

> Yellowstone River
> One hundred miles from Buford and
> a thousand from civilization

We have had a day and a half sail on this beautiful river, passing through a new and almost unexplored country, wild and picturesque. I find this a much finer body of water than the Missouri, rapid, deep and clear with its banks well lined with timber. Along its banks we see an abundance of game and water fowls.

We can only sail from daylight, which is now about three o'clock, until about six o'clock, as the Captains are obliged to get wood along the river banks. While that was being done last evening the Companies went out and had a skirmish drill. The scene was quite an interesting one, with the two steamers lying at the banks near a dense forest, the troops drilling, the horses and mules grazing and, later in the evening as camp fires were built along the bank, the men on the upper deck singing some jolly songs with the moon shining brightly over the clear waters. It was a scene for an artist.

They have on board some cavalry horses, rations and two Napoleon guns with about eleven hundred rounds of ammunition. These are unsuitable for this service and it is a shame that troops are compelled to go into such unequal fights half equipped when they could be better organized. The ordnance department is not supposed to know anything about this kind of service, for they are never here, and its head spent his time during the war at West Point. Sheridan represents the honor of the army without studying or confidence in anything but cavalry; and Sherman unfortunately does not take that interest or positive action in the organization and details of the army that it sadly needs. Such matters as clothing, shoes, horse equipment and ordnance are left to worthless staff officers or obscure clerks.

I hear many complaints that men who were in Custer's fight were unable to reload their pistols, that the shells stuck in their pieces and that from these defects many became disabled.

I hope to hear some news from the front by a steamer that we are looking for, and that I expect to send this by. I am very much afraid that we will be too late for the next movement, owing to the inexcusable blundering of someone sending us up the river from Yankton as the steamer was already at Bismark, and had we gone there we would have been a week ahead and in time for the next movement. The command is in fine spirits and every preparation made to make it very efficient. I had drills three times a day on shore and boat and have just had officers' instructions in the cabin. In fact the steamer, ever since we came aboard, has been as busy as a bee-hive, and I believe the command will be in fine condition when we arrive in the hostile country. If we succeed in driving the Indians, which I have no doubt we will, I presume they will retreat north, and in that event we will be a long way from communication. As it is now, there is no regular mail communication from Fort Buford. They pretend to have a mail about once a week, but sometimes I presume it is nearer six weeks then six days.

We may not be able to get this boat up this river, and may be compelled to march a part of the way. I shall be anxious until I can get some communication with or see General Terry, as I fear he may move before we get up there and we be left to look after the supply camp or posts. I understand that General Crook was going to get ready to move — he has been doing that for a year — on August 1st, and if he does Terry will not wait for us or the 22nd Inf. Another instance of sending troops into the field and fighting them in detail.

If your father will get me some data regarding our earlier relations with the Indians, from the days of Pontiac and Red Jacket to Sitting Bull, he will do me a very great favor. He has an abundance of time and the data is there, in the libraries of Cleveland.

Yellowstone River
Near Rosebud
August 2, 1876

We are nearing General Terry's supply camp which is said to be opposite the mouth of the Rosebud, on the north side. Last evening we met the "Far West" which left General Terry's command at two o'clock. Major Moore had two guns and two companies on board going down to the mouth of Powder River to look for Indians. It seems that there had been left about sixty tons of grain at that point without guard, which the Indians have since destroyed. The steamer "Carrol" that preceeded us with the 22nd Inf., was fired into there. As we passed we saw an army wagon thrown into the river, some scattered grain on the bank and signs of Indians about. Passing on a few miles we saw a party of four going in that direction. I doubt if Major Moore's party will be able to do any good. He informed me that there was no news at the front, that the command has fallen back to the Rosebud and I presume are waiting reinforcements. The officers seem to be very much stampeded and demoralized, but I trust the same spirit does not exist at the front, or at least if it does that this command will be able to reassure them. I doubt if General Terry will have over a thousand fighting men in line after taking out the guards for steamboats, supply camp and trains. Still that force, well organized and handled, ought to go through any body of Indians. I somewhat doubt if we find any Indians to the southwest, although that is the impression here. I somehow feel that the main body has gone northwest, possibly on the Musselshell. From all I can learn from the officers, General Crook makes no comments or gives General Terry any information. I think it almost a military crime that these two commands are not under one head and governed by the simplest principles of warfare. This river is the natural base for both commands, when operating so near together. I am really more than anxious to get up, for we ought to meet with a success within a few days or develop stronger resistence than anything that has yet been shown, and one little success would change the whole feeling in regard to those Indians. At almost every stopping place we have disembarked (in three minutes) and had battalion and scout drill, so that this command at least will be in fine condition and quite strong. The recruits are doing remarkably well.

CHAPTER VIII

I N SPITE OF what he had seen and heard, Miles did not share the terror that gripped the frontier as the result of Custer's defeat. Travel had ceased. Communications were cut. Settlers cowered in their homes. Terry and Gibbon clung together at the mouth of the Big Horn. The trooper who ventured out of sight of camp was apt to loose his scalp. Miles was sailing boldly up the Yellowstone on the 27th of July when Terry and Gibbon — after at last hearing from Crook — left the camp on the Big Horn to join Crook on the Rosebud. The men badly needed encouragement, especially Gibbon's force, which was designated the Montana Column. This force left Fort Shaw near Great Falls in March expecting to join Crook and Terry within a few weeks. The men suffered frostbite and snow-blindness. When they reached the appointed rendezvous on the Big Horn, Crook had returned to Fort Fetterman after his abortive attack on the Cheyenne village and Terry had not yet started from Abraham Lincoln.

"General Terry," Lieutenant Bradley of the Montana Column reported in his journal, "fears that the Indians may combine and get the better of us; and we are therefore to cease our advance for the present and remain in this vicinity until further orders, in a state of inactivity unless sure of striking a successful blow. Now for a tedious camp life and a long campaign."[1]

From the twenty-first of April until the ninth of June when Terry met Gibbon on the Powder River, the Montana Column remained inactive in the field.

After four days' hard marching from the 27th of July to the 30th, the commands of Terry and Gibbon, reinforced by the remnants of the Seventh Cavalry, reached the mouth of the Rosebud. On August 1, Lieutenant Colonel E. S. Otis arrived on the steamer *Carroll* with six companies of the Twenty-second Infantry, and on the day following the steamer *Durfee,* carrying Miles and the Fifth Infantry, reached the headquarters camp. The day was hot and sultry. The Sioux had burned the grass in their rear and smoke hazed the distant prairie and badlands. "The entire country seemingly on fire," wrote an eye-witness. Among the cottonwoods on the riverbank stood rows of tents. Horses, under the watchful eye of herders, grazed on the hills. Cavalry mounts stamped on the picket lines. Mules brayed in the improvised corral close by the lines of wagons. Some of the men inspected equipment; others gathered in groups to discuss the reinforcements and to speculate on the whereabouts of the Indians. Blacksmiths hammered on shoes which had been lost during the march. Recruits sweated, heaving supplies from the steamers to the riverbank. Men slept, wrote letters, read their mail and gambled the pay they had received three days before on the draw of a card. A general air of confusion and indecision permeated the camp. We can imagine Miles debarking from the *Durfee* with his troops from Leavenworth, well equipped and disciplined, and Miles himself, vital and confident, striding forward to Terry whom he had asked to be his groomsman seven years before.

The man who had not hesitated to storm Fort Fisher had lost his initiative. On the 4th of August, Miles wrote Mary from camp opposite Rosebud, Montana.

We arrived here on the 2nd and found everybody pleased to see us. I must say that I found matters entirely different from what I expected. I never saw a command so completely stampeded as this, either in the volunteer or regular service, and I believe entirely without reason. I expected to find everything on the other side ready to move, yet to my surprise I was ordered to disembark on this side, thereby losing at least two days. The same thing happened to the 22nd Inf., which today is marching down to the steamer to cross to the other side. As we lost seven days in coming up, we will lose at least five here, and during this time I presume Crook will make his move so that the same miserable lack of cooperation will be witnessed. No one here knows where Crook is or the Indians, although the latter seem to be hanging about the Powder River. The party that went down on the "Far West" recovered some fifty tons of the oats that had been abandoned there and scattered by the Indians. The corn had been taken. The steamboat captain and two scouts went out a few miles and met a small party of Indians. One scout was killed, and they killed one Indian with one of the Seventh Cavalry carbines in his hands.[2]

As the command is now crossing the river on steamboats I presume we will get over in time to start day after tomorrow or the day following. It is expected that we will move up the Rosebud and develop the Indians or find Crook.

General Terry seems very friendly disposed but says nothing about a command, although there are a collection of parts of regiments here under junior officers. He does not seem very enthusiastic or to have much heart in the enterprise. They begin to talk about going in, in October, and I shall be happily surprised if the thing is not a dead failure and results in the lasting disgrace of the army. If it does, Congress would be fully justified in disbanding the army next winter and reorganizing it again, for this campaign thus far would not have been creditable to a militia organization. These may seem singular statements for me to make, but I am prepared to back them up by overwhelming evidence of facts.

I do not wish to stop on this river and build posts unless I am allowed to continue active operations this winter. I certainly have no desire to go back to Leavenworth without doing anything. I should feel like going in the back way in the night. I know military operations would be far more effective and less expensive if matters of administration were not so much neglected. There is no trouble with the men, but with the officers, both high and low. It is now costing nearly one thousand dollars a day for steamboats on this river to do what a few pontoon boats would do. We have one curiosity here and that is an ordnance officer, the only one that has been in the field (except during the War) since the Utah campaign.

Camp at the Mouth of Rosebud
August 7, 1876

We are still at this point, sweltering in the sun, doing nothing, and I am supremely disgusted as this useless delay seems fatal to the success of this enterprise. I think General Terry lost his chance when he retreated after Custer's battle. From all accounts the Indians had had enough of fighting and were retreating as rapidly as possible, laden with their numerous dead and wounded and throwing away their packs, etc. But after that fight there seems to have been nothing done but retreat, and the worst kind of demoralization and timidity is displayed by the officers. Although I brought up a fine command in perfect condition and fully equipped, yet I find myself brigaded under Gibbon, and of course have nothing to do but creep along with the expedition. I think a little more enterprise and courage with this command would be valuable, even if there is no cooperation or communication between the two commands. I hope we may be successful, but it looks more like an organization for a walk-around. When they get tired of it I hope I may get a chance, as I would willingly undertake this affair with one third the number of troops now in the field. But it would require more energy and persistency than I see displayed. Gibbon is anxious to go to California, and I think it would be a good plan to let him go, and Terry would do better down south. If this kind of campaigning is continual it will last a year or two without much credit to the army.

We start with about forty days' supplies and draw a small amount in the supply camp. The river is running down very rapidly and it is somewhat doubtful if the steamers will get up again. They have been kept here ferrying us across, which should all have been done when we arrived here. All of these river men say that the Yellowstone is not navigable after this month, so that chance of our having to come in for supplies seems probable, if for no other reason.

I regret that I cannot write in better spirit, but as we have already lost fourteen valuable days it does not seem very encouraging. All are well and in fine spirits, though very impatient to get away. With the stores we brought up we have fitted out three battalions. I have not received letters yet and do not expect any for a month, as I presume the "Key West" will not be up until after we leave.

The more I see of movements here the more admiration I have for Custer, and I am satisfied his like will not be found very soon again.

How Miles chafed at being brigaded under Gibbon! The commander of the Montana Column, Miles felt, had failed like Terry. The slight bearded Colonel on the Yellowstone lacked the courage of the Major General at Reams Station. What had happened to the two commanders? Had they been intimidated by the vast and ruthless land? Confused by the darting, primitive foe? Miles could not have helped hearing how Gibbon had twice failed to attack a great village of Sioux which his chief of scouts, Lieutenant Bradley had discovered, once on the Tongue River and once on the Rosebud. The first time, Gibbon had prepared for the attack. The officers had written letters home; the Crow scouts had stripped and painted for war. Then, when the troops experienced difficulty crossing the river, Gibbon changed his mind and decided to leave the village alone.

"And so," Bradley wrote, "we failed to march against the foe.

There ever will be a difference of opinion as to the propriety of the course pursued, but as I am not writing a critical history I will not take this advantage of my fellow officers to record mine."[3]

A second time Bradley discovered a village, probably the same one which had moved to the Rosebud, but, although the troops camped only eighteen miles away, Gibbon made no move to march on the hostiles.

There is little doubt that, in his customary outspoken manner, Miles expressed his opinion of such tactics. Unmolested, the Indians in the village had combined with the Sioux Crook had failed to pursue after the Rosebud, to wipe out Custer's command on the Little Big Horn.

Miles was still "disgusted" when, on the eighth, the command resumed the march along the Rosebud to meet Crook. The weather remained sultry and the march was delayed by numerous crossings of the river which corkscrewed between sandstone bluffs. Gradually, the valley widened and the timber thinned out. At the end of the day, the troops had only gone nine miles. That night, the temperature dropped eighty degrees and the following day, the long line of infantry, cavalry and wagons marched in a cold, drizzling rain ten miles! Was this the way the command was going to conduct a campaign against Sitting Bull and Crazy Horse? Miles could hardly contain himself.

On the morning of the tenth, which was again clear, when the troops were marching up the valley a large cloud of dust was seen rising behind a spur of hills. Scouts whipped their ponies back to the column shouting, "Sioux! Sioux!" The cry flashed along the column. At last, they were going to have a chance to fight the elusive hostiles! The troopers of the Seventh, remembering the Little Big Horn, settled grimly in their saddles. Leaping from their ponies, the Crow scouts began to strip and paint their faces. Orders cracked along the line. Trumpets shrilled. The cavalry swung into a skirmish line across the valley with one wing resting on the bluffs and the other on the timbered riverbank. Infantry moved into position on the flanks while the wagon train raced into the protective rectangle.

Down the valley galloped a single horseman. White man? Indian? A white man showy in fringed buckskins, long yellow hair and goatee. William Cody, better known as Buffalo Bill, scouting for Merritt who had joined Crook on Goose Creek.

The dust? That was Crook's column. In a moment they were in sight. Men swore, feeling cheated. But perhaps, now they had met Crook, they'd take after the Sioux in earnest. Here they came, the dust hazing about the horsemen and fluttering guidons. As Crook's column approached, the cavalry leading Terry's advance at a rapid trot opened up like a fan launching a sheaf of skirmishers to the front. Who could fail to recognize the dash of the dead Custer's beloved Seventh? Hats were waved. Men cheered.

"Never before or since," wrote Lieutenant Charles King of the Fifth Cavalry, "has the valley of the Rosebud beheld such a gathering."[4]

Crook sent his aide to Terry to invite the General and his staff to visit his camp. A long strip of canvas was stretched on the ground beneath the cottonwoods. Eating utensils were borrowed from the pack train. Two huge coffeepots were set to boil on the fire and the cook busied himself preparing what rations were available. The meeting between the two commanders was cordial. Terry wore regulation blue uniform. Crook presented his customary disreputable figure in frayed trousers and shirt, his great beard straggling over his chest.

Bourke, Crook's aide, was impressed by Terry's scholarly air and gentle, charming manner. Terry was unaffected and affable in contrast to Crook who was "reticent and taciturn to the extreme of sadness, brusque to the verge of severity."[5]

Was Crook, too, haunted by the ghost of the golden-haired Custer? He would not concede defeat at the Rosebud. If he had pursued the Indians, he wrote later in his official report, his command might have met the same fate as Custer's. The Sioux were not ordinary Indians. ". . . With improved arms, I have seen our friendly Indians, riding at full speed, shoot and kill a wolf, also on the run, while it is a rare thing that our troops can hit an Indian on horseback . . . The Sioux is a cavalry soldier from the time he has intelligence enough to ride a horse or fire a gun . . . Even with their lodges and families, they can move at a rate of fifty miles per day."[6] The Sioux were familiar with the country. They had spies and hunting parties out all the time who reported on the number and movement of the troops. They could choose or avoid conflict as they wished. He had not, Crook wrote, requested reinforcements from the division commander because he had not wanted to embarrass him. "I mention this simply from the fact that there has been much of an unpleasant nature said in regard to the matter."

Sheridan cannot have been pleased by such excuses. The public was clamoring for punishment of the Indians who had murdered Custer. The newspapers demanded to know what was wrong with the military. (A familiar refrain by this time.) The dissatisfaction was reflected on the Rosebud by Colonel (brevet Major General) Eugene Carr, second in command to Merritt, who commented as Buffalo Bill introduced him to Grant Marsh. "Captain, I've heard of you and the way you do things and I told Bill I wanted to meet you. I'm mighty glad, sir, to know ONE LIVE MAN up in this country. They seem to be extremely rare!"[7]

Criticism of Crook was tempered by the news that Crook's one-time subordinate and greatest admirer, Rutherford B. Hayes, had been nominated for the presidency of the United States. An officer who had the backing of the President could afford to make a mistake, now and then, although to do Crook justice, he did not attempt to profit by this relationship.

Crook did not like to discuss the battle of the Rosebud. Was it because he could not prove victory? Crook was only one of the men who sought to justify himself in that sprawling camp along the tributary of the Yellowstone. There were other men tortured by doubt, by regret, by fear and frustration. Men like Reno, leading the remnants of the Seventh Cavalry, eyes bitter with memories of the Little Big Horn. Miles's criticism rubbed salt into wounds. Bourke, championing his hero, Crook, would not mention Miles in his report of the camp on the Rosebud. Others spoke of him briefly, which leads us to believe Miles was not popular. Critics seldom are liked and Miles was not hesitant about expressing his opinion of a bungled campaign.

Undoubtedly, Terry breathed a sigh of relief when Miles was detached to patrol the Yellowstone. Crook had brought word the Indians had left the Big Horn mountains and, passing around his right, had turned eastward toward the Tongue. The scouts found the trail over the low hills stamped into dust by the hoofs of thousands of ponies. Terry and Crook decided to follow this trail while Miles was to guard the fords of the Yellowstone to prevent the hostiles turning north to Canada.

On the 12th of August, Miles wrote Mary.

Headquarters Yellowstone Line

When I last wrote you I was very much annoyed at the delays and what seems to me to be a waste of important time. I expressed little confidence in the success of the movement. I was quite right, as we made only ten miles a day for two days, and then came on the third day on a trail Crook was following, some three to seven days old. Had we moved soon after our arrival, or thoroughly scouted the country south, we would have come upon the body of Indians in Crook's front. But as it is, it is well that the two commands have joined. General Crook and his command looked very rough.

It seems of little use to keep that large command together, which was the first idea, for the Indians could have fought Crook or Terry separately if they had wanted to fight. But I think poor Custer nearly broke their back.

I suggested to General Terry that it would be well that the fords of the Yellowstone be guarded to prevent the Indians going north; and after some consultation he gave me the order to "go." I took four companies of my regiment and made one of the most extraordinary marches ever made by infantry troops. We had just completed a most fatiguing and severe march of sixteen miles. We rested a couple of hours for coffee and then started until one o'clock, took a rest of two hours and a half and then marched to the Yellowstone, thirty-four or six miles. We made forty three miles in twenty-four consecutive hours, which is one of the best marches ever made, and as we were in the Sioux country we had to march prepared to fight, which was of course more difficult. The march was as hard as any I ever knew or have read of. The dust was perfectly blinding, and we must have left a cloud of dust equal to that made in ordinary times by a corps. The night was cloudy for part of the way and dark, and the ground rough and covered with cactus and sage brush. The men would stumble along and the troops go through their army shoes, yet they went through to the River in the best of spirits, though utterly exhausted. Nearly all of the officers held up until the last few miles. They will get rested on the steamer and at the station.

At the mouth of the Rosebud I established a ferry for crossing the supply train when it reaches that point. I organized a large scouting party to go down on the north side of the

Yellowstone, comprised of a detachment of cavalry and about 250 Crow allies, and also a small force to come down in small boats. I have stationed my troops near the mouth of the Tongue and Powder Rivers, and am patrolling the river to prevent the Indians escaping north if possible. I am of the opinion that some have already gone north, but this movement has been very rapid, and is in time for intercepting any force in front of Terry and Crook. They start with all the rest of their forces, with pack animals, in the hope of overtaking the Indians in their front. I find that it will not be safe to go over the rapids below this point with the expectation of getting back. Therefore, we will keep above this point for the present. I am just sending a scout through, and hope he will return with word from you. It is now time for him to leave and I must close.

Mouth of Powder River, M. T.
August 20, 1876

It is exceedingly gratifying to write you with the expectation of its going through and of receiving a reply, or as I hope many precious letters. As I told General Terry this morning, one of the misfortunes of this command was that it was commanded by a bachelor. There seemed to be no effort made to bring up the mail. I got tired of waiting, so I proposed to send Sergeant Mitchell and seven men down the river in a skiff, with directions to get a mount of horses at Buford[8] and return as speedily as possible. I expect them to return with a month and a half mail from my own precious darling.

Since I last wrote you I have been more than busy. On the tenth we met Crook's command making one of his magnificent scouts, as senseless and ill advised as it was fruitless. After a month of delay and preparation he leaves his train with fifteen days' supply. We met him, or he joins us, with his animals nearly exhausted on a trail fifteen days old, according to some scouts and to others ten or five days old, but anyway so old that he had not the remotest chance of catching the Indians. Had he not got some supplies from this command he would have been compelled to travel back on his own trail at the end of the seventh day.

When it seemed probable that the Indians would attempt to cross the Yellowstone and go north, I was sent out with my command to make a forced march to prevent such a movement. I had my command deployed for two hundred ten miles along this line. After six days march on the trail, the two commands came in here for rest and supplies without seeing an Indian or exchanging a shot, and this is what is called Indian campaigning! The truth is there is not a man here who has studied this question close enough or paid enough attention to his profession to conduct an Indian campaign. Terry means well enough, and is decidedly the best man, but he has had little experience and is too much under the influence of those slow, ineffective men like Gibbon to reap good results. This business to be successful should be conducted on sound military principles first, and then with great energy and persistency.

We expect to move south east in three or four days, in the hopes of finding the Indians. We start with fifteen days supplies and wind up at Lincoln or the Black Hills. As I said some time ago, when this proves a failure I hope I may get a chance, or be retired to Fort Lincoln where I can enjoy the most delightful domestic felicity.

I have written a long letter to Wendal Phillips,[9] in reply to his assault on Custer. I have two reasons for this. I think we ought to defend Custer. It gives me an opportunity to write something for him which I have desired to do, and then I do not think the Army should knuckle down and allow a man to hold it up to the world as below the level of humanity. I expect he will come back strong, but I do not propose to allow him to have it all his own way.

It now looks as if this campaign could not last long, as I think we will be out of supplies in twenty or thirty days. Everybody is in hopes the Indians will be so good as to return to their Agencies, which would surely be a great accomodation to us. I could then return in time to see the Centennial and to get my precious ones together before winter.

The time spent on these barren plains seems so much lost.

It is entirely different now with me from what it was during the War when I was a bachelor. I could afford the precious hours then, but I cannot now, and I believe this will be my last campaign in this kind of service. I would like the chance of closing this, but after that I have no ambition of engaging in another. You can have no idea of the barrenness of this country.

I have received no word from the other four companies of my regiment. The companies here are getting rested and will be in good trim for the next march. The Fifth has excelled all others in making their forty-three miles in twenty-four consecutive hours.

Miles's anger had become discouragement. He saw no chance of accomplishing anything in the Sioux country. The patrol of the river was the only bright spot in the campaign. Miles and Grant Marsh, on whose boat Miles made the patrol, got along famously. Marsh was impressed by the speed of Miles's march from the headquarters camp to the Yellowstone where the *Far West* waited at the bank, and Miles, in turn, appreciated how quickly Marsh got up steam and, within a short time, was steering his boat down the river with troops aboard. Marsh was a man after Miles's own heart, physically brave and aggressive. A friendship sprang up between the two men that was to last a lifetime. Marsh greatly admired Miles, who, he said, "never found any work too hard to be performed, any danger too great to be faced, when duty demanded it; who gladly shared with his men every privation and peril to which they were exposed, and whose watchful care for their welfare knew no relaxation."[10]

The pilot and the army officers gathered in the little house on the roof of the *Far West* to watch for Indians or signs of Indians on the wooded banks of the river. It was raining; the river had fallen and Marsh had difficulty navigating. For hours on end,

Miles watched the shores, asking questions about the country and the Indians. No detail was small enough to escape his attention. In the afternoon, the *Far West* reached the mouth of the Tongue River where Miles put a company ashore to guard the ford. The 13th of August, another company was debarked on the Powder, and a few days later Captain Rice was put ashore at the mouth of Glendive Creek with a company of infantry and a fieldpiece. At this latter point, the men on the boat saw small groups of Indians in the distance and signal smokes rising from the bluffs, which led Miles to believe the Sioux might be going to cross, or had already crossed, the river en route to Canada. This was significant news. Miles conferred with Terry, and, while he was in camp, wrote to Mary.

> Powder River
> August 24, 1876

We are just on the eve of another movement. The command came in here six days ago, and after what I think has been an unfortunate delay we are about to start again. I have only four of my companies with me as Captain Bennett has been left at the mouth of Tongue River and Rice at Glendive about seventy miles below this point. These I expect will go down by steamer. Rice's company with one rifle gun was left to guard the crossings below. He reported Indians in his vicinity two days ago, and I have been very anxious to take the rest of my command down there as I believe it is much better to go directly where we know the Indians are than to hunt up an old trail that has been made nearly a month. Besides I think this command of two departments should not leave one company alone with the Indians near it. But Rice is well entrenched and is confident of holding his own. I hope we may be successful in this movement, but I have little confidence in it. There is too much demoralization in these commands, and everyone is anxious to get home.

When Miles returned to his patrol of the Yellowstone, he was accompanied by Buffalo Bill. Cody, already famous as a show-man, was tall and remarkably handsome in his fancy fringed buckskins, high riding boots and broad-brimmed sombrero. At his hip he wore a revolver and a bowie knife. His yellow hair hung to his shoulders. His mustache and goatee were auburn. Cody was another man whom Miles appreciated, and while Marsh guided the *Far West* through the rapids, which were falling dangerously low for a steamboat, Cody recounted the story of his fight with Yellow Hand, the Cheyenne chief, a month before. To Cody, scouting by riverboat was a novelty which he enjoyed, although he was not to remain on the *Far West* for the entire trip. At Glendive Creek, Captain Rice reported that, the day before, he had fired on a party of Indians with the Rodman cannon. Miles decided to remain overnight at Glendive and to send Buffalo Bill to Terry with word of the attempted crossing of the river by the Indians. Marsh was concerned when he heard Cody was going to ride seventy-five miles through the badlands to Terry's camp and warned him about making the trip, but the scout laughed and, leading his horse down the gangplank, rode off into the fading twilight.

Late the following night, Marsh was awakened by someone shaking his shoulder. It was Cody who had delivered the dispatches to Terry and ridden back the same dangerous route. With his instinct for the dramatic, Cody grinned.

"Captain, have the steward get me something to eat, can you? I'm hungry."[11]

The news that Cody brought Terry caused the latter to change his plans. While Miles was patrolling the river, Terry and Crook were following the Indian trail which Crook's scouts discovered leading toward the Tongue. The Shoshonis were about to leave Crook's command but Frank Grouard, in whom

Crook placed so much trust, was still with him. In the bushes near the Tongue, the scouts discovered the skeletons of two miners who had been caught and burned alive by the Sioux. The remains of the murdered white men lay beside the tracks of Indian ponies and travois poles that led over a high divide onto a plateau tufted with grass and thence to Pumpkin Creek and on to the badlands where wind and water had erroded the chalky soil into weird and fantastic shapes. It rained and the horses bogged down in the mud. There was no grass. The water tasted of alkali. Mile after mile, the troops struggled through deep ravines and tortuous gullies. Not an Indian was to be seen. The citizen scouts insisted the trail was comparatively fresh. The Crows said the trail had been made at least nine days ago. Supplies grew low and it was decided to march to the Powder to recuperate and take on new stores.

In the camp on the 22nd of August, Terry told Matthew Carrol, his wagon master, that Crook was to be supplied and that the Montana Column was to meet its wagon train at Fort Buford and go home. No troops were to be left behind to pursue the campaign and unless he (Terry) received contrary orders, no post was to established at Tongue river.

Crook received his supplies and marched for the Black Hills. At Slim Buttes, Anson Mills, of Crook's command, surprised and attacked the village of American Horse. This was Crook's only engagement with the Sioux on the march and was not followed up due to the exhausted condition of the command. Terry, after receiving the dispatches brought him by Buffalo Bill from Miles turned obliquely to the Yellowstone, marching over high, hilly country seared black by Sioux fires. Just above O'Fallon's Creek, he went into camp. On the twenty-seventh, he crossed the river on the steamers *Carroll* and *Yellowstone* and took up the trail again which led through the empty, barren country of the Big Dry Fork of the Missouri River. Indian signs were plentiful — the ashes of old campfires, cast-off moccasins, broken trovois poles — but Sitting Bull and his hostile followers had vanished. On the 6th of September, the Montana Column was ordered home without having found the Sioux they had set out to fight nearly six months before. The country still belonged to the hostiles. Only one small detachment remained behind. Before Terry went back to his headquarters in St. Paul, he received an order from Sheridan directing him to designate Colonel Nelson A. Miles with the Fifth Infantry and Lieutenant Colonel Otis with six companies of the Twenty-second Infantry to establish a temporary cantonment at or near the mouth of Tongue River.

CHAPTER IX

MILES welcomed the order to build a cantonment on the Tongue. Give him, he said, additional troops and supplies and he'd clear the country of Indians before spring. Terry immediately discouraged Miles's hopes of commanding a major expedition against the hostiles. The troops, Terry said, could not endure the severity of the northern winters. Crook's expedition of the previous year had proved the costliness of fighting Indians after snowfall. This, to Miles, was like a red flag to a bull. He retorted that Crook's men had been ordered out from warm barracks onto the plains insufficiently clothed and equipped. The men of the Fifth Infantry were seasoned campaigners. The gentlemanly Terry lost his patience. Why should Miles think he could succeed where his superiors had failed? Miles presumed too much when he demanded fifteen hundred troops which was more than a colonel was entitled to command. Miles was allowed his own regiment of five hundred men and two companies of the Twenty-second Infantry. Six companies of the Twenty-second were given to Lieutenant Colonel E. S. Otis at Glendive Creek and six companies of the Sixth Infantry to Colonel W. B. Hazen at Fort Buford. The first camp was at the confluence of Glendive creek and the Yellowstone, and the latter was at the point where the Yellowstone flowed into the Missouri. The Montana troops, which included Miles's Fifth Infantry, were to construct and improve their cantonments and to provide a basis for a force to campaign against the hostiles the following summer. Terry, as commander of the Department of the Dakota, was Miles's superior. Terry, in turn, was subordinate to Sheridan who commanded the Division of the Missouri which comprised the Departments of the Platte and Dakota. Sheridan, Miles knew, favored winter campaigns. Crook, commanding the Platte, was preparing an expedition in Wyoming to go after Crazy Horse, and Sheridan was giving him full support. Mackenzie's Fourth Cavalry as well as infantry units had been assigned to Crook. The high-strung Mackenzie was a skilled Indian fighter. He drove himself and his troopers relentlessly. His temper had become unbearable — some said because of the pain of an old wound, others because of a blow on the head which had left him unconscious for days. As Miles knew from his experiences on the southern plains, Mackenzie was a commander who brought results. He'd give the necessary aggressiveness to Crook's force.

Miles had no intention of letting Crook steal all the glory. "They expected us to hive up," Miles snorted, "but we were not of the hiving kind."[1]

In a matter of weeks, Miles built the cantonment on the prairie where the Tongue River swirled into the Yellowstone. The bluffs beyond the camp were stubbled with pine. Cottonwood fringed the river. The energetic Grant Marsh brought most of the supplies upriver to the cantonment since low water discouraged other steamboat captains from attempting Wolf Rapids between the mouth of the Tongue and Glendive Creek. The remainder of the supplies had to be taken off the boats below the rapids and carried overland by wagons. The new post was primitive. Buildings were constructed of vertical cottonwood logs chinked with mud and roofed with poles; warm enough in winter, one officer observed, but damned uncomfortable in wet weather when the mud melted. At the end of a month Miles wrote his uncle-in-law, Sherman, that the cantonment was nearly complete and was already a better-looking post than Camp Supply, Indian Territory. He had, Miles told Sherman, scouted the valley, which he considered unlike any country he had seen — alkali cliffs and bluffs, high-level prairies, ravines, lava beds. Miles foresaw that one day, when Montana had been made safe for settlers, cattle would graze on the native bunch grass. There would be ranches and towns. What wealth this vast new Territory would bring to the Union! But Miles did not tell Sherman of this dream of the future. He concentrated on the present military aspect of the situation. The Indians, he said, could easily outdistance a command on wheels. Therefore he had asked for pack animals.[2] The use of pack animals was not original with Miles. Crook was famous for the reliance he placed on his mules, but Miles would not admit he followed Crook's example. The fact that Crook commanded a Department and he only a regiment still annoyed him. He made a crack at Crook and, indirectly, at Sheridan, by saying the "wise" decision to disarm the Indians at the agencies, a task that engaged Crook and Ranald Mackenzie the latter part of October, had driven more hostile rifles into the field than had been taken by the disarming. This statement would have been difficult to prove. It was true, however, that many Indians had slipped away from Standing Rock and Red Cloud to join the hostiles when they learned they were going to have to give up their guns and ponies. The middle of October, Miles wrote Sherman he'd had a report that a thousand lodges had left the agency for the Yellowstone.[3] Unlike Gibbon and Crook, Miles made the most of his Intelligence Service. Profiting from his experience on the southern plains, he employed Indian spies, runners and dissidents among the hostiles to inform him of the enemy's movements. From these people he learned that Sitting Bull with the Hunkpapas, Minneconjous and Sans Arcs was moving north of the Yellowstone to the Big Dry of the Missouri while Crazy Horse with the Oglalas and Cheyennes was traveling to the headwaters of the Tongue and Rosebud rivers. For additional information, Miles relied on the famous Yellowstone Kelly. Buffalo Bill, who had experienced enough adventures, had gone back east to stage a Wild West show. Kelly was as picturesque as Cody and, in the opinion of many on the frontier, a more able scout. Kelly saw Miles for the first time on the banks of the Powder during the confusion of equipping Crook for his departure for the Black Hills. Kelly admired the big infantry colonel with the icy blue eyes, "in the full vigor and flush of manhood."[4] Miles took to Kelly, too. The scout was a broad-shouldered, muscular man with shoulder-length black hair and black eyes. Well educated, he led the free life of the frontier because it appealed to him. He moved like an Indian and knew the country as did few white men. The preceding summer, he had been hunting in the Big Horns and knew nothing about the Custer Massacre. When rumors reached him of the military activities on the upper Missouri, he hurried to Tongue River to offer his services as a scout. Before he came into the cantonment, he killed an immense bear and, on the spur of the moment, sent the paw to the Fifth Infantry commander as his calling card, a flourish that appealed to Miles who promptly hired the scout. To enable Kelly to make long trips by himself, Miles gave him two of his best horses, one of them a thoroughbred.

It was not Yellowstone Kelly, however, or one of the Indian scouts who first discovered the hostiles, but a private of the Fifth Infantry named Cassidy who volunteered to carry dispatches from Tongue River to Buford. By a stroke of luck Cassidy ran across the Indians, although at the time, the trembling soldier considered himself anything but lucky. He was traveling by night and hiding by day as did all couriers in that part of the country and while he was lying on top of a bluff the morning of the second day out of the cantonment, he saw a party of Sioux crossing the Yellowstone. All day he watched them milling about among the cottonwoods and splashing into the water, ponies hauling baggage on travois poles, squaws, children, dogs and armed warriors. As soon as it grew dark, Cassidy started back to the cantonment to inform Miles, who was delighted to learn the whereabouts of the elusive hostiles. Cassidy was promoted and a message sent to Terry who ordered Reno and the Seventh Cavalry — temporarily patrolling the north bank of the Yellowstone — to cut off the Indians at the Missouri. Cavalry could move faster than infantry in this case. But by the time the Seventh arrived at Wolf Point the Indians had crossed the river and were sixty miles north. Feeling it was useless to pursue the Sioux further, the Seventh gave up the chase and, shortly thereafter, was ordered back to Fort Lincoln. Miles's opinion of Reno's failure to pursue the Indians can be imagined. Such a defeatist spirit had permeated the army the previous winter and summer. Infantry could not cover the ground like cavalry but it could, at least, try.

In a letter of October sixteenth to Sherman, Miles wrote, "Tonight I am somewhat concerned about a wagon train out from Glendive as it has been seven days enroute and should have come in today. I shall start down to meet it tomorrow morning if my scouts do not bring me word of it tonight."

Miles did not know that his scouts had encountered a large body of Indians and one of the scouts had been killed. The next morning, the seventeenth, Miles set out to rescue the wagon train with 394 riflemen of the Fifth Infantry. They marched all day in blowing sand and dust. When darkness closed over the prairie, the men boiled a cup of coffee and resumed the march. In the morning, they met the wagon train escorted by Lieutenant Colonel Otis and five companies of the Twenty-second. As Miles had suspected, the Sioux had attacked the train which had been forced to return to Glendive where Otis reinforced the escort and started out again, fighting off repeated attacks from the Sioux, who saw an opportunity to capture the animals and food in the commissary wagons. Setting fire to the grass, the Indians charged through smoke, yelping and shooting, but their aim was poor and Otis kept stubbornly on his way. The morning of the second day, Sitting Bull told Johnny Brughière, a breed, to write a note which he sent to Otis.

> I want to know what you are doing traveling on this road. You scare all the buffalo away. I want to hunt on the place. I want you to turn back. If you don't I will fight you again. I want you to leave what you have got here, and turn back from here.
>
> I am your friend,
> SITTING BULL
> I mean all the rations you have got and some powder. Wish you would write as soon as you can.[5]

To this arrogant and at the same time pathetically childish note, Otis replied: Nothing doing. He was going on to Tongue River and if Sitting Bull wanted to fight, he'd be pleased to accommodate him. Otis's courage was admirable. He used good judgment and did not lose his head. The train pushed on and the Indians renewed the attack. Eventually, Sitting Bull asked for another parley. Otis would not meet with the chief and Sitting Bull would not come to see Otis, so three chiefs came in Sitting Bull's place to explain to Otis that they were mad because the white men were driving away the buffalo. They were hungry and had no ammunition. Otis told them they had wasted enough ammunition for several hunts by attacking the wagon train, but, figuring compromise was better than fighting all the way to Tongue River, he gave the Indians one hundred and fifty pounds of bread and two sides of bacon, which apparently satisfied Sitting Bull, for the Indians broke off the fight and when Miles marched up a day later on Cedar Creek, not a Sioux was to be seen.

Miles listened to Otis's report, told him to continue to Tongue River with the train the following morning and himself went in search of Sitting Bull.

"As we had come this far," Trumpeter Brown of B Company observed, "General was determined to give the redskins a chase."[6]

They marched all that day northeast toward the Big Dry of the Missouri, that immense stretch of country between the Missouri and Yellowstone in eastern Montana where the last of the buffalo grazed on the open prairie and in the deep coulees — the country that, two months before, Terry had called "inaccessible." Indian spies informed Miles that Sitting Bull intended to remain in the vicinity for the winter; that he planned to establish a camp approximately one hundred miles from Crazy Horse, so that communication could be maintained between the two hostile groups. The Indians would then hunt buffalo and raid isolated settlements for plunder. Sitting Bull seems to have seen no reason why the whites would not agree to these terms. He had been the victor in the summer's battles with United States troops. The country should be left to him. In times past the army had, sensibly, gone into winter quarters at the same time as the Indians. In the spring, when the hostiles had replenished their supplies, warfare could be resumed.

Even then, Long Dog, whom Miles considered one of the most incorrigible of Sitting Bull's men, was at Fort Peck trying to get ammunition.

Sitting Bull did not know, or did not care, that Miles was on his trail, for he was concluding a successful and leisurely hunt when Miles caught up with him on Cabin Creek, a stream fringed with cottonwoods in an empty, barren land. The Sioux had killed a quantity of buffalo and eaten well of roasted ribs. With the supplies taken from Custer's troops and from Black Hills citizens, they were fairly well supplied. Miles was still some distance away when his presence was discovered. The alarm was given and the warriors seized their rifles. One moment the dun colored prairie over which Miles was advancing lay silent and empty beneath the autumn sky. The next moment the bluffs surged with painted and befeathered warriors. Undaunted, the little force of men in blue deployed into line of battle and, with Miles in the lead, marched steadily forward. If Miles had stopped or ordered retreat in the face of superior numbers — he estimated there were over a thousand warriors to his 394 infantrymen — the Indians would have been on them like wolves, but the self-possession of the troops impressed Sitting Bull. As the soldiers drew nearer, one of the Indians galloped forward with a flag of truce. Sitting Bull wanted to meet and talk with the commanding officer. Miles, remembering the naked body of his friend on the hill above the Little Big Horn, did not trust the Sioux chief, but he decided to parley with Sitting Bull anyhow. During the interview, he might learn more about the condition and numbers of the hostiles. There was also the possibility he could persuade Sitting Bull to surrender without bloodshed. He agreed to a conference but a hitch developed when Sitting Bull insisted Miles come to the Indian lines to talk. Miles sent word that was impossible, the chief must come to him. In the end, it was

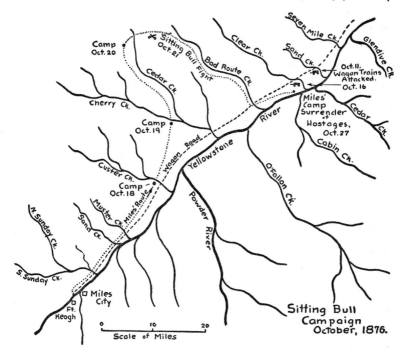

Sitting Bull
Campaign
October, 1876.

decided to meet between the lines. Miles went forward accompanied by Lieutenant Bailey and five enlisted men. Sitting Bull walked to meet him in company with five chiefs. Soldiers on one side and the mounted warriors on the other side watched as the Indians spread a buffalo robe on the ground. A cold wind stirred the dried grass of the prairie. The darkened skies threatened snow. Miles wore a coat trimmed with bear fur and, when the Indians noted this, they whispered in Sioux, "Bear Coat" — which was, ever afterwards, their name for Miles. Sitting Bull wore moccasins and leggings and a blanket wrapped about his waist.

Later, Miles described the distrust shared by the two leaders in a letter to Mary.

I have had two interviews with Sitting Bull under the flags of truce and a good opportunity to study his character. He is a man apparently forty-five or fifty years old. He has a large broad head and strong features. He is a man evidently of great influence and a thinking, reasoning being. I should judge his great strength is as a warrior. I think he feels that his strength is somewhat exhausted and he appeared much depressed, suffering from nervous excitement and the loss of power. Of course he was anxious to make the best terms possible, and had some absurd requests which were not listened to. I endeavored to explain to him the requirements of the Government and the advantage it would be for him to make peace. At times he was almost inclined to accept the situation, but I think partly from fear and partly through the belief that he might do better, he did not accept. I think that many of his people were desirous to make peace . . .[7]

"Big Leggins" Brughière acted as interpreter. Evidence suggests that he added to the mistrust by either deliberately or unintentionally mistranslating the conversation between the two men. Miles was suspicious enough already, as he wrote Mary.

In one of your letters you enquire if I thought of my darling little girls. I assure you that I did, almost constantly, as I thought he might become desperate and contemplate something like the Canby affair.[8] But I had been forewarned the night before. I can not explain the very singular dream that I had, but I woke up with a shock as I seemed to have been struck directly in the forehead by a ball or some powerful instrument. Of course I thought what could be the meaning of such a strange dream, and, without being alarmed, I thought, in view of meeting the Indians, I would take it as a warning from my guardian angel to avoid unnecessary danger. Therefore I took every precaution to have the ground covered by the guns and rifles of the command, and to show the Indians that any act of violence would result in their destruction. While sitting on my horse waiting for the line of savages to come up I thought of my darlings far away.

During the council I thought of the warning I had received. I endeavored to watch Sitting Bull all the time, as well as to keep my arms handy. At one time the young Indians continued their line until they had nearly formed a circle around us. I told Sitting Bull he must send them back, or the council would end at once. After that warning and my caution I was interested to learn from his interpreter that Sitting Bull had designed to kill me, or at least to make the attempt, but that he was persuaded from it by others, or what is quite likely was not given a good opportunity. I had no confidence in him but believed I could convince some of his chiefs that it was better for them to surrender, and in that I was successful. I created a dissatisfaction in their numbers, and made the results more easily attained. I formed quite a liking for Bald Eagle and Red Shirt,[9] and believe they had confidence in me.[10]

Significantly, no pipe was smoked at this parley. The reports of the council are sketchy. The Indian story differs from that of Miles. Suspicion distorted words and actions.

The heavy-set Indian and the lean, mustached officer eyed each other warily. Sitting Bull, Miles said, demanded to know why the troops had not gone into winter quarters as was their custom. Miles replied the soldiers were out to bring Sitting Bull into the agency. He — Miles — did not wish to continue the war but if Sitting Bull refused to co-operate, the war would be continued and would end, as all Indian wars ended, with the subjugation of the Indians to the government.

Then, according to Miles, Sitting Bull wanted to know how he knew where to find him. Miles, ignoring the direct question, replied he not only knew where to find Sitting Bull but where he had come from and where he was going.

Sitting Bull demanded, "Where am I going?"

"You intend," Miles said, "to remain here three days, and then move to the Big Dry and hunt buffaloes."

The answer appeared to infuriate the Sioux, who apparently suspected treachery on the part of his people. "His whole manner," Miles said, "appeared more like that of a wild beast than a human being; his face assumed a furious expression; his jaws were closed tightly; his lips were compressed, and you could see his eyes glistening with the fire of savage hatred."[11]

Miles had no arms except the revolver in his belt. Lieutenant Bailey was similarly equipped. While the two men were talking, a young warrior stepped up to Sitting Bull and slipped a carbine beneath his buffalo robe. A number of other Indians joined the six who had originally accompanied Sitting Bull between the lines. The soldiers, fidgeting with the strain of standing face to face with a thousand warriors who had taken part in the Custer Massacre, shifted position. The Indians, quick to see how the line of troops extended forward and around the council group, moved ahead. Tension mounted.

Move all Indians back to their original position, Miles told Sitting Bull sharply, or the conference will end at once.

The demand was reluctantly complied with. At any moment, a warrior might shoot Miles through the heart. Miles, fully aware of this, faced Sitting Bull outwardly calm. The slightest sign of fear would be fatal. He could not, Miles told Sitting Bull, continue to raid the settlements. The ultimatum angered Sitting Bull who was puffed with pride over his victories of the summer. The country, Sitting Bull retorted, belonged to the Indians and not to the white men.

The Sioux chief refused to compromise. Feeling that further talk was useless, Miles broke off the conference. He was angry and so was Sitting Bull. However, arrangements were made to continue the parley the following morning. Miles withdrew the troops three miles to the nearest timber and water. In the morning, soon after daylight, he moved back toward the Indian camp and, after a march of ten miles, discovered the Sioux tepees and pony herds. Sitting Bull again sent forward a flag of truce and the conference was resumed. With Sitting Bull were Pretty Bear, Bull Eagle, John Sans Arc, Standing Bear, Gall, White Bull and several others. According to the Indians, the more moderate chiefs had argued during the night for acceptance of government terms. Miles, on the contrary, seems to have decided a fight was inevitable and Sitting Bull impossible to deal with. This was borne out when Sitting Bull said he was anxious for peace but peace must be on his own terms. The soldiers must leave the country to the Indians. Military posts, lines of travel, settlements — all but a few trading posts where the Indians could obtain ammunition and supplies — must be abandoned. In other words, the Indians were to be the victors. The terms, Miles retorted, were out of the question. Sitting Bull must surrender to the government and put himself under government protection or accept the consequences. The conference was at an end. No advantage, Miles told the Sioux, would be taken of him under flag of truce. He would be allowed to return to camp, but, if he had not accepted the government terms within fifteen minutes, the troops would open fire.

Of course [Miles wrote Mary], his non-acceptance of our offer had to be considered an act of hostility and he was so informed.

I immediately started the command forward, and the Indians commenced burning the prairie. We opened the fight, they returning fire at once, and for sometime there was considerable fighting and maneuvering for position. I think their design was to draw us on to a position they had selected, and then, if they succeeded in occupying and holding it, they would make another Big Horn affair of it.[12]

Trumpeter Brown described the fight from the point of view of the soldier.

> The Indians started to move out, so General moved up . . . One of the Indians was setting the prairie on fire to our left. The General ordered one of the scouts to go out and stop him. The scout rode out and as he reached the point of the bluff he yelled at the Indian but fired at the same time. The Indian rolled over on the burning grass. We did not stop but kept straight ahead for the redskins on the bluffs. The opera had commenced . . .[13]

The fight continued most of the day among swirling clouds of smoke. Occasionally a warrior threw up his hands to sprawl from his racing pony. Soldiers were glimpsed, the upper parts of their bodies visible in the acrid fog, rifles leveled to fire, then the smoke obscured them from view. The fighting had a nightmarish quality. Flames flickered along the grass. Coughing, swearing troopers struggled to fix their sights on Indians who appeared and disappeared in the smoke like painted fiends. Most effective was the big gun which Miles brought to bear on the main body of Indians, but the fire power of the gun was offset by the mobility of the hostiles who were mounted while the soldiers fought on foot. At one time, the command was surrounded by Indians. Quickly Miles formed the troops into a hollow square. "Not a single man left his place," Miles observed proudly, "or failed to do his full duty."[14] Doggedly Miles kept after the hostiles, driving them from the hills and bluffs, through their camp and down Bad Route Creek. When darkness fell, Miles ordered the men into camp, selecting a circle of hills with the wagons corralled in a valley in the center. The fighting, so far, had been indecisive. Who could tell if the Indians would rally and stage a concerted attack on the little body of troops? In every man's mind were the stories he had heard of the scalped and mutiliated bodies on the Little Big Horn. Exhausted soldiers slept fitfully on their arms. Every so often a shot cracked from the picket line where a hostile had tried to sneak up on a sentry.

"All night long," Trumpeter Brown observed, "they [the Sioux] could be seen dancing and yelling in the flames like so many demons."[15]

At daybreak, the fighting was resumed. But the Indians seemed to have had enough. Circling the troops, they fired into the ranks, wounding two men, and then withdrew, and within a short time could be seen retreating in the distance. Miles kept after them across the blackened prairie forty-two miles to the ford on the Yellowstone the Indians had crossed a week before. The persistence of Miles's pursuit dismayed the Indians. This was not warfare as they understood it — glory in counting coup, attack and run to fight another day. The big, cold-eyed officer meant business.

"It was a good thing for the regiment," Miles wrote Mary, "as it was all engaged, every company, and the fact of whipping and routing Sitting Bull's body of Sioux has inspired them with great confidence and spirit."[16]

The night before the command reached the Yellowstone, Miles sent an orderly to shake Yellowstone Kelly awake. The stars glittered, clear and cold, above the silent camp as Kelly approached Miles waiting in his military greatcoat. About the Colonel lay the sleeping forms of his staff. Others might slumber. Miles, anticipating the morning, had too much on his mind to rest. He fired questions at Kelly. How far was it to the river? How shallow was the ford? What was the probable course of the fleeing Indians?

The troops caught up with the hostiles at the river. The main body of Sioux were on the opposite bank. Miles sent across for them and a number of chiefs returned under a flag of truce. A council was held beside the river with the chiefs sitting in a semicircle facing Miles. The sky was a deep blue. The October sun was warm. Golden leaves fluttered from the cottonwoods. This time Johnny Brughière, the half-breed interpreter who had been with Sitting Bull, was in the soldier camp. He had come over to Miles at Cedar Creek and Miles had commissioned him a scout. Sitting Bull did not appear, but Gall arrived late at the council and Yellowstone Kelly noted the wild look in his eyes. Two thousand of the hostiles agreed to go to their agencies and surrender, giving up five of their principal chiefs as hostages. But the prize, Sitting Bull, escaped. With Gall, Pretty Bear and approximately forty lodges, Sitting Bull broke away from the main camp and fled north.

Writing from camp near Camp Fire on the Yellowstone twenty miles above Glendive, Miles told Mary:

Yesterday Bald Eagle, a powerful chief of the Indians in the south, came in and said he would now surrender. He did not want to fight any more. I expect to see him again today.

I will endeavor to write oftener, but of course you will understand that when we are moving about with very little or no tentage and contending against these formidable Sioux, when a mistake would result in a massacre, my time is more than occupied. I sleep very little at night, and of course am very anxious. I have lost flesh and am now as slender and lithe as a greyhound, almost.

I have had an opportunity of meeting the noted Sitting Bull and putting his formidable force to flight, and I am satisfied that it will do much to end hostilities.

It was the largest engagement and the *only* time that Sitting Bull has been fought and followed up in the last two years, if he ever was before then. His movements were discovered and counteracted. From the reports of the disgraceful failures of late I judge that the country sooner or later will understand the difference between doing something and doing nothing.[17]

Miles felt he was, at last, accomplishing something. Now let the public see how an aggressive officer waged a campaign against the Indians as compared to Crook who wasted his time in dilatory maneuvers.

If, Miles told Sherman, he'd had the mounted troops that Crook had, Sitting Bull would not have gotten away.

As I wrote you before I could have captured the whole outfit if I had one battalion of cavalry but so much has been said about that arm of the service and the army almost disorganized to strengthen it that as an infantry officer I do not propose to ask for a single trooper. I can hunt them on foot but it is not easy for ten small infantry companies with broken down mules and four scouts to capture the whole Sioux nation. If you expect me to be successful see that I am supported or give me command of this whole region and I will soon end this Sioux war, and I would be very glad to govern them afterwards for the more I see of them the more respect I have for them and believe their affairs can be governed to their entire satisfaction as well as for the interests of the government.[18]

Blunt talk from a Colonel to a Commanding General of the Army. But Miles knew that Sherman, and Sheridan, too, would be glad to hear of the surrender of the Indians. Commissioner Manypenny had not been far wrong when he had observed the army needed a victory to restore its prestige.[19]

Miles was concerned about the Indians who had given up their arms and wrote Terry that he hoped they would be fairly treated ". . . While we have fought and routed these people and driven them away from their ancient homes, I cannot but feel (it is not) right they are compelled to submit to starvation, for I fear they will be reduced to that condition as were the southern tribes in 1874."[20]

The next day he wrote ". . . Fearing you may not fully understand just the conditions upon which these chiefs surrendered, I wrote you again . . . What is to be accomplished will depend on the manner in which these chiefs are treated, and the reception their people receive on their arrival . . . Bull Eagle understands he is to turn in his arms, particularly the Springfield carbines."[21] Unfortunately, Miles said, the interpreter at the Cheyenne agency had told the Indians that they would be terribly punished and, as a result, they were "very suspicious." Sitting Bull, Miles continued, was a bad influence. His band was the wildest on the continent and there were Indians in his lodges who had never seen a white man. As long as Sitting Bull was free, the country would not be safe for settlement. Therefore, Miles notified Sherman, he would start back for Tongue River, get supplies and start immediately for Fort Peck and the Big Dry after Sitting Bull.

CHAPTER X

Anxious to capture the prize himself before winter set in, Hazen set out from Fort Buford after Sitting Bull. Hazen was a West Pointer, eight years older than Miles, who had been the Kiowa agent during Custer's Washita expedition. The capture of old Bull would bolster a career temporarily retarded by exile to Buford. Hazen hoped to accomplish his objective before the snow deepened. Unlike Miles, he would not wage a winter campaign. His Sixth Infantry was fresh from barracks and well supplied, giving him an advantage over Miles who had to return to Tongue River completing a march of 300 miles, part of which had been made during the running battle with the Indians. At the cantonment Miles organized a command of 434 riflemen and a small detachment of artillery, although the term "organized" was misleading. The troops were the same with the addition of a few companies. Much of the equipment had to be improvised. Winter was approaching and Miles knew he must be prepared for the terrible cold of the northern plains. Winter on Llano Estacado was mild compared to winters in the remote Northwest. The men cut up wool blankets for underwear. Over their buffalo overshoes they tied grain sacks and wool masks covered their faces. Miles had asked for Sibley tents. These had not arrived. One third of the small number of horses sent by the Department Quartermaster had been declared unfit by a board of survey. Footsore mules and horses had to be replaced by captured Indian ponies.

In contrast to Miles's little force was the expedition Crook was outfitting at Fort Fetterman to go after the same Indians Miles and Hazen were pursuing. Bourke, Crook's admiring aide, declared, "The organization with which Crook entered upon his second winter campaign was superb in equipment."[1] Nothing was lacking that money could provide or previous experience suggest. There were eleven companies of cavalry, four batteries of artillery, six companies of the Ninth Infantry, two of the Fourteenth and three of the Twenty-third, comprising a force of over fifteen hundred men. In addition, Crook's personal staff included a chief medical officer, aides, and chief of scouts. Friendly Indians included 155 Arapahoes and Sioux, ninety-one Shoshonis, fifteen Bannocks, one hundred Pawnees under the renowned Major North, and four interpreters. There were also four hundred pack mules with sixty-five packers, 168 wagons and seven ambulances. About the time Miles was reorganizing at Tongue River, Crook was taking time out to pursue his favorite sport of hunting on Laramie Peak where he killed a great number of deer and a cinnamon bear. There is no record of what Crook thought of Miles's determination to wage a winter campaign. He kept his thoughts to himself, this brooding, taciturn man, but he cannot have attached too much importance to Miles's understrength regiment. Miles commanded a small area while Crook was a brigadier general and a department commander.

Trumpeter Brown, that hardy, good-natured member of B Company, noted in his diary: "November 3. Back at Tongue River for supplies. November 5. Out on trail again."

Miles wasted no time. In a letter to Mary, he wrote:

We are again starting out for twenty or thirty days and perhaps longer. It is a cold frosty morning. The ground is covered with snow.

I shall endeavor to follow the Indians as long as possible,

even to their retreats where they think we can not go, for it is only in that way that we can convince them of our power to subjugate them finally. I presume you may hear from us up north, unless Hazen has already succeeded in capturing Mr. Bull. Possibly, the latter may go into the Agency and give Hazen a chance to seize him. I could have done that or destroyed him and his party when they were within range or under our guns. But that would have been violating a flag of truce and the whole civilized world would have denounced it. Still I think we will be able to wear them down in time, or we will encounter much stronger force than has already been met.

I am very well provided for against the cold as I have all the clothing I can well carry. I leave this comfortable cabin with its cheerful fireplace with less regret than I would if I were leaving my precious darling here during my absence, for I fear you would be very lonely waiting here for me during these long dreary days and weeks. I presume it will be nearly a month before we return and then it will be quite cold.

I shall take only my Regiment with one piece of artillery, in all about 475 men.[2]

On the Big Dry the scouts found the trail of the Indians. The little force dwindled to antlike size as it marched across the frozen plain. Miles, impatient as always, rode in advance of the troops with a scout and a few soldiers. When he saw a butte or a high bluff, he rode to the top. Often he had to dismount and climb over the rocks. From the summit he swept the country with his glasses for a sign of the hostile camp. In every direction, the land undulated endlessly to the horizon — bleak and gray and streaked with snow. The treeless plain was broken by clay bluffs and sandstone cliffs eroded by the wind. The loneliness stirred the troops to uneasiness. Like the sea, it was elemental. Men could die, their bones be scattered by the wolves and no one the wiser.

It began to snow. Within a few hours, the Indian trail was obliterated. The wind rose, driving icy particles into the faces of the men and horses so that it was impossible to see more than a few feet ahead. Fingers and toes numbed when the temperature dropped below zero. Breathing grew difficult as the moisture from eyes and breath froze on the wool face masks. Heads down, the men trudged against the shrieking wind. Their cumbersome clothes weighted their weary limbs. At last, a halt was called in the shelter of a bluff. Ice had to be broken on a stream for water. Horses and mules foraged for the sparse grass beneath the snow. The cooks cursed to get a fire going in the wind. Canvas ripped in the gale. Exhausted, the men threw themselves in their blankets. All night long the pickets stamped their feet to keep from freezing. Before daylight, reveille sounded. Breakfast was frozen beans, frozen bacon and cold coffee, and, then, back on the trail again. To hold to a northerly direction, Miles resorted to a compass. That day, the tenth, they made twenty-five miles.

On the Forks of the Big Dry, Miles wrote Mary, November 13.

> For seven days we have been moving north over a very rough country and in the face of a driving snow storm. I have thought of your wish and my design to keep a journal and write you every day but we have reveille at four-thirty and after that my time is entirely occupied either with the details of the march or camp and with the plans of my movements. I really do not have time or opportunity to write, except occasionally.
>
> We are bundled up to the eyes, on account of the extreme cold. Last night the thermometer ran down to ten degrees below zero, which is quite cold for November . . .
>
> This is one of the wildest and least known counties on the continent. We have moved in the heart of the hostile Sioux

country where a command has never been before and where we have to explore without accurate maps or guides, as no white man that I can find has ever dared to come into this country before. The country is all cut up with rivers, caverns, cliffs and bluffs, making it very difficult for a command to move. We are however in position to move in any direction, and I presume you may hear from me on the Missouri. I am sending this with a dispatch to General Hazen. The couriers will take it through across the country to Fort Peck, a somewhat hazardous ride as they may encounter a camp of Indians, and there being some three inches of snow on the ground, it makes it more difficult for them to move unnoticed.

Two days after this letter was written, Crook moved out of Fort Fetterman with his large and well-equipped force for the Powder River country and the Tongue where Crazy Horse was wintering and where, rumor had it, Sitting Bull intended to establish communications with the Oglala chief.

The same day Miles reached Fort Peck after crossing the divide, where for three days the command camped without wood to build a fire and melted snow for water. The troops were not many hours behind a portion of Sitting Bull's band which mixed in with friendly Yanktonais camped about the Fort. Since the agency was under Hazen's command, the Indians came under his jurisdiction. Miles no longer had authority to deal with them. But he did not feel the march to Peck had been wasted. "I believe," he wrote Sherman, "we have divided Sitting Bull's people and that his strength and influence is fast breaking down. I think he as well as they are satisfied we can whip him every time and that has a very damaging effect upon his people."[3]

Sitting Bull had discovered that Bear Coat was unlike officers he had known in the past. The constant harassment was beginning to show effects.

Miles had no intention of giving up now, although Hazen had withdrawn his force some weeks previous. The cold on the northern plains was too much for the commander of the Sixth Infantry.

Leaving Peck, Miles proceeded west, reconnoitering the country for a hundred miles to the confluence of the Mussel-shell with the Missouri. Here, the river crossing presented a problem. Chunks of ice floated, half submerged, in the black water. Miles solved the problem by cutting cottonwood logs and roping them together into rafts. The raft that he was on broke loose and swept downstream to catch on a snag. Miles could not swim well enough to get to shore. Attempts to throw him a rope failed. After eight hours of being marooned on a water-logged raft in subzero weather, a hardy volunteer rescued Miles by swimming out with a rope. The soldiers thought the incident a great joke. "Our shipwrecked colonel," they called Miles. Miles grinned with them, although not as heartily as the men, who loved the rough, frontier type of humor. Being stuck on the raft was no joke; he was wet and chilled to the bone. Nor did Miles like to be caught in such a helpless position.

He did not tell Mary about the incident in the letter he wrote from the camp on the Musselshell, November 30.

> We have made a wide detour in endeavoring to keep between Sitting Bull and the point where he expected to obtain ammunition. We crossed the Missouri on the ice and after five hard days marches we arrived at this point, intending to recross to move south, but this country is entirely different from any other, for when we expect cold we get warm weather and vice versus. It grew warm during our march from Peck and broke up the ice in the river.
>
> Since we have been here we have built two rafts, but the great fields of ice floating down makes the crossing extremely

dangerous. The thermometer falls to zero at night and then goes up to 54 during the day, keeping every thing in this unsettled condition. If it does not change for the better very soon I shall change my plans and move elsewhere. This long continued scouting away from winter quarters is wearing away this winter of our discontent, and will I trust make it seem shorter to me. We are almost out of the world here and up to this late date we have not learned who is elected President.

Crook's friend Rutherford B. Hayes was elected President. Another bit of news that Miles had not heard was that, five days previous, Mackenzie struck the Cheyenne village of Dull Knife on the Powder and wiped it from the face of the earth. The vengeful cavalryman set fire to the lodges; seven hundred ponies fell into the hands of the captors. The Indians were driven onto the wintery plains. Half starved and freezing, they killed their remaining ponies for food. Old men and children put their legs in the steaming entrails to keep warm. One officer and six enlisted men were killed and twenty-five wounded. The attack was considered a great victory and head-lined in eastern newspapers.

In order to cover more country, Miles decided to divide his command into three columns. Retaining one himself, he gave the other two to Captain Snyder and Lieutenant Frank Baldwin who had served him so well on the southern plains and who was with the Fifth when it came north from Leavenworth in July. To Baldwin, Miles said. "Now, Baldwin, do the best you can. I am responsible for disaster, success will be to your credit; you know what my plans are and what we are here for."[4]

The responsibility of commanding a battalion in that terrible country in the winter nearly unnerved Baldwin. It was now December, the month the Indians called the time of the "cold moon." The snow lay two feet deep and the temperature seldom rose above zero. At one time on Poplar Creek it fell to sixty-six below zero. The horses were growing weak. A number of mules died of starvation. The men, bearded and gaunt, somehow kept going. On the seventh of December, Baldwin caught up with Sitting Bull eight miles below Fort Peck on the river. Leaving his wagons and pack mules and taking only five days' rations, Baldwin marched to within a few miles of the hostile camp and lay over until morning to make the attack. Baldwin did not know Sitting Bull was aware of his coming and that he had sent his women and children to safety and entrenched himself with his warriors against the coming attack. At daylight Baldwin came in view of the camp, which consisted of nearly a hundred lodges, equal to five hundred warriors. This was a larger force than Baldwin had counted on. He had only a hundred and six men in his three companies. It was also obvious that the Indians had prepared for the attack. "The Indians," Trumpeter Brown observed, "did not seem desirious of fighting and motioned the troops back. Lieutenant Baldwin being a very prudent man withdrew while he had a chance."

Baldwin was luckier eleven days later when he again caught up with Sitting Bull at the head of the Red Water. Joe Culbertson,[5] Baldwin's capable scout, was sure that the Sioux chief was somewhere in the vicinity. The unknown country of the Big Dry was the great feeding ground for buffalo that came down from the north at the approach of winter to seek the shelter of the ranges along Bear Paw Mountains and Milk River. The Indians had to camp where they could kill plenty of game and the women could dress hides to trade for ammunition, sugar, salt and cloth and, occasionally, rum from the Red River breeds. The officers with Baldwin protested that it was too risky to go south toward the Yellowstone. Baldwin overruled them, saying the risk was justified by the chance to catch

Sitting Bull, although he was well aware that his command was nearly exhausted. Many of the men were ill. There were less than two days' rations for the troops and but three sacks of oats for the eighty mules and four horses. The march, Baldwin said, was the most hazardous of his not uneventful life. Not only did he have to watch out for Indians, but he had to march across country as desolate as the Arctic. At night, unable to sleep, Baldwin visited the pickets and the men in their tents at least once every two hours to be sure they did not freeze to death. The stock, after the grain was gone, subsisted on cottonwood limbs. When Culbertson at last found Sitting Bull on the Red Water the men were more fit for a hospital than an attack but, disciplined and hardy campaigners that they were, they tightened their grip on their rifles, ready to go. Not a man asked to be excused. Perhaps hunger was an incentive. They hadn't eaten much the last few days and they knew there was meat in the Indian camp. Baldwin decided to employ the same tactics he had on McClellan Creek in 1874. He sent the wagon train charging down the icy slope toward the Indian lodges. The Indians, caught by surprise, fled before the soldiers. There were no casualties on either side and Baldwin's force was too weak to pursue Sitting Bull, but the Indians lost sixty head of horses and mules, which was a severe blow. That night the troops feasted on buffalo ribs, and in the morning started back to Tongue River. Yellowstone Kelly, who was one of the few persons with whom Miles could relax, was with the Colonel when Baldwin arrived at the cantonment. Miles had a fire going in his log hut and was telling Kelly about the battle of Chancellorsville when a tap sounded at the door and Baldwin entered. Miles greeted Baldwin warmly. Discreetly, Kelly departed to let the Lieutenant make his report.

Baldwin had to tell Miles that Sitting Bull had once again escaped the troops. After the engagement on the Red Water, the Sioux turned southeast to the Powder and was presumed to be on his way upriver to the Big Horns to find Crazy Horse. Although Baldwin had not captured Sitting Bull, Miles was pleased that he had driven the elusive chief from his camp. The Sioux were in bad shape now. They had been unable to hunt; they had lost their ponies and provisions. Perhaps they would come into the cantonment to surrender.

That there was some justification for this hope was proved a few days later when a party of Sioux from the hostile camp on the upper reaches of the Tongue approached the cantonment. To the left of the Indians lay the log huts of the command. On the right a number of Crow lodges were pitched by the frozen river. The Crows, who were serving as scouts, ran out to meet their bitter enemies, the Sioux, as they trotted toward the cantonment, making signs of friendship. Deceived by the welcome of the Crows, or else confident the soldiers would protect them from harm, the Sioux made no attempt to evade the Crows who advanced with outstretched hands. But instead of shaking hands the Crows pulled the visitors from their ponies, shooting and stabbing five of them.[6] The rest turned and whipped their horses back the way they had come, while the Crows, sure of the retribution that would follow their act, fled to the hills in the opposite direction where they hid from pursuing officers. Miles was furious at the treachery of the Crows. The Sioux delegation had not been from Sitting Bull's camp but word of the murder would spread among the hostiles, checking further attempts at negotiation. To make matters worse, one of the murdered Sioux was Bull Eagle, whom Miles regarded as the finest specimen of a real chief that he had seen and whom he had intended to recommend as head chief of the upper Sioux when the hostiles had surrendered.

There was nothing to do, now, but continue the campaign.

CHAPTER XI

MILES wrote Sherman that he was starting out on a new campaign under great disadvantages. Terry and Sheridan were not supporting him. What few mules he had were nearly dead. Sometimes, they had grain, sometimes not. There was no hay. Many of the men lacked stockings. Miles intended to buy them from the traders and trust the government would pay for them afterward. "The way this command had been supplied would be a disgrace to the worst militia organization in the land."[1]

Sherman would have preferred Miles to make his charges through official channels. He did not disregard Miles's complaints, but he felt the Colonel was harming his career by stirring up controversy. He had infuriated Pope in 1874. Now, he was angering Sheridan and Terry. His continued criticism of Crook was particularly tactless. Rutherford B. Hayes, the new President, had called Crook the brains of the army when he had served under Crook in the Civil War. Hayes would not appreciate denunciation of the officer he considered the most capable in the army.

Two days after he wrote Sherman, Miles wrote to Mary. He had been away from Mary for nearly six months and missed her affection and understanding. Without her, fancied slights loomed larger, sensitiveness to criticism increased.

> I am about starting out again for those hostile people. One part of my command started today up the Tongue River to be followed by the remainder in a few days. I expect to over-

take them some sixty or seventy miles up the river, and then we make a fresh start from there. I do not think we will be gone as long as we were during the last movement. From all I can learn through the papers that Great Powder River expedition must have been out nearly a month and I suppose would be on the headwaters of Powder, Tongue and Rosebud. I see by the papers that Crook has had everything given him and the resources of a large department. My lot has been quite the reverse. He is moving against the same body of Indians as my command, and has thirteen hundred troops while I have four hundred and twenty, a difference of nearly a thousand men. I hope there will be no investigation of this Indian business this winter as my testimony, I fear, would not be favorable to the authorities.

We have been having intensely cold weather. The mercury one morning ran down to forty below, but as it was clear and calm it was not too hard to endure.[2]

Mary, who was in Washington, was not reassured by this letter. More important to her than Crook was her beloved husband's welfare. To her, the frontier was a terrifying country and the Sioux a terrifying enemy. Years later, she was to tell how she had to wait — "all through the long hours of the day — wait simply for interminable time to pass; to lie and listen through the dark hours of the night and think until thought itself becomes a terror; to sleep, and waken with the dull pain still at my heart, and the ever present question uppermost, 'Will today bring the news that he has been killed?' "[3]

The sorrowing figure of Elizabeth Custer was much in Mary's mind. Mrs. Baldwin had heard rumors that her husband had not returned from his expedition. Now Mary learned her husband was proceeding, once again, against the Sioux.

Miles did not help matters by writing in a later note that "many here who have been in this country and among these

Indians for years predicted the command would never return and that it would be another Custer affair."[4]

But one of the old scouts remarked as the command started up the valley of the Tongue, "Your men seem to think they can whip any number of Indians."[5]

The men had confidence in themselves and in their commander. Miles had not mollycoddled the troops. They had marched hundreds of miles, been ill fed and half frozen, but they had seldom failed in their objective.

This time they needed all the encouragement they could get. The military had great respect for Crazy Horse who defeated Crook on the Rosebud and led the Oglalas on the Little Big Horn. He was no ordinary Indian, this strange, pale-skinned leader of the Sioux. He had a large force of warriors reinforced by the Cheyennes from the village that Mackenzie had destroyed. The men of the Fifth had less than a week to recuperate at the cantonment before they started out again.

The Indians precipitated the campaign when a band of Cheyennes ran off two hundred and fifty head from the cantonment beef herd. Such boldness suggested the hostiles were short of meat. Immediately Miles organized a force of 436 men — the same tough, stringy troops who had marched a thousand miles after Sitting Bull — figuring the cattle thieves would lead the way to Crazy Horse's camp somewhere between the Tongue and the Big Horns.

The snow measured a foot deep and the temperature registered thirty below zero. Ice edged the cottonwoods and willows along the Tongue. Over the gray land lowered a gray sky. The boots of the men, who were muffled in greatcoats, crunched on the frozen crust. After the men jolted the wagon train which included two pieces of artillery camouflaged with canvas to deceive the Indians who were watching the progress of the column. The lower valley of the Tongue widened to high, bare bluffs. As the command advanced southwest, the valley narrowed and the country grew rougher and more broken. The command could easily be marching into a trap.

Yellowstone Kelly, accompanied by Liver Eating Johnson and a number of other scouts, rode in advance. Some distance up the valley, the scouts discovered a collection of shacks hastily knocked together from rocks, turf, posts and slabs, apparently shelters the Cheyennes had built to keep from freezing to death after Mackenzie drove them from their lodges.

There were signs of Indians everywhere. Liver Eating Johnson could smell them. In the willows of a river crossing, the strong scent of Indian tobacco lingered in the cold air and pony hoofs had chipped the ice. Frequent river crossings slowed the troops and, as the valley closed in, the snow deepened. Sandstone cliffs ran down to the stream. Ravines slashed the timbered foothills. The temperature rose and it began to rain. Miles scanned the sky with concern. If the ice rotted on the river, the wagons would have to be forded with the aid of ropes and poles; submerged floes would have to be cut away. Feed grew scarce as the grass that the animals had been able to paw through the snow gave place to cactus and sagebrush. Just before reaching camp, the scouts exchanged shots with a small Sioux war party. Miles quickly threw a skirmish line across the valley and on the bluffs but the Indians vanished into the rough, snow-whitened wilderness.

Later, Miles wrote to Mary.

You can have no idea of my anxiety when engaged in active operations against these wily savages far out in this remote country, or of the responsibility of a command of this kind. There was not ten minutes of the day that my mind was not absorbed by the most intense interest in the success of this enterprise. We are not engaged in one where error can be corrected.

Our days on the march are something like this; The bugle sounds reveille if we are not very near Indians at 4:30 o'clock. We have breakfast about 5:30 or six o'clock. If the Indians are very near, whenever we can. I march an hour and a half before daylight, but if there is danger of marching into an ambush I wait until the day dawns, about seven thirty o'clock. From the time we wake in the morning there is not a moment when I am not anxious about my command. About fifteen minutes before we march, the advance guard and flankers are thrown out, and the pickets withdrawn. The advance guard and flankers and rear guard cover the command during the day. Their numbers are changed as the character of the country or the appearance of Indians demands. Passing over a new country, like the mariners of the ocean we are obliged to follow the compass and select the most direct and best route for the command, requiring constant watchfulness and tireless activity.

As we approach the end of the day's march a good locality must be selected, good ground for fighting, with water, timber and grass. As we go into camp the pickets are thrown out, and the scouts and flankers withdrawn, the troops posted, the animals turned out to graze, the snow cleared away and our tents pitched. Dinner or supper about four o'clock, and as soon as it is dusk all the animals are gathered up and cottonwood cut for them. If there is no timber or grass they graze on wagon poles, sage brush and anything they can get during the afternoon and evening. A tracing of our day's march is made up and orders issued for the march the next day. Frequently the scouts are sent forward to spy out the land. Sometimes they do not return until midnight, and in fact they are liable to return any hour during the night. We are so thoroughly chilled and stiffened up that it would be almost impossible to write even if the ink did not freeze. When not too cold I get several hours sleep, for the responsibility, the anxiety and the planning occupies my thoughts as much at night as by day.[6]

The necessity for vigilance was proven at dawn of the sixth day when a band of warriors swept down on the ox drivers who, assisted by two soldiers, were driving in stray cattle. One of the soldiers was killed. The scouts and Baldwin's company turned back at the sound of firing but the Indians eluded the pursuers amid the snowy rocks and pines. The command halted while the soldier was buried on the trail. The grave was shallow since the ground was frozen too hard for digging. With bowed heads, the men stood in the chill light as the earth was shoveled over the body. "To rest from the cares of the world," wrote Trumpeter Brown, "no more to resume the rough marches of the campaign."

When the burial detail was finished, the troops marched over the grave to obliterate it so the Indians would not dig up and mutilate the dead soldier.

The valley of the Tongue was, now, no more than a wide gulch. Sandstone cliffs to the river's edge necessitated frequent river crossings on softening ice. Down timber, impeding the passage of the wagons, had to be chopped away. A cold, steady drizzle churned the snow to slush. The trail, which was well worn, was used by the Indians en route north and south to hunt and to raid. The command was getting deep into hostile territory. To the southwest lifted the white peaks of the Wolf Mountains. In the gray light of a January afternoon, the scouts came on an abandoned Indian camp. Examining the blackened embers of fires, the holes made by lodgepoles, bits of buckskin and other debris, the scouts determined the village had been recently occupied and that it was a large one — more than a mile long, which meant hundreds of warriors. Miles, knowing his small force was greatly outnumbered, kept on the alert for ambush as the column struggled up the canyon. The horses found grass beneath the snow, a godsend to the starved

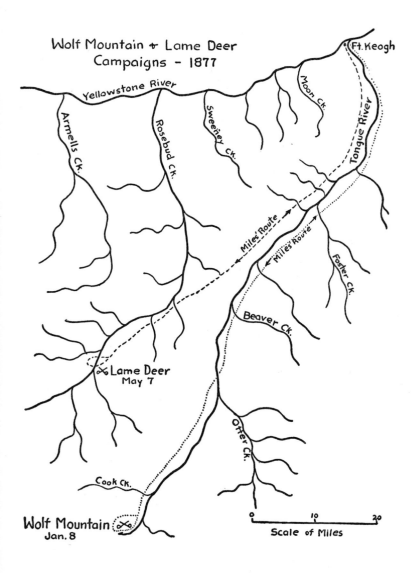

Wolf Mountain & Lame Deer
Campaigns - 1877

Ft. Keogh

Yellowstone River

Moon Ck.

Tongue River

Armells Ck.

Rosebud Ck.

Sweeney Ck.

Miles' Route

Miles' Route

Foster Ck.

Beaver Ck.

×Lame Deer
May 7

Otter Ck.

Cook Ck.

Wolf Mountain ×
Jan. 8

0   10   20
Scale of Miles

animals. Ash grew among the cottonwoods, pine darkened the hills and ravines. On Hanging Woman's Creek the scouts discovered another large Indian camp, fires still smoldering. An emaciated pony stood in the trampled snow. Kelly informed Miles the Indians must be just ahead.

The nearness of the hostiles nearly cost Kelly his life when he rode ahead of the command with three scouts and paused to rest in an open place in the timber. Foolishly, the men posted no pickets. Having had little sleep for the last week, they began to drowse. A shot startled them to wakefulness. Three allied Crow scouts and a Bannock crashed through the scrub pines into a Sioux war party creeping up on the unconscious Kelly. The Crows ran, flat to their ponies, but the Bannock and the scouts, leaping on their horses, spurred through the timber and onto a ridge. In the blue-black shadows of the ravine below moved hundreds of warriors.

Beating a safe retreat, Kelly reported the encounter to Miles. The scout's breath fogged in the icy air. He spoke in the educated English that contrasted so oddly with his shoulder-length black hair and buckskins. Miles, knowing that at last he had caught up with Crazy Horse, was elated and also anxious. Crazy Horse had launched a surprise attack on Crook at the Rosebud. He could do the same in the canyon of the Tongue.

Later, when the men went into camp, they could see Indians watching them from a shale cliff. Making no attempt at concealment, they stood in plain view of the soldiers, blanketed, motionless figures. Miles felt they must be very sure of themselves. At dusk, the Indians disappeared.

It grew colder. The wind blew in gusts down the canyon. Snowflakes swirled in the darkness. Miles had little sleep that night. The strain of months of campaigning were beginning to tell. He was twelve years older than he had been during the

Civil War. Occasionally, he'd been able to relax in Virginia. In this menacing land, he could not let down his guard for a single instant. He was edgy, tense. He listened for sounds above the wind, going over and over in his mind the position of the troops and the probable disposition of the Indians. On him alone rested the life and death of 436 men — 435 since they had lost Betley[7] back on the trail. When he closed his eyes he saw the never ending frozen plains between the command and the nearest army post in case of disaster. If he were to lose a large number of men in a blizzard or if Crazy Horse were to outwit him, he would be better dead like Custer than alive to be court-martialed. He'd receive scant sympathy from Terry or from Crook or Pope. A number of people were waiting for him to make a mistake.

Still he pressed stubbornly up the valley, sending Kelly and his companions ahead of the column to reconnoiter. From behind a snow-laden cedar, Kelly examined the black ridges running down from the peaks. Movement caught his eyes. Figures moved on a trail that switchbacked down a mountain spur — three women, a boy, a girl and a child apparently unaware of the nearness of the troops or that Crazy Horse had moved his camp.[8] When the women neared the cedar, the scouts rode out in front of them. Terrified, the women began to cry, making no move to defend themselves when the Crows touched them with their coup sticks. But Kelly did not intend to let the Crows kill the women as they had the members of the peace party who had come into the cantonment. The squaws' dresses were heavily beaded and fringed, their blankets the best the trader could supply. Kelly surmised the women were of some importance and that they had been on a visit and were returning to their village. Without protest, they allowed themselves to be taken to the soldier camp where Kelly presented them to Miles. With the courtesy he exhibited to all females, red or white, Miles ordered a tent prepared for the women and food brought to them.

That the captives might prove valuable hostages was soon apparent. The hostiles had seen the scouts ride off with the women, and within a short time an alarm was sounded as a number of warriors showed themselves on the crest of a ridge. Mounting their horses, the indefatigable scouts galloped up the river bottom. The first Indians were bait to lead the scouts toward a higher ridge behind which waited ten or fifteen warriors. Kelly, who considered himself a match for any number of Indians, decided to charge, although the warriors, resting their guns on crossed gun sticks, were aiming directly at the scouts from a range of less than sixty yards. The shots exploded in the thin air. A scout's horse buckled at the knees as blood poured from his nostrils. Another horse neighed wildly. Yelling to his comrades to follow, Kelly jumped his mount off a rocky shelf into a timbered hollow where he dismounted and taking shelter behind a scrub oak, fired back at the Indians. Shrilling the war whoop, the Sioux closed in on the scouts, taking advantage of every bush and rock. A feathered scalp lock, a drift of smoke from a gun — the scouts aimed with deadly accuracy but the original fifteen warriors were joined by eighty or a hundred more. Kelly might have ended his colorful career in that icy hollow if Miles, always alert, had not realized the dangerous situation of his scouts and ordered Lieutenant Hargous to advance up the valley on the double with his company, taking care to avoid ambush. At the same time Miles directed a shell fired from one of the guns at the ridge behind which the Indians were hiding. The blast of the shell coupled with the sight of the soldiers advancing through the frozen willows bordering the creek forced the hostiles to break off a charge. In the moment of confusion, the scouts withdrew down the canyon. There was no doubt, now, that Crazy Horse, like a wolf, was turning at bay.

The pickets, that night, could sense the Indians about the camp. Some of them crept close enough to the tent of the women captives to speak to them in the Cheyenne tongue. Shots echoed at intervals during the night, but it was difficult to see in the snow-driven darkness and more difficult still to hear above the wind. By daylight, the troops were up and swallowing a hasty breakfast. A man could not fight on an empty stomach in subzero temperature. In the faint gray light, horses neighed; a bugle clamored amid the hustle of men and animals. Miles, with a switch in his hand, directed the placement of one gun in the valley and the three-inch Rodman cannon on a sloping bluff above the camp commanding a view of the canyon. Sporadic firing broke out. Glancing at his watch, Miles noted it was 7 A.M. Lieutenant Baldwin, seeking to cheer the men, rode along the line of skirmishers deployed among the willows of the river bottom. By this time the Indians were all around, slipping like shadows among the rocks and trees. A number boldly showed themselves on the ridges, taunting the troops with an early death. Kelly, who understood Sioux, shouted back a challenge to the hostiles. They were all women! Women were afraid to fight!

Take courage, Baldwin told the troops as he reined in his horse along the skirmish line, meet the enemy like men! The Indians are going to charge!

Single shots became a fusillade mingled with the high-pitched, ululating war whoop as the Indians swarmed down the valley to be met by the fire of the skirmish line. A shell burst in the snow. Did Crazy Horse lead the charge? If so, he was not identified but his skill could be seen in the Indian tactics. Seeing the troops commanded the valley, the Indians changed their method of attack. Abandoning their attempt to charge, they concentrated on taking the command by the flanks and the rear. The thunderous report of the cannon was punctuated by the whooping of the warriors as they galloped their ponies along the crest of the ridges. Miles, standing with his little switch beside the Rodman gun on the ledge, heard the bullets whine past his head. One hit the spoke of the cannon wheel with a sharp ping. Kelly, who had joined Miles, feared for the Colonel's life. The cannon was a target for the hostiles and one of the mules which hauled it had been killed, but Miles refused to take shelter. From his elevated position he saw a large number of Indians gathering in the upper end of the valley with the obvious intention of taking the ridges back of camp. Quickly Miles issued his orders. The troops reached the ridge in time to drive the Indians off, but the hostiles succeeded in gaining possession of a high bluff further to the rear and to the left. Two companies, A and C under Captains Butler and Casey, were sent to dislodge the Indians — a difficult task for the warriors from their superior position could fire down at the men. The face of the bluff was nearly vertical, drifted with snow in the ravines and icy in the open. The men were encumbered by rifles and heavy coats. Their boots slipped on the ice. They sank in the drifts. In places the bluff became so steep that they had to grab sagebrush to haul themselves upward. The Indian fire grew more accurate. Ammunition ran short and Miles ordered Baldwin to carry a fresh supply to the hard-pressed companies. With a box of rifle ammunition in front of his saddle, Baldwin galloped across the trampled snow to the bluff, waving his hat and crying to the men to come on!

Inspired by Baldwin, the men redoubled their efforts to scale the bluff. The summit was level, swept clean of snow by the wind. By this time it was below zero and threatening a storm. Several men had been wounded. The shooting in the narrow canyon exploded like strings of firecrackers. Men cursed, taking shelter behind clumps of sage or rocks. The cold ached in their laboring lungs. They were still struggling upward when a weird and wonderous sight met their eyes. Against the gray sky of the summit appeared a Medicine Chief in a feathered cloak and war bonnet. In full view of the astonished troops, he began to dance. He danced forty yards along the ridge and turned and danced back, the little bells tinkling on his feet and the eagle feathers tossing with his movements.[9] Surprise held the men open-mouthed. Only Yellowstone Kelly guessed that the Medicine Chief was trying to draw the fire of the troops and that the hostiles, in his life or death, hoped to read their fate. In an instant the men recovered themselves. They were hardened realists. The Chief's pathetic act of bravado did not impress them. They begun firing, but their numbed hands could not steady the barrels of their rifles and the Medicine Chief presented no easy target with his bold, high-stepping rhythm. Back across the ridge he danced and then turned and danced the other way, his shrill whooping rising above the shooting. A soldier, sighting carefully, pulled the trigger. The Medicine Chief tottered, the high steps slowed to a shuffle. The gorgeous scarlets and yellows of feathers and buckskin sank against the snow and disappeared. Yelling, the men surged upward and over the crest, driving the warriors from the summit and across the hills toward the main body of Indians. The death of the Medicine Chief panicked the hostiles. After he fell, they failed to rally and retreated up the river toward the Wolf Mountains. Miles immediately set out in pursuit although it had begun to snow and the flakes closed like a shifting white curtain across the canyon. A dead pony lay among the rocks. In a ravine, the trampled snow was stained red with blood.

Later, Miles wrote to Mary about the fighting at Wolf Mountain.

> With a New Year's greeting I would salute you, for I really feel grateful that a merciful Providence has spared me to return again to this place and communicate with my own Precious One, even in this way.
>
> My New Year's was spent far up in the canyons of the Tongue River, and the year opened with a lively skirmish with the Indians under Crazy Horse, below Otter Creek. On the third we had another affair with them, and on the 7th captured one young warrior and seven women and children of the Cheyenne tribe. The scouts, in their endeavor to capture a still larger number, or to develop the strength of the Indians, were surrounded by about 250 Indians, and saved themselves by getting into heavy timber. The Indians fought hard for them, but were driven away when the main command came up.[10]

In a second letter describing the Wolf Mountain fight in more detail, Miles told Mary:

> On January 8th we had a fair stand up fight at Wolf Mountain for nearly five hours in the snow, and part of the time in a severe snowstorm. I think the Indians were very confident of their ability to whip us, and even intimated that we had had our last breakfast by calling out that we "would eat no more fat meats." The country was roughly mountainous and the heaviest fighting was done by Captains Carey's [Casey's?] Butler's, and McDonald's companies, where it was impossible for a horse to go. The enemy was fighting on foot, like Infantry, and even charging on foot, something seldom if ever done by Indians. They were well whipped, the fighting ending very suddenly by their retreat. They seemed to have

lost some one of their principal men, as they were seen to carry him away, followed by quite a concourse of his friends. The snow where the principal body of Indians fought was crimson with their blood, and for five miles up the valley pools of blood were found. As the engagement progressed and as the bullets were whistling about me, I often thought of my precious ones and wondered if I would ever see them again, for we were far away in that remote country where the least mistake meant defeat and defeat disaster. Yet the Indians were out-manoeuvered and defeated at every point. This tribe of Indians has whipped Crook twice and have never before been defeated and followed up.

I never saw troops behave better or fight with more coolness or pluck. They have an idea that they can whip anything, and they always get away with anybody they meet. I knew that I would meet very strong force of the best fighting Indians on the Plains, and went prepared for it. I took out two pieces of artillery disguised as wagons, and ran them around behind ambulances. At the proper time the covers were pulled off and the ball opened for the edification of the Indians.[11]

Still later, Miles wrote again to Mary.

I have never seen Indians handled as well as at Wolf Mountain, or show more boldness, and I believe they found in us a different mode of fighting than any they had ever met. They soon realized that with such a command it was a losing game. As soon as Big Crow [the Medicine Chief] was killed the news seemed to run along their line. They quickly abandoned the field, followed by a few bursting shells from our rifle guns.

Our lines were then very much extended. The snow was deep and falling rapidly. I concluded that the tired soldiers who had been climbing steep bluffs and rugged hills had done well enough for one day, and that it was useless to try to catch mounted men on the run with foot soldiers. I was satisfied in having whipped the Indians in a fair and open fight when they outnumbered my forces two or three to one.

With a slight advance that day we rested until morning

when the command moved forward up the Tongue River five miles. From the high bluffs the scouts could see further up the valley, but not a sign of an Indian could be seen for fifteen miles from the scene of the fight. They did not stop retreating until they reached the Big Horn Mountains. To have followed them there would have run the risk of losing my whole command; not from Indians but from the intensely cold weather. Had a part of my supplies been sent up the Yellowstone, as I had requested six months before, I would have followed them to the Big Horn Mountains and remained with them. But all there was left for me to do was to return to the cantonment. We had not captured or killed Crazy Horse's entire tribes, but we were masters of the situation and had taught the destroyers of Custer that there was one small command that could whip them as long as they dared face it. They have told different stories about their losses, but I believe their report about twelve or fifteen killed and twenty five or thirty wounded would come very near the fact. We have shown them our strength, and we will now show them our kindness. That is one reason for keeping the women and children captured by the scouts the first day. They seem quite contented and pleased with the ways of the white people. They say that their people will come in and give themselves up.[12]

CHAPTER XII

THE VICTORY in the Wolf Mountains lightened the arduous march back to the cantonment. Miles felt he had done well. He had driven Crazy Horse, who had defeated Custer and Crook, from the field. The chief had not been captured but the battle would play an important part in the surrender of the hostiles.

When the Indians surrendered, as the captive women were certain they would, Miles wanted them to come into Tongue River and not to the agencies. He had asked that the Minneconjous who had surrendered on the Yellowstone be well treated. The request had been ignored. It was the old story of the southern Cheyenne after the campaign of 1874. Miles was determined that this time he would assume the responsibility for the welfare of the Indians. The Indian Bureau and Department Headquarters could object if they pleased. Tongue River was a long way from St. Paul and Washington.

Miles's elation did not last. At the cantonment he found an order for the immediate discharge of all his scouts but two, his teamsters, wagon masters, guides, packers and blacksmiths. His wagons were to be limited to thirty in number.

To Miles this meant frustration at the moment of victory.

Furious, he protested to Sherman. "I am sure there is command neglect of duty at St. Paul."[1] The cut in his personnel, Miles raged, would force him to do what Sitting Bull wanted him to do — go into winter quarters.

He was keyed up, running like a hound on the scent. He

would not be checked as he had so often been checked before. He would not see it was time to go into winter quarters. The large hostile bands were broken up. The Indians were coming in to surrender. Congress had cut military appropriations. There was no money to pay teamsters and scouts at the Tongue River cantonment. On the march back from the Wolf Mountains, a number of men froze toes and fingers in the bitter cold. Baldwin had such fits of coughing that his tent mate had to hold him in his arms until the paroxysm passed. Miles of the superb physique could not understand the physical limitations of others. When an old wound pained him, he ignored it. Discomfort was to be expected — and endured — on a campaign. The job, as Miles saw it, was unfinished. Sitting Bull was still at large and the wild bands had not yet come in. No, Terry and Sheridan were discriminating against him in favor of Crook. He was to receive no recognition unless he fought for it in Washington as well as on the Yellowstone. In this mood of bitter disappointment and anger, he scrawled to Sherman:

> If I am not allowed to move again this winter you may look for Indians west of the Big Horn Mountains next spring. Now if I have not earned a command I never will and if I have not given proof of my ability to bring my command into a successful encounter with Indians every time I never will besides I now have a better knowledge of this country than any other white man and unless you can give me a command it should be no less than a department you can order my regt out of this country as soon as you like for I have campaigned long enough for the benefit of thieves and contractors. If you will give me this command and one half the troops now in it I will end this Sioux war once and forever in four months.[2]

Rash, foolhardy words! Fortunate, indeed, for Miles that the tough, rusty-haired general in Washington knew how Miles hated the check rein. Miles did not need to tell Sherman how well he had done. Sherman appreciated the work of his subordinate. But no matter how successful Miles had been, Sherman could not give him a command. The army was limited to eleven general officers and, at present, no vacancies existed by reason of death or retirement. Miles was well aware of this and his demand for promotion exasperated the Commanding General.

In his bitterness, Miles intensified his attacks on Crook. Once again, he declared, Crook had failed in his objective. The first of January, Crook had given up his expedition against the Sioux and returned to the cantonment. Mackenzie's raid on Dull Knife's village in November had been the only encounter engaged in by the elaborately outfitted Powder River expedition.

As was his custom, Miles expressed his resentment to Mary in a letter written from the cantonment on the Yellowstone, dated January 19, 1877.

> This campaign has been one of the most successful in history of Indian warfare, in spite of the difficulties which had to be overcome. But it is simply outrageous the way I am supported, or rather not supported. I do not believe that General Terry ever reads my reports or pays any attention to my requests. He is determined that I shall do nothing, for I receive no more encouragement from Department Headquarters than I do from Sitting Bull. I find here an order from Department Headquarters directing me to discharge all my scouts but two, all my civilian packers and send all my wagons but thirty to Buford. This virtually compels me to abandon the campaign and do just what Sitting Bull wanted me to do two months ago, to go into winter quarters and there remain. Instead of having fifteen hundred men as I was expected to have, and as I am prepared to prove before any investigation or committee

of Congress could have wintered at this point, my force has been cut down to about four hundred fighting men, outside of the guard necessary for the protection of property here. Fortunately the country has been pretty well cleaned of Indians, and there are now no large camps within striking distance of this command. If I could have proper support, or was even allowed to supply my command from this point, I could clean this country entirely in four months and open it for settlement. But there seems to be a determination that this war shall not be ended this winter, or that it shall not be ended by this command.

I find that a few days rest will be very enjoyable, for the weather was very cold and we were chilled through. The snow is about one and one half feet on the level, but the command waded through it and came in in good condition and fine spirits. It was quite an affecting scene as the command came marching across the plain, the band playing "Marching through Georgia." A wintry scene indeed. It is very gratifying to return after a successful campaign.

Ensuing letters to Mary indicated Miles's gradual acceptance of the cut in his forces. He heard from Sherman. The cut was necessary. It was not dictated out of personal vindictiveness by Terry or Sheridan. Sherman could exercise his authority with Miles when necessary. But Miles was not to think his work was unappreciated. Reinforcements and action in the spring were hinted at.

But Miles's feeling about Crook remained unchanged, as he showed in his letters to Mary.

Cantonment on the Yellowstone
January 21, 1877

In 80 days we have cleared this vast country of thousands of savage Indians marched a thousand miles and in every engagement we have been successful.

On returning I find orders from Department Headquarters which will cripple my command so that I can do nothing, or very little this winter. But fortunately I have beaten both my friends in the East and Billy Bull and Crazy Horse as to time. I do not think there is a large hostile camp now within one hundred miles of my command. The home of the Sioux has been shifted. If they retreat west of the Big Horn Mountains it will be necessary to place supplies at more distant or western stations than this.

I hear there was a rumor that Baldwin and his command had been destroyed. Mrs. B. will be very anxious and much distressed until she hears of his victory. He is a very safe and gallant officer and I have great confidence in him. He is one of those officers that I am willing to trust a long way out of my sight.

I will make a request that Congress grant a gratuitous issue of clothing (one suit) to my command, for they have actually worn theirs out in their tremendous marches, and the severity of the climate is such as to make their allowance of clothing insufficient.

Headquarters Yellowstone Command
Montana
February 5, 1877

The band is a source of great enjoyment to the garrison, and I think they play nearly as well as they did at Leavenworth, although the surroundings are quite different. At first, when they played those beautiful melodies, some said that it sounded almost sacreligious [sic] out in this wild camp. But as we have become somewhat civilized and the cantonment is beginning to look a little more like civilization, their music is appreciated. They are putting up quite a music hall, and will have a fine minstrel company and considerable fun, I have no doubt, either this week or next. We have three large stoves here and a fair supply of goods of all kinds.

I am considering the plan of making another move this

winter, but have not yet fully decided. The fact is we have driven the Indians so far away, except for small parties, that it is almost impossible to reach them. The last time we had to go almost into the back door of Crook's command.

I am surprised to learn that he turned his back on that very large Indian camp; it must have been within forty miles of his camp, and had been there for weeks. I think his official annual report is the most extraordinary document ever signed by a Brigadier General.[3] If I believed the Indian such a terribly formidable enemy, I would not risk myself in this country a week! "Ten thousand times more formidable" than when armed with the bow and arrow! What chance has a command against those Indian monsters? Such statements only intimidate a command.

Headquarters Yellowstone Command
February 19, 1877

Today I have plenty of business as my interpreter [Johnny Brughière] returned with twenty-nine hostile Indians. I sent him out after the Wolf Mountain fight to see if there were any of the Indians who had had enough of the war and were disposed to accept the terms of the government. I sent one of the captive Indian women with him.[4] They were well received in the Indian camp and seven of the prominent Indians came in to know what would be expected of them. As we had shown them we could whip them in the field, we now show them that we can treat them fairly in camp.

At first they seem disposed to talk strong, but they were given to understand that that would be of no use, that there could be but one big chief in this part of the country, and that I proposed to occupy that position. White Bull, one of the seven, is a man who has never been in any Agency, has never shaken hands with any white man and is a friend of Crazy Horse and Sitting Bull. He seems to be a man of importance and influence in the hostile camp. He is half Cheyenne and half Sioux, and is the Chief of four tribes when they are at war. The Indians seemed very much pleased with everything they saw, and went back evidently with the information to bring in their people. I sent word to Crazy Horse and Sitting Bull that if they did not come in I would go out after them.

I think White Bull was very much impressed with our strength and with the ways of the white man. He had never heard a band play before and was much amused. They are the wildest kind of Indians. Unless something happens or evil councils prevail, I think quite a large number of their people will come in and give themselves up.

They claimed that they whipped the troops from the Department of the Platte [General Crook] and followed them nearly to Laramie. They are not willing to admit that they lost many in the fight at Wolf Mountain, but their stories do not agree as to numbers. They all admit that they met a command they could not get away with, and that their big medicine man was killed and left on the field.

The next thirty days will show. They may give up or I may try and go out again for them; but I have been cut down so much and crippled by those in the rear that it is next to impossible.

I give Generals Terry and Hazen, Colonel Otis and Major Card the full credit for this. My animals are living on about one half or one third the ordinary allowance of forage and I will be entirely out in a short time. If I do not succeed in ending this affair this winter, it may be the same thing over again next spring and summer.

I shall be very closely confined here for several weeks to come. The weather is getting warmer and the snow is disappearing.

> Headquarters Yellowstone Command
> Montana
> February 28, 1877

Enclosed I send you a little picture of what is known as the "bad lands." You can get no idea of the character of the country, even from this photograph, as the ground is so cut up by ravines, canyons, bluffs and cliffs. If any one thinks it an easy task to take a command through Indian country and fight two or three times your number of hostile Sioux, I am quite willing they should try it. Much of the country is so rough that no animal could enjoy traveling over it unless it be a mountain sheep. There are thousands of square miles of such Indian country where it is almost impossible for a command.

On the 15th of March, Miles wrote two letters to Mary. Both were dated from Headquarters, Yellowstone Command. The first was brief.

"We are patiently waiting for the return of our Indians who went out to the hostile camp to inform them upon what terms they could come in."

The second letter was longer.

I see that some Indian Agents and jealous people who have been comfortably housed all winter have been trying to belittle what we have accomplished, and to make out that we have not killed enough Indians. I wish to goodness they would try it themselves.

I would be very glad if Crook would explain why he turned around, marched the other way and remained in camp fourteen days when the Crow scouts offered to take him to Crazy Horse's camp in six days. The fact is [he] scarcely thought it possible for me to reach Crazy Horse's camp at all with my poor mules. But I was determined to cross sabers with that Indian. He had sent word to Sitting Bull that he had nearly as many warriors as he had had in the Custer fight and could fight any command that might come against him. I thought I would at least take that notion out of his head . . .

Miles gives no indication, at this time, that he was aware the military who controlled the agencies were trying to persuade Chief Spotted Tail to negotiate with the hostiles. Spotted Tail was Crazy Horse's uncle, and the Indians had told Crook, under whose jurisdiction the agencies fell, that the hostiles would listen to Spotted Tail with more respect than any other man. Consequently in February, Spotted Tail set out to visit the wild bands on the Little Missouri and Crazy Horse's people on the Little Powder with the goal of persuading them to surrender to Crook. Spotted Tail arrived on the Powder at the moment the Indians were debating Miles's terms.

By March, Miles had been informed of the rival peace emissaries, and wrote to Mary in a letter dated March 17, 1877.

Today my interpreter returned bringing with him two Indians and reporting that about one hundred and fifty Indians were following. He reports that when the party that was here returned to camp, the camp was harangued and the criers announced that the war was over and that they must not send out any more expeditions against the whites. The camp moved at once from near the Big Horn Mountains, on the Little Horn, and he traveled with it to the Tongue River and down it to near the mouth of Otter Creek. At the field of our engagement at Wolf Mountain they found the body of the big medicine man and head warrior of Crazy Horse's camp.[5] He was the greatest leader among them. There were two prominent men killed there, and some of them admit that they lost fifteen killed and forty-five wounded. But any way the fact is that Crazy Horse's camp has never been struck nor have they had a fight since the Custer affair, except that at Wolf Mountain. And now they seem anxious to accept the terms of the government. I presume that if they go south, Crook will go out to meet them and claim the credit of bagging them. Yet he has had no more to do with it than if he had been in Egypt.

With my interpreter came a young warrior, Hump, the finest specimen of an Indian. He has not the intelligence of Bald Eagle, but is evidently as bold and enterprising as he is represented to be. He is very young, yet he is the head of the warriors and has perhaps more influence than any of the tribe, for in war the warriors rule the camp. I have known of him for sometime. He has stolen more than a hundred horses from the Crows this winter!

White Bull returned. He is the leader of the Cheyennes and has fifteen prominent chiefs with him, so that communication is established and I will now test my ability to manage this matter. As they were moving in this direction down Tongue River a runner came in saying that Spotted Tail was on his way, but travelling very slowly, bringing a great many presents, including two kegs of powder, and that General Crook had sent them some powder. My interpreter says that the runner showed him a bag of the powder. I do not believe they got powder from Crook, but that the traders sent it out with word that the Indians could trade for all the powder they want if they go in. I will write you about it, but at present I have my hands full and have Indians on the brain.

Miles demanded unconditional surrender from the hostiles. Spotted Tail had been authorized to offer more lenient terms. The Indians, he intimated, would be given a reservation in their own country. Crook's reputation would receive a big boost if the chief who defeated him on the Rosebud surrendered to him at the agency.

On the 20th of March, Miles wrote Mary from his Headquarters, Yellowstone Command.

The Indians have remained here and we have had several talks. I think we will become sufficiently acquainted to understand each other, although they are very wild. Many have never shaken hands with a white man or been in any agency or post. They are very curious and very much amused by the band. I think there are some that will have to take another good whipping. But I believe there is a large percentage that are now willing to give up and accept the terms of the government. The prospects look well now, and I am playing my last card.

Owing to lack of supplies, I am forced to remain quiet but I will keep up as bold a front as possible.

Headquarters Yellowstone Command
Montana
March 22, 1877

You can not imagine how very much I have been worried during the past few days, for the results of these consultations with these representations of the hostile tribes will result either in peace or war.

It is very difficult to deal with these wild savages. First, to make them have confidence in you, and then you have to use the greatest discretion in placing confidence in them. Next you have to reason with them and convince them that it would be safe and better for them to place themselves and all that they have in life in the hands or under the control of their enemies. It is far easier to fight with them successfully than to council with them with success. Yet I believe we will be successful.

I think if it had not been for the diversion caused by a runner from the Spotted Tail Agency, a good part of them would have come in here, as they were on the way. But it is perfectly understandable that when they are about to give up they should want to go where they will be best treated. If they go to their Agencies it is all right, only I want to be sure that they go. For three days I have had men sounding them to see how they felt and what their disposition was. Today I had a talk with them and told them it must be the last for I could not allow any more to come in unless they came to stay.

I think they do not know just what is best for them. They are very suspicious and distrustful of the whites, and they lie to each other. That is one reason why so many come in to learn for themselves.

There is a division of feeling among them. Some are disposed to remain on the warpath and fight it out to the bitter end. Others are disposed to accept the terms and do as I tell them. I think this feeling may prevail. I will test it tomorrow.

I would like to retain them all; but it might look like bad faith. Although I would be justified in my own mind in so doing as they have not come in just as I told them to. But it might not be the best policy as it might prevent others from coming in. The management of these people just at this time, considering the condition of my command is a difficult question. But whether they come in or go to their Agency it would make no difference to my movements, for I have been feeding my animals on half to one third forage and I have no grain or hay enough for a five days' march.

I will have difficulty in keeping my animals alive until the boats come up, thanks to the mismanagement of Lieutenant-Colonels Otis and Hazen and a few others in the rear who have consumed 1,500,000 lbs., of grain in getting up about 500,000 lbs., to my command. I anticipated this three months ago and requested authority to supply my command in Montana, but no answer has ever been received. Had it been approved, I could have had grain all the time and have kept moving.

Whether these Indians come in here or go to their Agencies, one thing is certain; no other commander can claim credit for it, for the work was done by this command in the early days of January in driving them up into the deep snow of the Big Horn Mountains.

I learn from your letter that I may have a large command. But I would prefer a small command with the means of placing supplies where I know I will want them, and of keeping my command effective than having a large command and having it supplied by the incompetency or indifference of others. I can not possibly get away now until I know the result of this important work and may not be able to then if the Indians do not come in, for I have a good command and do not intend that it shall be idle. I must make the best of my opportunity. You know it is so seldom that there is even a chance to do anything in the army. I think it best to make the most of it.

Headquarters Yellowstone Command
March 24, 1877

I have had several conversations with the Indians and gave them their final terms. They must decide at once. If they chose to remain hostile we will move against them. Or they may leave a few warriors as a pledge of their good faith, take part in the council on Powder River and then determine whether to go in to their Agencies or to return here. But they must do one or the other without delay. They again declared their good intentions and the peace elements at once came to the front. They abandoned their extravagant demands, and White Bull came forward and said he would remain. He is a Cheyenne Chief and head warrior, a man of thought and strength. Following him came Little Chief, another Cheyenne Chief, and five others.

Then I said I would like the same assurance from the Sioux, and as Hump had been a great leader in war I wanted him to lead in peace and make for himself the name of being as wise in council as he had been valiant in arms. He very manfully said he would remain, also his brother Horse Road, another Sioux chief. Hump is a famous leader among the warriors of the hostiles. He is evidently very popular with the fair ones of the tribe, for that night they were all singing praises to him for being so brave as to remain with the whites.

It is amusing to see how curious the wild Indians are about the ways of the white man. Many of them declare they have never been in any Agency or Post and never shaken hands with a white man. But the most amusing thing of all is their love affairs, for there is really a "woman in it." When the Cheyenne chief, White Bull, first came in he said that the brother of one of our captive squaws had promised her to him, her warrior having been killed in the Custer affair. I told him all right, when he brought in his tribe I would give him a fatherly consent to such an alliance. But after they went away she appeared rather sad and I learned that she did not want to be given to White Bull but was in love with Little Chief!

There was a complicated question, but I thought I would let them settle it themselves. It seems that the mother of this buxom widow had formally been White Bull's squaw, and I think used her influence against his approaches.

When they received their final terms, I said that if they, or a few of them would remain I would release the captives, which they seemed very anxious to have done. White Bull has always appeared friendly and places great confidence in me, but Little Chief has not fully gained my confidence. He was the spokesman and orator for the Cheyennes. Possibly White Bull thought that, in addition to showing his good faith, it would be an act of gallantry to remain. But Little Chief, his rival in more ways than in war or the council, promptly said, "I will remain." In one of the most anxious hours of my life I was somewhat amused and at the same time pleased as I thought that, if they both remained and the widow went away with the others, it would settle that love affair for a time. But I was mistaken. In the evening, I had prepared a little feast for those that were to remain and two prominent men of the tribes that were to return. I learned that the widow had said she would remain with Little Chief. I feared matters might be again complicated, but I asked White Bull about it or got the interpreter to, and in the magnanimity of his heart he said it was all right. He gave her up cheerfully but evidently not without pain for he appeared very thoughtful that evening. He however soon threw it off and had no idea of committing suicide on account of the unappreciation and fickelness of a woman. He evidently braced himself up for thoughts of more serious importance to himself and his people. But he did not care to be a witness to nuptial felicitations, and being half Sioux and half Cheyenne he abandoned the Cheyennes and took up his abode with the Sioux. The next evening a few of us went up to see how the Indians were. They have two large hospital tents. We found Sioux and White Bull talking very contentedly, and in the Cheyenne tent we found five of the men playing cards "for all that was up," while over in the corner was Little Chief that famous warrior who a few hours before had stood in the area of the council, a perfect type of the American Indian, defending the rights of and declaring the wrongs done to his race, and pleading for the welfare of his people. There he was, breathing soft and fascinating words of love in the whispering accents of the Cheyenne tongue, while the blushing widow sat close beside him on a log, playfully listening to his assurances of devotion. It was quite a picture and one of the most amusing courtships I have ever witnessed.

Little Chief seems more peacefully disposed now, and they all seem quite contented and happy. I have no guard over them during the day and believe they have fully made up their minds to leave the warpath. They are much pleased and interested in hearing the band play and are very anxious to go to see the minstrels. They have heard the others talk about them. They also want to see a herd of sheep that is owned in the neighborhood, and I am trying to make them understand how much better it would be for them to own domestic stock than to chase the buffalo.

Headquarters Yellowstone Cantonment
March 31, 1877
Tongue River, Montana

Winter is rapidly disappearing and the mild warm winds from the west are rapidly changing the cold and bleak scenery to one of new life and cheerfulness. The days come and go very much alike and I am now enjoying quite a respit from the cares and exposures of the campaign. Although I find enough to occupy my entire time, yet I am taking it very easily, and although I do not feel at liberty to go away, for something is liable to occur at any time requiring my presence, yet life is nothing like so wearing as it was a few months ago. I am enjoying perfect health and have gained fifteen pounds since I came in from Wolf Mountain, but I expect to lose it again when I take the field. The responsibility of having an independent command and contending against these wiley savages in such a country as this is very wearing, and I expect I will grow grey even if I have nothing else to trouble me.

My Indian friends seem very contented and say and appear very sanguine that their people will come in. It is rather amusing to watch them, particularly Hump who is about the brightest and most enterprising Indian I have ever seen, and a natural leader. Everything seems to him a revelation.

They are greatly amused with Marshall's concert and variety troop, and much pleased with the white man's music. They would not believe that the acrobatic feats were real, and insisted that the performers were medicine men or had no bones. But I convinced them the next day by calling up the men and telling the Indians to examine them for themselves. That is one reason why it is difficult to manage them, as they are governed by all the savage instincts of their nature and superstitions and constantly suspicious of evil. They are much amused in looking at the London Graphic with its pictures of the Prince of Wales' visit in India, the military displays, the rulers and the tiger hunts. As I wrote this they are singing, which they do most every night and frequently break out in the dead of night, or two or three o'clock in the morning, with their songs.

Headquarters Yellowstone Command
April 5, 1877

As the spring opens I presume it will bring into this country numerous settlers and gold hunters, and of course the mail deliveries will increase as the demand for it is increased. We may, by next fall or winter, have a mail twice or three times a week.

Four companies of the 2nd Cavalry are to report to me by the 10th. They will have about 335 cavalry-men and it is possible that quite a large number of the Crows may come down as allies. This force, with the 7th Cavalry, would make some two thousand men to occupy the Posts, and with that force I believe I could whip all the Indians in the country. In fact

I believe that with the Fifth Infantry alone I could go any-
where, for I am sure the Indians could do nothing to stop us.
The men of the regiment have an idea that they can whip any
number of Indians. This arises from the fact that they have
always been successful and do not know what it is to turn
their backs to the enemy. They have confidence in each other
and in their officers, which is one half the victory.

The days are passing rapidly and everybody is getting their
houses in order, or rather their log and mud huts, to receive
their wives and families. The command was in the field so
early and constantly that it has never had time to finish the
cantonment, and as the ladies are expected on the first boat
(everything is coming up on the first boat!) everyone is busy
getting their little shelters as comfortable as possible. My
house will be completed very soon and will have four good
sized rooms besides a small dining room and kitchen. My
movements are so uncertain that I scarcely anticipate occupying my house, for if the Indians do not come in I shall be out
after them, and if they do give up the war path I shall probably go East, at least for some distance.

Headquarters Yellowstone Command
Montana
April 15, 1877

I would gladly go down to meet you, but I do not feel at
liberty to leave for a single day, as I am looking for the Indians
to come in every day, and must prepare to move against those
who remain out. I should judge from a telegram received
from Department Headquarters that General Sheridan was
afraid they would surrender here. But it makes very little difference where they surrender, it will be the result of our efforts
during the winter, and not of those troops who turned back on
account of the "Inhospitable country." Sitting Bull said a
short time ago to his brothers in council, "My friends, I have a
great mind to go North (meaning to the British possessions),
for the whites have a chief down here who is leveling down the

Bad Lands and making trails so that they will catch us surely next summer." Besides gaining a knowledge of the country, we have kept him so constantly moving that he finds it very uncomfortable and unsafe.

I presume you see all the mean little squibs thrown out to the papers from Crook's Department and from Agency officers. It is very annoying for every officer above the rank of Captain seems to be terribly jealous and envious of me, for some reason I know not what.

I do not expect to be able to move for several weeks on account of not having any grain, but when I receive it I will endeavor to make it lively for the Indians.

On the 22nd of April, three hundred hostiles, mostly Cheyennes, surrendered to Miles at Tongue River. Among them were Two Moons, White Bull, Hump and Horse Road. By far the greatest number of Indians, influenced by the easy terms promised to them by Spotted Tail, turned toward the agencies. By the end of April over two thousand hostiles surrendered at Spotted Tail and Red Cloud Agencies. Touching-the-Clouds led the Minneconjous, Red Bear and High Bear led the Sans Arcs. The first part of May, Crazy Horse surrendered with over two thousand of his people. The Indians' guns and war ponies were taken from them immediately. So much for the easy terms promised them by Spotted Tail. In fairness to Crook — which Miles seldom was — the commander of the Platte did his best to keep his promises to the Indians whom he had told he would try to locate on their old hunting grounds near the Tongue. But despite repeated trips to Washington, Crook failed in his purpose. The Sioux were transferred east to agencies near the Missouri River.

PART FOUR

*Chief Joseph and
the Nez Percés*

CHAPTER XIII

O NE BAND of approximately 51 lodges,[1] mostly Minneconjous under Lame Deer, refused to surrender. As the Sioux were moving up the Powder, Lame Deer and his band broke away and turned west. Lame Deer told the peace emissaries he would never surrender to the white man. He would go where and when he pleased, in this instance, to hunt buffalo on the Rosebud. He was not afraid of the soldiers coming after him. He had good scouts. The soldiers would not find his village.

If Lame Deer had known "Bear Coat" better, he would not have made such a statement. This was the sort of challenge Miles liked.

Lame Deer left the Powder on the 22nd of April. Miles's supply of hay and grain was gone and he had to turn his stock out to graze on withered grass and cottonwood brush. Without feed for his stock, he could not move against Lame Deer. But Baldwin — the ever reliable — had gone to Bismarck for supplies and on the twenty-eighth, returned with a wagon train of grain. May 5, Miles started after Lame Deer with four companies of the Second Cavalry that had arrived from Fort Ellis the previous week, two companies of the Fifth and four of the Twenty-second. Miles experienced none of the misgivings he had felt on the march up the Tongue in January. Snow still whitened the mountains but the valley greened to spring. The creeks rushed full and clear between their banks and the mornings were filled with the songs of meadowlarks. Good-naturedly, the men of the Fifth taunted the "yellowlegs" as recruits. Miles's lips twitched beneath his mustache. There would never be another regiment like the Fifth Infantry. He was glad to be in the field again, relieved that the delicate negotiations with the Sioux were finished. White Bull and Hump, the handsome, six-foot Oglala, were serving as scouts for the command. The only disappointment was that Crazy Horse had not surrendered with his fellow warriors. The news stories provoked Miles. The eastern journals and officers close to Crook intimated the Sioux had surrendered because of the Dull Knife fight. Little mention was made in the Department of the Platte of the Wolf Mountain battle. How much of this was due to Crook and how much to his subordinates is difficult to say. Miles felt Crook was to blame.

Sixty-three miles from the Yellowstone (see Map 3, p. 143), the Sioux scouts found Lame Deer's trail leading west to the Rosebud. Knowing the hostiles were watching, Miles pretended to show no interest in the trail. Passing over it, he made camp on the Tongue River. Lame Deer's scouts saw the normal preparations for a military bivouac. Picket lines were strung, tents erected in neat rows. Smoke from the cooking fires hazed the spring twilight. The scouts retired, satisfied the soldiers were safe for the night. As soon as it was dark, the camp stirred to activity. Leaving his wagon train under guard of three infantry companies, Miles marched on Lame Deer's trail. The country was broken by canyons and hills, rocky and in places timbered. It began to rain. Boots slipped in mud. Sweat of men and horses steamed in the wet blackness. By a forced march, the men covered thirty miles to a high divide between the Rosebud and the Big Horn. The sky was beginning to lighten when Miles called a halt in a meadow surrounded by bluffs. At dawn, scouts were sent to reconnoiter and, from a high peak, discovered Lame Deer's village fifteen miles distant as the crow flies. That day, the troops remained in concealment. When it grew dark they continued their advance, keeping to the shelter of the gulches and the hills. Eight miles from the village, the command halted until one o'clock the following morning when they again moved cautiously up the valley of the Rosebud. In the first gray light of day, Miles glimpsed Indian lodges along the Muddy, a tributary of the Rosebud. The Indians, unaware the soldiers were in the vicinity, slept peacefully. Ponies grazed on the lush grass starred with wildflowers. Returning to the command, Miles directed mounted infantry and scouts under Lieutenants Casey and Jerome[2] to stampede the pony herd by charging up the valley. Simultaneously, after a shouted order to surrender had been ignored, a battalion of cavalry attacked the village. The pounding hoofs of horses, shots and the yells of the soldiers startled the Indians to panic. Screeching squaws fled from the tepees. Old men and women hobbled to safety. Warriors, seizing their rifles, fired back at the troops. Four soldiers and one officer were killed. The Indians lost nearly twice that number.[3]

The suddenness of the attack completely unnerved the hostiles. As Miles galloped up to a group of warriors, they dropped their weapons on the ground. Lame Deer and a younger Sioux whom Miles identified as Iron Star but whom the Indians claimed was Lame Deer's son or nephew, were among the warriors. Lame Deer, Miles said, was "wild and trembling with excitement."[4] Anxious to secure the surrender of the Indians without further bloodshed, Miles extended his hand to Lame Deer, saying "how-how-kola" — the Sioux word for friend. Adjutant Baird, also, extended his hand to Iron Star. In a few more moments, a surrender would have been effected. Unluckily, a white scout rode up just at that moment and, fearing treachery, drew his rifle to cover the Indians.[5] Lame Deer, seeing the scout raise his gun, wrenched his hand from Miles and, grabbing his rifle from the ground, fired point-blank at Miles. Sensing his danger, Miles yanked his horse back on his haunches. The bullet missed his chest by inches, striking and killing an enlisted man in the rear. Immediately the soldiers began shooting and within a few seconds both Lame Deer and Iron Star were dead.

The death of the chiefs ended all resistance. The Indians, breaking up into small bands, fled toward the Little Missouri but they could not escape the tenacious commander on the Yellowstone. In the ensuing months, the bands were trailed four hundred miles across eastern Montana, western Dakota and northern Wyoming until they surrendered at the agencies.

The morning of the Lame Deer fight, Miles was concerned mainly with the destruction of the village and dispersal of the pony herd. Without horses and supplies, the Indians were crippled. The village was one of the richest Miles had seen. The lodges were heaped with robes, furs, beaded buckskins, war bonnets, bells and ribbons, cooking utensils, saddles and ammunition. The soldiers were allowed to take what they wanted for souvenirs and the rest burned. Two hundred ponies were selected from the herd and presented to the foot soldiers of the Fifth as mounts. Among the horses were some that bore the brand "7th U.S." — animals captured on the Little Big Horn.

The destruction of Lame Deer's village left only a few hostiles still roaming the Yellowstone country. In May, Sitting Bull, stubbornly refusing to surrender, crossed the line into Canada after attacking a party of white men on Milk River and running off some of their horses. Miles felt the British had no right to offer Sitting Bull refuge and that the wily old chief would continue to cause trouble by raiding across the border. He would also be a rallying point for other hostiles. Determined to prevent this as far as possible, Miles ordered details to scour the country for small bands of Sioux.

In late May and June, the Yellowstone Command was reinforced by eleven companies of the Seventh Cavalry, four companies of the First Infantry and two companies of the Eleventh which were later ordered to a post in the Big Horns. The Seventh was commanded by Colonel S. D. Sturgis who had been on detached duty when Custer commanded the regiment as a lieutenant-colonel. Sturgis was an older officer, cautious and hide-bound. His son had been killed on the Little Big Horn and his death had embittered Sturgis against Custer and the Indians. When one of his officers remarked that there were a good many Indians in the vicinity, Sturgis pointed toward an Indian burial scaffold on the prairie. "The good Indians are up there on those poles."[6] Sturgis resented serving under the command of Miles, who was a younger man, and showed it by a cranky disposition. The men of the regiment, on the contrary, were delighted. Trumpeter Mulford of M Company, short and blond and high spirited and with an active imagination that sometimes led him to exaggerations, declared: "General Miles is waiting for our Regiment to join his command, which our men are anxious to do. He is a success as an Indian Fighter."[7]

"Custer's Avengers" was the name given the Seventh. The men were spoiling for a fight with the savages who had wiped out their comrades and the man who had ironically become a hero, Custer, "brave and manly . . . a fighter, kind commander and gentleman in every sense of the word."[8] Old timers told how Custer, when he led a charge, called, "Follow me, boys!" Comparisons were constantly being made by the men between

Custer and the unfortunate Sturgis with the latter getting the worst of it.

Miles, too, could not help comparing the two commanders. He had to keep telling Sturgis to hurry up. Custer would never have needed urging.

Miles was on a scout when Mary arrived at the cantonment on the eleventh of July on the steamboat *W. T. Sherman*. Mary's disappointment was keen when she scanned the dock and did not see Miles's six-foot figure among the uniformed men greeting their wives. After nearly a year's separation, Mary had hoped her husband would welcome her to their new home. How could she explain to her sister, Elizabeth Sherman, and to Cecelia why Miles was not present? She would have been less than woman if tears did not sting her eyes. She was tired and afraid. The country was wild and strange. Indians swarmed about the post. The quarters were primitive. The trip upriver had been an ordeal. Mary, Elizabeth Sherman and Cecelia had boarded the steamboat *Don Cameron* at Leavenworth with a number of Fifth Infantry wives and their household baggage. The *Sherman* which accompanied the *Cameron* also carried passengers and baggage for the Tongue River cantonment. Forty miles below Sioux City, Iowa, the boat hit a snag and sank. The crew of the *Sherman* rescued the passengers but the women saved only what they wore.

When at last Miles returned to the post on the sixteenth of July, Mary forgave him everything. But they had little time together. Miles had arrived at the cantonment with General Sherman who was making an inspection trip of the Northwest. The General and his party, traveling on the *Rosebud* captained by Grant Marsh, had stopped at the mouth of Glendive Creek where they encountered Miles. The meeting, Grant Marsh said, was a surprise. It might have been unexpected by the

Nelson Miles in the famous fur cap and bear-collared coat. *Photograph by Huffman.*

Lieutenant General Nelson A. Miles.

Command headed by Captain Baldwin, in December 1876, in search of Sitting Bull. Painting by Frederic Remington. *By permission of the Remington Art Memorial, from the Remington Collection of the Rockwell Gallery of Western Art.*

Sitting Bull, the Sioux chief. *Courtesy of the Montana Historical Society.*

Miles and his staff, in 1876, before starting on the Wolf Mountain
Campaign. *Courtesy of the Montana Historical Society.*

Fighting over the captured Nez Percé herd in 1877. Painting by Frederic
Remington. *By permission of the Remington Art Memorial, from the Remington Collection of the Rockwell Gallery of Western Art.*

Surrender, in October 1877, of Chief Joseph of the Nez Percés. Painting by Frederic Remington. *By permission of the Remington Art Memorial, from the Remington Collection of the Rockwell Gallery of Western Art.*

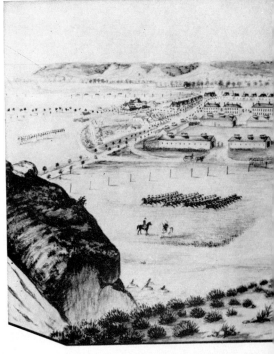

Sketch of Fort Keogh, Montana, made about 1878 by H. Steiffel of Company K, 5th US Infantry. *Courtesy of the Montana Historical Society.*

Chief Joseph of the Nez Percés.
*Courtesy of the Montana
Historical Society.*

Captain Lawton's command in pursuit of Apache Chief Geronimo in 1886. Painting by Frederic Remington. *By permission of the Remington Art Memorial, from the Remington Collection of the Rockwell Gallery of Western Art.*

Geronimo, chief of the
Chiricahua Apaches. *US
Signal Corps photo in the
National Archives.*

Troop C, 8th US Cavalry, in camp on the Big Cheyenne River during the
Indian trouble of 1890–1891. *Courtesy of the Montana Historical Society.*

Crazy Horse, chief of the Oglala Sioux. Although some doubt exists that a picture was ever taken of him, this photograph is purported to be authentic. *Courtesy of the Montana Historical Society.*

Gathering up the dead of the battlefield at Wounded Knee, South Dakota, in 1891. *Courtesy of the Montana Historical Society.*

visitors but not by Miles, whose efficient intelligence service kept him informed of the progress of the Commanding General up the Yellowstone. Leaving his command on the eighth, Miles rode across country with a small escort to greet the *Rosebud* at Glendive Creek. Boarding the boat, he proceeded upriver with Sherman to the cantonment.

Sherman's visit was the occasion for dress parades, balls and conferences. Miles insisted that Sherman stay at his quarters the first night at Tongue River, which meant that Mary, who had arrived only a few days previous, had to act as hostess. She rose beautifully to the crisis knowing how important Sherman's visit was to her husband. Elizabeth, her attractive sister, helped to entertain the formidable uncle. Both young women were fond of their famous relative but they were closer to the Senator Shermans than to the General. In fact, Mary had named Cecelia after the Senator's wife.

Terry was with Sherman and Major Card, the Department Quartermaster whom Miles had castigated in his letters. No record exists of conversations between Miles and Sherman, but Miles undoubtedly reiterated his opinion that aggressive action was necessary against the Indians. And he probably brought up the matter of his promotion. Miles was no man to beat about the bush.

Touring the reservation, Miles showed Sherman the new post being constructed a mile and a half west of the cantonment which was to be called Fort Keogh after the Irish troop commander who died with Custer. (Evermore the ghosts of the Little Big Horn were to haunt the Yellowstone and its tributaries!) At the dress parade, thirty enlisted men were called forward to receive the Medal of Honor for heroic deeds performed during the winter campaigns. Afterwards, Companies B, F, G and I passed in review on their captured ponies.

Miles's activation of his own cavalry unit was most un-official. So, too, was the Indian camp about the post, which Sherman inspected. Miles had taken the Indians' guns and war horses and was teaching them how to farm; not without difficulty, for the Sioux and Cheyenne preferred hunting to plowing. The Indian Department had told Miles there were no funds to feed the Indians, so he supplied them from his own scanty stores. To supplement their diet, Miles allowed them to hunt in the vicinity of the post, usually under the care of Johnny Brughière. The Indians were healthy and happy and showed no disposition to join the disaffected under Sitting Bull. Objections by the Indian Bureau to the "agency," over which they had no jurisdiction, were ignored by Miles. So, too, were Terry's misgivings. Terry felt Miles was overstepping his authority in regard to the Indians, but Terry was no match for Miles, and Sherman, who could handle Miles — it might be said, he was the only man who could — was impressed by what his nephew-in-law had accomplished in the short time he had been on the Yellowstone. Temporarily, at least, he was willing to let Miles have his cavalry and Indians. While the Command-ing General was at the cantonment, he wrote McCrary, Secre-tary of War for Rutherford B. Hayes, that he now regarded the Sioux Indian problem, as a war question, as solved by the operations of General Miles the previous winter and by the establishment of the two new posts on the Yellowstone. "Boats come and go," Sherman continued, "where a year ago none would venture except with strong guards. Wood yards are being established to facilitate navigation and the great mass of the hostiles have been forced to go to the agencies for food and protection or have fled across the border into British Terri-tory."[9]

When Sherman left the cantonment, he continued his trip

to Fort Ellis, at Bozeman, Montana, by way of the Custer battle-field. Disquieting reports were coming from the West where General O. O. Howard, whose aide-de-camp Miles had been during the Civil War, commanded the Department of the Columbia. The Nez Percé Indians had risen against the whites. Miles read the reports with interest but the Nez Percés were too far west to engage the troops on the Yellowstone. Continuing his scouts, Miles rode across the Missouri and the vast, empty plains of northeastern Montana.

On the 25th of July, 1877, Miles wrote Mary from "Camp on trail immediately south of Boundary." (U.S. boundary.)

We have followed the trail of Sitting Bull and a large body of Indians to the Canadian line and cleared the country again of hostile Indians *for the fourth time*. We have had our usual success in not losing a single soldier and accomplishing our object. I could have killed or captured more Indians if it had not been for some lying half breeds who said that all the hunting parties had gone north; but I would have lost lives doing it.

Lieutenant Tillason came through the [Indian] lines day before yesterday and Major Walsh visited our camp yesterday. He states that there were 5,000 Indians in their camp and 2,000 fighting men. This is confirmed by Lt. Tilliason and others who passed through this camp, although their force has been belittled and poo-pooed at by those who do not want our Indian troubles closed at once.

The troops rode back to the cantonment, lean and rank with sweat, their horses "ganted" by the sparse grass of the badlands. Beards stubbled the cheeks of the troopers. Their hair hung to their uniform collars. For twenty-two days they had followed the Indians across hard baked earth and alkali. Often there had been no wood or water and the ration of salt bacon had to be eaten raw. Major James S. Brisbin of the Second Cavalry complained, "I never saw, even during the war, harder or more dangerous service."[10]

It took a tough man to keep up with Miles.

Returning to the cantonment was a pleasure it had not been during the winter. Miles looked forward to holding Mary in his arms again as keenly as he had during the first months of their marriage. His was the demanding love of a strong, self-centered man. Mary's love was giving and understanding. This time, apprehension mingled with Mary's joy to have her husband back again. The Nez Percés had evaded Howard and were moving east across the mountains to Montana.

CHAPTER XIV

MILES kept informed of events, not only in his own immediate area, but in other military departments as well. He would not read a novel; he lacked the imagination to enjoy fiction, but his interest in anything that concerned his profession was insatiable. He had a great respect for history and historians. Current events he was apt to interpret on his own terms. Long before the Nez Percés outbreak, he was familiar with the tribe which had been friendly to the whites since the advent of Lewis and Clark in 1805.

An intelligent, industrious people, the Nez Percés had asked only to be left alone on the high plateaus and valleys of northwestern Oregon and western Idaho, but settlers coveted the country, particularly the rich Wallowa valley which had been set aside for the non-treaty Nez Percés led by Chief Joseph. Numerous outrages were committed against the Indians by the whites and, eventually, political pressure forced the creation of a commission of which General Howard was a member. The one-armed, bearded Civil War veteran who had become known as the "Christian general" because of his religious fanaticism was no match for Joseph when the chief testified before the commission. Joseph was about thirty-five, tall and powerfully built, quiet and proud in manner. His arguments against annexation of the land by the whites were too logical to be answered. With no legal basis whatsoever, the commission ordered the Nez Percés to move onto a reservation at Lapwai, Idaho, or be placed there by force. The young warriors wanted to go to war. Joseph counseled peace. Sadly, the Nez Percés gathered their herds and prepared to move from their beloved valley, but before they reached the reservation, young warriors, bitter and resentful, killed four white men. Joseph still advised against war and Howard might have prevented further trouble if he had met with Joseph, but instead he sent two troops of the Second Cavalry to punish the Indians. The result was the battle of White Bird Canyon where the whites lost thirty-four dead and retreated in confusion before the Indian fire from bows and arrows and muzzle-loading muskets. Horrified, Howard called for reinforcements from other military districts and set out after the Nez Percés himself, committing still another mistake when he divided his forces and sent two troops of cavalry to attack a peaceful Nez Percé village under the erroneous impression it was hostile. This brutal attack sent the villagers, under their famous chief, Looking Glass, to reinforce their kinsmen. All told, the Nez Percés numbered approximately seven hundred and fifty. After an arduous march, Howard finally caught up with the Indians on the Clearwater River in Idaho where he fought an indecisive battle in rugged country, losing thirteen men killed and twenty-seven wounded. The Indian losses were slight. Breaking off the fight, the Indians continued east to the rock-pinnacled Bitterroot range. The Lolo trail that crossed the mountains was steep, choked with windfalls and boulders. Encumbered by women and children, baggage and two thousand head of horses, the Nez Percés managed to keep ahead of Howard who struggled along behind with his guns and camp equipment. At the eastern end of the pass, the Indians evaded a fortification erected by volunteers and a company of infantry from Missoula and continued their march up the Bitterroot valley. Their intention was to join the Crows in eastern Montana or, if that failed, to cross the border into

Canada with Sitting Bull. By this time, the country was in an uproar. Terrified citizens a hundred miles away in Deer Lodge, Montana, locked themselves into the penitentiary. Troops loaded in San Francisco to reinforce Howard's command. The press, in banner headlines, censored Howard for his failure to capture the Nez Percés, and enlisted sympathy for the Indians by telling how they did not scalp or multilate their enemies but fought by the white man's code of honor. Sherman, traveling about Montana at this crucial moment, felt that Howard could handle the situation and that the press was unfair to criticize the General who had no remounts for his cavalry. McDowell,[1] commanding the Division of the Pacific, wrote Sherman he thought Howard should have left the preliminary dealings with Joseph to the Indian Bureau and not tried to get his name in the papers. Howard, McDowell said, was too much influenced by what the press said about him. A Montana scout expressed the general opinion of the volunteers when he wrote that Howard was an old man, slow to move and unfamiliar with Indians.[2]

Meanwhile, the Nez Percés, leaving the clover-scented meadows of the Bitterroot, climbed the timbered ridges that led to the Big Hole country where they paused to rest beside a placid stream. At dawn, their sleeping camp was attacked by a force of soldiers and volunteers under Colonel John Gibbon who had made a forced march from Fort Shaw, Montana. Children, old people and squaws were ruthlessly slaughtered in the initial charge, but the Nez Percés rallied to drive the soldiers back to the timbered hills from which they had made their attack. Gibbon was wounded, a mule carrying 2000 rounds of ammunition was captured and a howitzer rolled over a bluff. Only the rumor that Howard was coming up with his brigade saved the troops from annihilation. Thirty-one soldiers were killed and thirty-eight wounded. The Indians suffered severely, losing nearly two hundred who were killed at the time of the battle or who died later. When Howard arrived, the wounded Gibbon exclaimed in wonder, "Who could have believed that those Indians would have rallied after such a surprise, and made such a fight?"[3]

The Nez Percés were indeed proving themselves a foe to be respected.

Up to this time, Joseph had hoped to treat with the whites for the recovery of the Wallowa. The killing of women and children at the Big Hole disillusioned him. After the battle, he took an active part in planning aggressive action with Looking Glass, White Bird and Alokut, the war chiefs. Further disillusionment awaited the Indians when the Crows refused them refuge and combined with the army to fight against them. The only course left the Nez Percés was to join the Sioux in Canada. Burdened with wounded, they crossed southwestern Montana to Targhee Pass at the entrance to Yellowstone Park. Howard, reinforced by volunteers, was drawing close again. Turning back on their trail, the warriors struck Howard's camp at night and drove off his mule train, necessitating a layover while the unfortunate Howard scoured the countryside for animals to carry his supplies.

Sherman began to lose patience. He did not want to interfere with the operations of his old comrade-in-arms but the citizens of Montana were daily growing more vociferous. Leaving Yellowstone a few days before the Nez Percés entered the Park, Sherman continued his tour to Fort Shaw, where he wrote Howard that if he was tired, he should give the command to some younger man. The Nez Percés must be pursued to the death and Miles was too far away to be of help. Howard answered quickly that he was not tired. Stung by criticism from the press, he prayed for guidance from the Lord and set off again after the elusive Indians.

Sherman underestimated Miles. Howard's struggles had been carefully noted by that observant commander some hundreds of miles distant on the Yellowstone. From newspaper stories and "unofficial reports" — Miles's intelligence system at work again — Miles decided that the Nez Percés would, if they continued to evade Howard, try to reach the Judith Basin and, if pursued, would go north of the Missouri. Without waiting for orders from Department Headquarters, Miles, acting on his own initiative, ordered Lieutenant Doane, Second Cavalry, with Company E. Seventh Cavalry and Crow allies to the Missouri at and west of the Musselshell to ". . . intercept, capture or destroy the Nez Percés."[4] Seven days later on the 10th of August, Miles ordered Colonel Sturgis with six companies of the Seventh Cavalry to Judith Gap to intercept the Indians. Miles did not go himself, for at that time he feared Sitting Bull was about to cross the boundary into the United States. Should the Sioux join the Nez Percés, the Northwest would face a general Indian uprising, or so thought Miles.

The men of the Seventh were disappointed that Miles did not lead the expedition. The weeks of scouting with him had increased their admiration.

There seems to already be a different look on the way things are to go [Trumpeter Mulford noted admiringly]. We now have a *man* at the head who is not afraid of his shadow and who we think will make others hump themselves to keep up with the procession. General Miles, although a young man seems possessed of fine judgment, and does not put on as much style when at war, as a clerk in the Adjutant's tent. He is as brave as was General Custer, though we miss in him that dash that caused General Custer's death. He wants to see where he is going, but when he sees he goes. He is called "Buffalo Soldier" by the Indians and they say that no bullet can hurt him. We hope that none ever will.[5]

With little enthusiam for their commanding officer, whose age and lack of aggressiveness they deplored, the troopers of the Seventh pushed west to the Clark's Fork Canyon not far from the northeastern border of Yellowstone Park. The Nez Percés were trapped between Sturgis and Howard coming up from the rear, but again the chiefs outwitted the army by escaping through the dry bed of a river shut in by towering walls of rock. The long retreat was beginning to take its toll. Dead and crippled horses marked the Indian trail. An old squaw, left to die in camp, was killed and scalped by Crow scouts. A wounded warrior met the same fate. The Indians were too exhausted to care for those who could not care for themselves. The escape through the gorge brought the Indians behind Sturgis. Furious at being outflanked by the Nez Percés, Sturgis turned around and pursued the Indians to Canyon Creek ten miles north of the Yellowstone near where Billings now stands. Before he began his pursuit, he and Howard agreed to send a message to Miles appraising him of the situation. If neither Sturgis nor Howard succeeded in stopping the Indians, Miles might be able to head them off before they reached the border.

The two commanders hated the necessity of seeking help from the younger man but, at that point, they were desperate. Sturgis later blamed Lieutenant Doane for not guarding the lower canyon of the Yellowstone to prevent the flanking movement of the Indians, while Howard blamed Colonel Gibbon for countermanding orders to Sturgis. Whatever mistakes were made, Sturgis did not hesitate to admit he had been outwitted by the Nez Percés. Sherman, deciding to keep out of the affair, prepared to depart for the District of Columbia and San Francisco. If he started issuing orders, he felt he would confuse the issue.

The courier to Miles was riding hard for Tongue River when Sturgis, unexpectedly, caught up with the Indians on Canyon Creek. Dismounting his force of three hundred and fifty men, Sturgis attacked the Indians at the moment they discovered the troops were on them. A hot fight ensued while the warriors held off the soldiers so the squaws, old men and children could escape with the horse herd through a narrow canyon. Sturgis, Trumpeter Mulford reported disgustedly, instead of leading a charge, stationed himself on a bluff to view the battle through his field glasses. Mulford was too hard on his colonel. It was not entirely Sturgis's fault that the Nez Percés escaped through the canyon during the night. The men and mounts of the Seventh were exhausted. The country was rimrock, cut by gullies and boulder-strewn gulches. All the next day the Indians fought a running fight with their treacherous friends the Crows, being forced to abandon over five hundred horses — a severe blow, for the horses enabled the Nez Percés to keep ahead of their pursuers.

On the Musselshell, Sturgis gave up the chase. Feeling that the men had done well, he issued a card of thanks which was read by the Adjutant. The troopers, angry that they had not vindicated their honor lost on the Little Big Horn, growled, "We do not want wind pudding; give us something solid!"[6]

At Tongue River, Miles heard rumors of the continued discomfiture of the army. Anxious for news, he was standing on the bank of the Yellowstone looking west when he saw a man on horseback traveling across the hills. Miles watched as the horseman descended the bluffs to the ferry that brought him across the river. When he reached the opposite side, the horseman rode up, dismounted and saluted. Miles, recognizing him for a Seventh cavalryman, demanded quickly, "Have you had a fight?"

"No," the trooper responded, "but we have had a good chance."[7]

Ripping open the dispatch, Miles read the report from Sturgis and a letter from Howard. General Howard wrote that the Indians had passed him and were reported going down the Clark's Fork to the Musselshell; that they would probably cross the Yellowstone near the mouth of Clark's Fork and make "all haste to join a band of hostile Sioux . . .

"I earnestly request you to make every effort in your power to prevent the escape of this hostile band," Howard begged, "and at least to hold them in check until I can overtake them . . ."[8]

The dispatch was five days old. The cantonment was a hundred and fifty miles from where the Nez Percés crossed the Yellowstone. The chances of intercepting the Indians was slight, but Miles did not waste time on the possibility of failure. He drafted a reply to Howard, which he sent off immediately, saying he was starting out; that he expected to be about six or seven days to the Musselshell and two more to the Missouri. "If you get any information that shall change my course," Miles told Howard, "please send me word."[9]

While Miles was dictating the dispatch, an order had been issued to round up all the available men at the cantonment. During the night the men were checked in, supplied and ferried across the river so that by sunrise the next morning the troops were equipped with thirty days' supplies, ammunition, pack trains, wagon trains, artillery and scouts. Couriers were sent to Forts Buford and Peck over a hundred miles distant with requisitions for supplies to be sent up the Missouri for

Howard and Sturgis. At daylight, the command wound its way up the trail from the river to the high mesa on the north bank to intercept the Indians who had, so far, eluded every force the United States Army had sent against them.

CHAPTER XV

THE WIVES at the cantonment watched until the last pack mule was out of sight and then returned to their quarters for the long days and sleepless nights of waiting. It would have been easier for Mary if Miles had not been so eager to take the field, although this did not occur to her. Her husband's interest was her own. While Miles was gone, she wrote to Senator John Sherman, one of the most prominent men in the Senate and Chairman of the Military Affairs Committee.

Cantonment M. T.
October 4th, 1877

Dear Uncle John;

I take the liberty of enclosing you some scraps cut out from the N. Y. Herald complimentary to Genl Miles. You will observe that Genl Sheridan gives Genl Miles the credit for clearing this country of the Hostile Sioux and ending the war . . . There is so much said now in favor of increasing the Army. In case that should be done there will be probably an increase of general officers. I hope you and Uncle Cump will not forget General's claims for promotion.[1] You know that it is recommended, and his successful campaigns in Texas and the Indian Territory, together with the one just closed, certainly entitles him to a great deal of consideration. There will of course be great many applicants for the commission and doubtless many will personally press their claims. We are now so far away and cut off from communications that I hope Generals friends will not forget him. There will doubtless be opposition on the grounds that he is a volunteer but I trust the President would not be influenced by such prejudices. I trust you and Uncle Cump will forget that Genl is any way connected with the family but think of him as a hard working energetic soldier who deserves promotion.

Genl Howard sent a courier in fifteen days ago asking Genl Miles to come out to his assistance in his pursuit of the Nez Perces. Genl started with his command in less than twelve hours, and when I heard from him last he was crossing the Missouri River in close pursuit; driving them toward the Canadian line.

I hope you are all well this Fall. We hoped to have spent this winter east but until Sitting Bull is disposed of Genl felt that his work was not finished. We like this country very much. Celia and I are both better than we have been for several years. Give much love to Aunt Celia . . .

Sitting Bull and the Sioux were very much on the mind of the military. At the Missouri Agency, Crazy Horse was growing sullen under the restrictions imposed on him. His guns and horses had been taken away. He was not allowed to choose an agency in the Powder River country, as Crook had promised. The last part of August, Crook had started for Fort Brown[2] to oversee the massing of troops who were to head off the Nez Percés, but, fearing an outbreak among the Sioux, Sheridan telegraphed Crook to return to Red Cloud. Thus the Commander of the Department of the Platte took no part in the Nez Percé campaign.

Miles's force numbered approximately three hundred and fifty men; five companies of the Fifth, four of whom were Miles's mounted infantry, three companies of the Seventh Cavalry, three companies of the Second Cavalry, a company of scouts and thirty Cheyennes. The artillery consisted of a twelve-pound Napoleon gun and a Hotchkiss single-shot breech loader. Miles, hoping he could intercept the Indians south of the Missouri, headed for the juncture of the Musselshell with that river. The command pushed across the sage brush and prickly pear of the high plains. This was prairie dog and rattle-snake country. A cold wind rattled the leaves of the cotton-woods in the coulee bottoms. Sodden, gray clouds drifted across a leaden sky. On a distant bluff, a smoke signal spiraled up-ward. Sioux? Sitting Bull's band was reported to be moving south. Miles took no chances. Scouts rode far in advance and to the left — John Two Moons, son of the chief and High Wolf of the Cheyennes were among the scouts. The remainder of the Cheyennes trotted beside the column, a motley crew in cast off hats and parts of white men's clothes, but they took good care of their war horses which they drove before them, while in their buckskin pouches they carried all the para-phernalia an Indian needed for war.

A forced march of fifty-two miles in twenty-four hours brought the column to Squaw Creek near the confluence of the Musselshell and the Missouri. Miles needed a more thorough knowledge of the area and, if possible, a way to cross the Mis-souri which was too swift and deep to ford. Lieutenant Biddle of the Seventh volunteered to reconnoiter. Luck was with the command. As Biddle drew rein on a sandbar, the *Benton* churned downstream, the last boat of the season en route to Bismarck and points south. Fifteen minutes later it would have been out of sight. At Biddle's hail, the *Benton* reversed its engines and headed into the bank. Baldwin, who had been Miles's right-hand man in so many campaigns, was on board en route east for rest and recuperation. The next morning, regretting he was not on active duty, he watched the column come down to the rocky shore of the river. A battalion of Second Cavalry under Captain Tyler was ferried across with orders to move along the left bank and prevent the Nez Percés from fording upstream. Miles, with the remainder of the com-

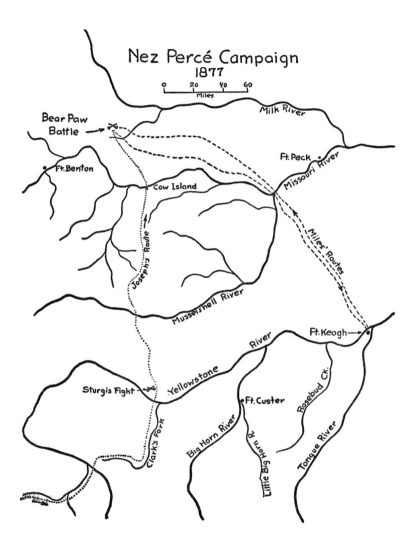

Nez Percé Campaign
1877

mand, stayed on the south bank. His scouts had reported seeing the Nez Percé "flankers" which led Miles to believe the Indians were still fifty to seventy-five miles south of the river.

There then occured another phenomenal stroke of luck. The steamboat, after aiding the military, dropped downstream to take on firewood preparatory to resuming its journey, and the troops, before beginning the day's march, were eating breakfast when a Mackinaw boat floated down the river. In the boat were two men who gave Miles the startling information that the Nez Percés were not still south of the river. Two days before, they had crossed at Cow Island and were on their way north after plundering a store of supplies at this point on the Missouri.

This necessitated an immediate change of plans. Somehow the troops had to get across the river and get across fast. The *Benton* was too far away to hail, but a shot from an artillery piece could be heard for a great distance. If Baldwin caught the sound of firing, Miles was sure he would make the boat turn back. Twenty minutes after the first shell exploded, a soldier shouted, "Here she comes!"[3]

The black smoke streaming from the stack of the *Benton* was a welcome sight to Miles. With a grin, he told Baldwin he was glad to see him but hadn't expected the meeting to be so soon. Baldwin replied he knew something was up and that if it was a fight, he wanted to be in it.

No time was lost ferrying the column across the river. The *Benton,* with Baldwin reluctantly aboard, resumed its interrupted journey while preparations were made for a fast march. Excess baggage was dispensed with, ammunition given out and the packs on the mules redistributed.

While the packers tugged at the ropes and the soldiers heaved supplies into the wagons, Miles scribbled a hasty note to Mary.

Opposite the Mouth of the
Musselshell Montana
September 26, 1877

I learned that the Nez Perce destroyed the Cow Island depot the day we arrived at this point, and moved north. They are reported in strong force and moving together. I judge they can not have been very badly whipped.

We start right north for the Little Rocky and Bear Paw Mountains with the hope of heading them off or getting on their trail. I intend to move as rapidly as possible.

Miles meant what he said about moving fast. The wagons and Napoleon gun, assigned to the command of Captain D. H. Brotherton, were left to follow as best they could. With ten days' rations on the pack mules, the cavalry and mounted infantry started across the paririe at a trot. The men were eager for a fight. The Cheyennes perked up as they scented the enemy. Long after dark, the command halted at some pools of muddy water which had to be boiled and strained before it was fit for coffee. The men slept in a blanket on the ground with their heads on their saddles. At daybreak they were on the march again, northwest across the swelling roll of plains to the Little Rockies. The grass was stirrup-high, and buffalo, antelope and deer grazed within rifle shot, but Miles had issued strict orders against hunting for fear the shooting would alarm the Nez Percés. On the twenty-eighth, the command camped in a gulch at the northern end of the Little Rockies and was again on the march before daybreak, after first covering the cookfires carefully with earth. From a lookout high in the Little Rockies, the scouts had seen smoke to the southwest in the direction of the Bear Paw Mountains, a chain of hills fifty miles distant. Miles surmised the Nez Percés intended to cross the two mountain ranges by a low pass and that they were coming up from the west. Therefore he would move along the eastern base of the mountains, which would enable him to keep his command concealed from the enemy and to intercept them at the pass.

The night of the twenty-ninth, camp was made in a valley near the Bear Paws. It began to rain, and by morning men and equipment were wet and cold. In the darkness a courier rode in with a dispatch for General Miles from Howard. The General had ordered his cavalry back to Idaho and was taking over command of Sturgis's troops. Howard had this privilege. He was outside the District of the Columbia which he commanded, but he was senior officer.

Miles's troops had been on the move only a short time the next morning when three Nez Percés were sighted in the distance. Not long after, the Cheyenne scouts whooped as they discovered marks of travois poles and unshod pony hoofs deep-cut into the earth. The hostile village was just over the ridge. Immediately the Cheyennes threw off their clothes, stripped the saddles and blankets from their horses and threw them into a cache. In a space of minutes the warriors, painted and naked except for breechcloths and moccasins, were mounted on their war ponies.

From trooper to trooper passed the word: "Nez Percés over the divide." Miles halted the column. Arms and cinches were quickly inspected. Wheeling by columns of fours, the command changed course from south to north.

The trumpets blared their brassy notes. The pulses of the men quickened. The horses plunged, fighting their bits. The recruits in the Seventh, licking dry lips, thought of Custer on the Little Big Horn. The Seventh rode in the lead down a coulee where the pack mules tangled with the mounted infantry, up and across the hills. By the time the infantry had disentangled itself from the pack string, the Seventh was out of sight. The trot became a gallop. One mile. Two miles. Eight miles. At a gallop, the Seventh shifted into line of battle. Captain Hale, commanding the cavalry, led his battalion on a snorting gray, his wide brimmed hat aslant his handsome head. One of the officers hummed, "What Shall the Harvest Be?" Seasoned non-coms joked and laughed. At last the Seventh was going to vindicate its honor. No one doubted victory would be easily won.

The Nez Percé lodges were pitched on a stream that wound through a crescent-shaped valley shut in by bluffs on the east and west. The camp was already astir. A number of lodges had been taken down and the squaws were loading the pack animals. The Seventh thundered down on the camp from the south, the troopers shouting and firing their carbines. Simultaneously, the battalion of the Second Cavalry under Captain George Tyler swung to the left and rear of the village to cut off the pony herd.

The troops were overconfident. Two hundred yards from the village, Nez Percé rifle fire exploded in the face of men and charging mounts. Like professionals, the Indians waited until the cavalry was almost on them before they began shooting. They'd had short warning of Miles's approach, but in those minutes they had taken position among the bluffs which enabled them to fire directly on the attackers.

Checked by the fusillade, the Seventh fell back. Captain Hale and Lieutenant Biddle were killed. Moylan and Godfrey were wounded. Many of the first sergeants were killed, including one who had had a premonition of death when he bade his wife goodbye months before at Fort Rice.

The Fifth, galloping up the ridge from which the Seventh retreated, executed a left front into line. They too were overconfident. Leaping from their horses and throwing themselves prone, their mounts' lariats tied to their wrists, the men began shooting into the village. From clumps of sagebrush and coulees, the fire was returned with devastating effect. The Indians, so near their goal of freedom in Canada, fought with desperation. They had thought themselves safe when they paused to rest in this sheltered valley in the Bear Paws. Howard was far behind. Who would have thought that Miles could bring his troops up so quickly?

Miles, galloping across the battleground, drew rein in dismay to see the bodies of Hale and Biddle. Dead men and animals were scattered about the ridge. The Nez Percés were not to be routed by a single cavalry charge. Altering his tactics, Miles issued order to take shelter and make every shot count.

The Second Cavalry was more fortunate in its task of securing the pony herd. Galloping down the valley, the battalion broke up into details. Captain Tyler captured three hundred horses. Lieutenants Jerome and McClernand rounded up many more. As they were moving back up the valley, a party of Indians who had escaped the village tried to recapture the ponies but without success. In a short time, the entire Nez Percé pony herd was corralled in a sheltered hollow under guard of the soldiers. Without their horses, the Nez Percés could not escape. Their only recourse was to fight.

The Indian fire was murderously accurate. "From their concealment," Lieutenant Henry Romeyn said, "they sent shots with unerring aim at every head exposed by the troops."[5] The officers and senior non-coms were their special targets. Lieutenant Eckerson, saluting, told Miles, "I am the only damned man of the Seventh Cavalry who wears shoulder straps alive."[6]

Miles had hoped for a quick victory. Time was important, for Joseph had sent messengers to Sitting Bull's camp less than fifty miles distant requesting help. If the Sioux came to the aid of the Nez Percés, the Indians would have a fighting force that far outnumbered the soldiers. In order to guard against surprise by the Sioux, Miles ordered a constant lookout to the north.

With the time element in mind, he ordered a second charge to cut off the Nez Percés' water supply. Troops A and D of the Seventh, whose officers had been wounded, were placed under the command of Lieutenant Henry Romeyn who had G Company of the Fifth. These three companies attacked the village from the southwest. The troops cheered as they began the attack. Within the space of a few yards, the cheers were lost in a spate of bullets. Romeyn stumbled, shot through the lungs. A few men reached the enemy's rifle pits where they fell. Company I on the southwest succeeded in crossing the coulees, and a handful of soldiers fought their way to the Indian lodges, but they were driven out, losing a third of their number. This second repulse convinced Miles that the Nez Percé camp could not be taken by direct assault and that he would have to resort to siege. The Indians were holding out stubbornly although they, like the soldiers, had lost heavily. As it grew dark, both sides dug in. The wind rose, driving snow before it. Cold numbed the wounded. Indian and white. There was no wood for fires, and Miles could not spare men to cut fuel several miles away. He'd posted the troops in a thin line around the Indian camp to prevent escape. In the storm and uncertainty of that night, he slept little. What few moments he had to rest were haunted by thoughts of Sitting Bull's two thousand Sioux less than a day's march to the north. He had sent a courier to Sturgis on the thirteenth to bring his troops up with "caution and rapidity,"[7] but it was doubtful if Sturgis could reinforce him in less than five or six days. Dispatches had also been sent to Howard telling him the Nez Percés were cornered in the Bear Paws, and to Terry informing him of the battle.

By dawn, snow covered the Indian lodges in the valley, and the rifle pits on the ridge. The dead lay where they had fallen, still shapes whitened by drifting flakes. It continued to snow all that day.

In an attempt to hasten the surrender, Miles sent a messenger to Joseph under a white flag requesting a parley. After some difficulty a meeting was arranged, and Joseph came to see Miles, cheered by the soldiers who hoped the parley meant an end to the fighting. Joseph walked to Miles's tent where Miles met him and shook hands. "Come," Miles told Joseph, "let us sit down by the fire and talk this matter over."[8]

Joseph was accompanied by a number of his warriors and, at first, they seemed inclined to surrender. Joseph told Miles that Too-hul-hul-sote (Tuhulhulsut), Looking Glass and Alokut, all leading chiefs, had been killed. Miles said he did not want to continue killing the Indians and that if Joseph would give up his guns and his horses, he would escort the Nez Percés to Tongue River where they could stay until weather permitted them to return to Idaho. Miles's impression was that the Indians were waiting for the Sioux to come to their rescue.

While the parley was going on, Lieutenant Jerome of the Second Cavalry, acting under Miles's orders, was scouting the village, but instead of doing his reconnoitering from a safe distance he went down into the village where two Nez Percé warriors dragged him from his horse. One Indian wanted to kill him, but the other would not allow it. "Treat him right! He is one of the commanders."[9]

Miles, meanwhile "detained" Joseph when the Chief refused to accept his terms. Miles did not explain why he did this. The logical explanation is that he felt Joseph could be used as a hostage to bargain with Sitting Bull if the Sioux entered the fight. The fate of Custer lingered in his mind; he had no intention of risking his command. That he was justified was born out later by Joseph, who said if he had held the troops until the Sioux arrived ". . . neither the generals nor their soldiers would have ever left Bear Paw Mountain alive."[10]

In a letter to Mary written on the 3rd of October from "Camp near Bear Paw Mountains," Miles refers briefly to the matter.

We have been again successful. We surprised the Nez Perce camp at 8 o'clock Sunday morning and captured almost their entire herd. The fight was a very severe and desperate one, as they were caught and of course fought for their lives. Our loss was great although not large in proportion to theirs, considering they fought on the defensive and in ravines. We have a very large herd and many of their prominent men were killed, including Looking Glass. I had Chief Joseph in my camp one night and I believe he was acting in good faith, but unfortunately Lieutenant Jerome got detained in their camp, White Bird was disposed to fight it out, and Joseph had to be exchanged for Jerome. At present we have them closely surrounded and under fire, and they may yet give up. Lt. Baird was quite severely wounded, but is doing very well and is in good spirits. I am very well and comfortable. I can not tell how long I shall be detained in this country.

Joseph was exchanged for Jerome on the afternoon of the second. The evening before, Captain Brotherton arrived with the wagon train and the Napoleon gun, which eased the situation. Tents were pitched for the wounded and a detail was sent to cut wood for fires. By morning, Miles had the Napoleon gun mounted west of the Indian camp out of range of hostile rifles but, when the shells exploded in the valley, the Nez Percés abandoned their positions and took refuge in the coulees where the shells could not reach them.

The third day of the siege the report that Miles had dreaded was brought him by a scout who raced in to say that a large number of black objects were moving down from the north. Miles's mittened fingers gripped his field glasses as he raised them to his eyes. The rumor of approaching Sioux spread among the officers and men, and they joined Miles in the attempt to pierce the spinning flakes that obscured the hills. Miles figured quickly how he would place the troops to meet the attack and where he would put his artillery. He did not for a moment consider retreat. He was watching the figures draw closer and closer when a scout on the ridge shouted, "Buffalo!"

Miles lowered his glasses, the tension easing from his muscles. All about him, tightly held breaths exploded in relief.

This did not lessen the danger of attack from the Sioux. Again Miles resorted to the twelve-pounder. Changing the position of the gun, he ordered the trail sunk in a pit which enabled the piece to be fired like a howitzer. This time a shell exploded in a dugout which had been considered safe by the Nez Percés. Casualties grew in the Indian camp.

The siege was still going on the evening of the fourth when Howard rode in out of the storm. Miles met him on horseback wrapped against the cold in his fur-collared coat. "We have the Indians corralled down yonder in the direction of the firing," he told the General.

Howard was accompanied by his two aides, Lieutenant C. E. Wood and Lieutenant Guy Howard and a small escort of enlisted men. Howard was no help to Miles. What Miles needed was Sturgis's cavalry to reinforce his troops, but Howard had left Sturgis on the Missouri. Miles suspected Howard had come to assume command of his force at the moment of victory as he had assumed command of Sturgis's troops. He had no intention of giving up his command if it could be avoided. Howard promised he would not take over, and Miles relaxed. Howard's bearded face was lined with fatigue, and Miles felt genuine pity for his old wartime commander.

Howard had brought two Nez Percé scouts with him, and in the morning they went down to the village under a flag of truce to try to persuade Joseph to another parley. Joseph knew further resistance was useless and agreed to capitulate. His surrender speech, which was to be so widely quoted later, was simple and moving.

> . . . I am tired of fighting. Our chiefs are killed. Looking Glass is dead. Too-hul-hul-sote is dead. The old men are all dead. It is the young men who say yes or no. He who led on the young men is dead. It is cold and we have no blankets. The little children are freezing to death. My people, some of them, have run away to the hills, and have no blankets, no food; no one knows where they are — perhaps freezing to death. I want to have time to look for my children and see how many of them I can find. Maybe I shall find them among the dead. Hear me, my chiefs. I am tired; my heart is sick and sad. From where the sun now stands I will fight no more forever.[11]

Joseph handed his rifle to Miles. Trumpeter Mulford was to write later that the Chief wore beaded leggings over blanket trousers, beaded moccasins and a blanket. His features were regular, his "piercing black eyes like an eagles." His long black hair was ornamented with feathers. Long braids hung in front of his ears. His bearing was "calm and deliberate." He was indeed, Mulford said admiringly, "a Brave!"[12]

Howard stood beside Miles to accept the surrender.

The Nez Percés were still coming up the hill in sad little

groups to surrender their rifles when Miles wrote to Mary, his first thought, as always, of her.

> Headquarters District of the Yellowstone
> North of Bear Paw Mountains on Snake Creek
> October 5, 1877

I know you will be delighted to learn that we have kept the Nez Perces in a state of siege until this morning, when Chief Joseph surrendered to me. The camp is now about to do the same. We had a very severe engagement, but everything at the present time looks very favorable. I can not give you particulars but Brughier can tell you something about it. I trust it will all end as favorably as it looks now. Lt. Baird was wounded, but is doing very well and will be all right. Captain Hale and Lt. Biddle were killed and Lt. Romeyn and Capt. Godfrey wounded.

General Howard arrived last night.

Miles won the gratitude of the half-starved, freezing Indians by giving them fuel and food. Yellow Wolf, one of the Nez Percé warriors, said the "little boys and girls loved him for that."

The dead were buried and travois made for the wounded. Two days after the surrender, Miles started back with his command and the Nez Percé prisoners for the cantonment on the Yellowstone. The Sioux and Cheyenne scouts went on ahead, each with five captured ponies. Miles moved slowly. The weather continued cold. The country was rough. A number of the wounded died. On the 14th of October, Miles wrote Mary from "Headquarters District of the Yellowstone, Missouri River opposite Lynn Creek."

We arrived here last evening and are crossing today to the south side. I intend to cross the Fifth Infantry, the Indians and two companies of Cavalry, leaving the remainder of the Seventh Cavalry here for the present. I expect we will be obliged to move slowly, as our stock is somewhat reduced for want of grain and the Indian ponies are very poor. I hope to arrive at our new post in ten or eleven days. I may take a small party and go through quicker, but I have not decided. We have Chief Joseph and about 275 to 400 Nez Perces.

Three detachments are still out, to gather up the scattered parties of Indians. The Assiniboines are killing the Nez Perces as I sent them word that they could fight any that escaped and take their arms and ponies.

I have a bit of bad news to tell you, and that is the loss of your white horse. He got loose on the night of the battle, during a very severe snow storm, and wandered off. I expect the Indians got him, as I heard of a horse of his description in their hands, and I have sent for him, but may not recover him. I am very sorry and know you will be, but hope you will not mind too much. You shall have horses enough.

I have great reason to be thankful to have passed through such a terrible fire alive. For five days we were within range of their rifles. The fight was the most fierce of any Indian engagement I have ever been in. The Nez Perces had whipped or evaded at least 3000 troops, and were whipped and captured by 300. We took them completely by surprise. Their herd was grazing along the mountain stream for four miles. We captured about 500 ponies and left 100 dead on the field. Five of the prominent chiefs were killed, out of eight. Chief Joseph surrendered like a man. He is a very superior Indian, far above any others I have met in intelligence and ability, and a fine looking, mild mannered man. Everybody seems to respect him.

The night before the formal surrender General Howard came up with a small escort, but did not assume command or give any directions. He had really nothing to do but witness the completion of the work. I was very glad to have him come up as he has been so badly abused that I am willing to give him any help or share any credit with him.

Miles moved with an advance guard, flankers and a rear guard. He was still wary of the Sioux. Not until weeks later did he discover that the Sioux, when they heard Miles was fighting the Nez Percés at Bear Paws, instead of planning a rescue of their fellow redmen, packed up and moved back into Canada. They'd had too much experience of "Bear Coat" to want to tackle him again.

On the twentieth, Miles wrote Mary again in a letter headed "North of the Divide about 56 miles from home . . ."

> We are moving by short marches toward home. Tomorrow I hope to be on the bend of Sunday Creek and to get to my darlings in three days, possibly four. We have to move slowly on account of the weak condition of the Indian ponies and our own stock. We have Chief Joseph and the main body of the Nez Perces. I have sent out three detachments to bring in any of the scattered Indians that are still out, but they have not returned and I presume will not overtake us before we reach the Tongue River. The wounded were sent down to Buford. The Seventh Cavalry were left at Camp Hale opposite the mouth of Lynn Creek. Lt. Baird is coming with us, but Mrs. Baird should not expect to see him slightly wounded for he received a very bad shot through the left arm and left ear, which will lay him up for several months. He is doing very well and will get along without any trouble, and probably go in in advance of the command, possibly day after tomorrow. It was a very fierce fight, the death struggle by the Indians and gallantly fought by the troops. The whole Nez Perce movement is unequalled in the history of Indian warfare.

Mary received a fright, as did the other wives at the post, when the Sioux and Cheyenne scouts arrived ahead of the command, whooping and chanting their war songs. The captured ponies showed the command had fought a successful engagement with the Nez Percés but the wives were alarmed by the scouts making signs some of the officers had been killed. To Mary's relief, the scouts soon assured her the Big Chief was all right. Not until Johnny Brughière, the interpreter, arrived did the women learn that the two officers who had been killed were the two bachelors.

Once again, Miles wrote Mary.

> Headquarters District of the Yellowstone
> Head of Sunday Creek
> October 21

> Your sweet letter of the 18th reached me today. I am very happy to realize that I am so near home and have the bright anticipation of being with my precious ones so soon again. I think this will be one of our happiest reunions, for I have everything to make me perfectly happy and am receiving congratulations every day. Our victory was indeed very complete, but it was won with great difficulty and true gallantry by the troops.

> I have Captain Hale's sorrel horse, but his beautiful white horse fell on the field, a short distance from where the gallant officer met his death wound. I passed them both several times during the engagement.

> I have named the camp opposite the Musselshell after Hale and presume a post will be built there.

Two days later, the command reached the Yellowstone.

CHAPTER XVI

MILES could well be pleased by the victory at Bear Paws. His reputation was now established. Newspapers across the country carried the story. Terry praised Miles's prompt action. Sheridan telegraphed congratulations. Sherman expressed approval, although publicly he divided his praise between Miles and his old comrade-in-arms, General Howard.

"Of course Colonel Miles and his officers and men are entitled to all honor and praise," Sherman wrote, "for their prompt, skillful and successful work; while the others, by their long, toilsome pursuit are entitled to corresponding credit."[1]

A version of the battle, purported to be Miles's, appeared in a Chicago newspaper. Lieutenant Wood, Howard's aide, felt it gave too much glory to Miles and wrote what he termed a "true" version, making Howard the hero. Sheridan was furious. The result caused dissension. A year later, Howard was still trying to justify the "charge of slowness so freely imputed to my command."[2] Miles, for once, did not enter the argument, perhaps because by this time he was involved in another controversy, indeed, in several of them.

The more immediate concerned the Nez Percés. A few weeks after Miles returned to Tongue River an order arrived to ship the Indians south. Miles had intended to care for Joseph's people as he had the Sioux and Cheyennes who surrendered after Wolf Mountain and who continued to camp about the post, happily overgrazing the country and trying the patience of the citizens of the town that had grown up near the Fort and been named Miles City. In the spring, when the snow melted, the Nez Percés would be escorted back to Idaho. But the settlers in that state, secure on the lands they had stolen from the Indians, refused to allow the Nez Percés to return to their home and Sherman sided with them. "They [the Nez Percés] should never again be allowed to return to Oregon or to Lapwai."[3]

The Nez Percés were loaded on boats, taken to Bismarck, then to Leavenworth and, finally, to the hot lowlands of Indian Territory where, under the auspices of the Indian Bureau, many of them died of malaria and malnutrition. This, Miles stormed angrily, was a violation of the surrender terms. He had assured Joseph he could go back to Idaho. The government had broken his word to an honorable foe.

The fight to allow Joseph and his people to go back to their home was to continue for a number of years, to the annoyance of Sherman, the Secretary of War and various Congressmen.

Meanwhile, another disagreement arose between Sherman and his nephew-in-law. Miles felt the Canadian government should not give refuge to his old enemy, Sitting Bull. The Chief was a focal point for dissatisfied Indians all over the Northwest and, in 1878 and 1879, there were many dissatisfied Indians. Conditions were bad at the agencies. Crazy Horse was dead, bayoneted in the guardhouse at Camp Robinson.[4] Spotted Tail and Red Cloud Agencies were moved east toward the Missouri where the contractors flourished by providing maggoty flour and diseased beef to the Indians — and very little of that. When Congress appropriated funds to feed the Indians it was thought the rations could be supplemented by game, but the game had disappeared. The same thing was happening in the Northwest that had happened in Kansas and Texas. The vast areas that had once been free to the buffalo and the nomad

Indian had become farming land. Cattle had replaced the buffalo. Railroads traversed the prairies. "A more violent and radical change than any like space of the earth's surface," wrote Sheridan, wonderingly, of the Division of the Missouri which he commanded.[5]

For some months, there was danger of an uprising from the starving tribes penned up on the reservations. Crazy Horse's old band broke away from the agency and made for the Powder River which their dead chief had loved and lost. From the Powder River, the Oglalas rode north to join Sitting Bull. At intervals they slipped back to raid American territory, which justified Miles's claims that as long as Sitting Bull was free, the Sioux would continue to fight.

Miles did not blame the Indians for trying to leave the reservations. Like every other officer, he blamed the Indian Bureau for much of the difficulty. Sheridan accused the Indian Department of "wretched mismanagement."[6] Gibbon, temporarily commanding the Department of Dakota in Terry's absence, wrote that most of the Gros Ventres and Assiniboines were starving. The agents were interested in the Indians' souls, the military in their bodily wants. The agents, Gibbon said, were so busy preparing the Indian for heaven, that he made hell for him on earth. The military, not the agents, suffered in the resulting warfare. "The Bannocks, poor wretches, had to starve, turn hostile or appeal to the military for protection."[7]

The Bannocks, who were in Idaho, were mainly Howard's concern, but a small band broke away and, after raiding several ranches, headed east through Yellowstone Park. Unfortunately for the Bannocks, Miles was vacationing in the Park. It was one of the few sightseeing trips he had taken. Mary and Cecelia were in the party as well as a number of other ladies, three children, ten officers and a hundred enlisted men. The soldiers were veterans of the recent campaigns and Miles was rewarding them by the trip through Yellowstone. When Miles received word of the approach of the Bannocks, he sent the women to Fort Ellis, made a forced march to Clark's Fork Pass and, catching the Indians by surprise, defeated them in a short but brisk battle. The trip was then resumed, although the members of the party were more subdued than they had been before the Indian skirmish. One of the officers had been killed and several men wounded. Mary was visibly shaken.

Governor Potts of Montana Territory, hearing of the battle on Clark's Fork, telegraphed Sherman in Washington that Miles had "struck" the Bannocks and that "our people are clamorous for Miles to command all Montana troops."[8]

Miles approved of the people's request. Montana, he felt, could be made a Department, similar to the Department of Dakota, with himself in command. The northern Territory had a great future with its "vast area of rich grazing, agricultural and mineral lands . . . The natural grasses of Montana will give more strength to horses and mules than those found in any territory between this and the Rio Grande." The climate was healthful. ". . . The natives of this section, I think are as vigorous and hardy a race as can be found on the globe."[9]

No wonder Miles was popular in Montana when he made such a report to the Secretary of War. However, the creation of a military Department was not within the jurisdiction of the people. The decision rested with the Commanding General of the Army and, at that moment, relations between Sherman and Miles were somewhat strained due to the argument over Sitting Bull.

In February of 1878, Sherman reprimanded Miles sharply. He wrote that he was always glad to hear from Miles.

. . . but of late you have introduced into your letters too much important official matter, to answer which I might overlook the great principle that you hold a subordinate tho most important position and that it is not right that we should correspond on subjects direct ignoring Generals Sheridan and Terry. Were I either of these I would resent such acts on the part of others, and I will not be guilty of it myself. Therefor I must insist that on all official subjects you address me through Department Commander. . .

I have [Sherman continued] already paid you compliments almost fulsome, but I cannot make you a Brigadier General nor can I advise a new Department for your special command, nor can I modify my opinions found on a more comprehensive survey of the northern Frontier than you have made. I advise you to do nothing rash but leave to time to accomplish much that you now think can be done by you exclusively. I doubt if you should carry winter operations north of the Missouri River and most undoubtedly were you without the positive orders of the Government here in Washington to cross the British line, on the theory that the Canadian authorities are not acting in good faith, you would endanger the high reputation you now possess . . .[10]

Mary felt Sherman was unfair and, in a letter dated March of 1879, expressed her indignation to her Uncle John. She had, she said, been to Uncle John's house and her Aunt Cecelia had told her that there was to be a Cabinet meeting that afternoon and

the subject I have so much at heart may be brought up. The President told Genl Miles and myself that he had been so strongly petitioned to send Genl back to Montana, he had determined to do so. The Postmaster General as well as yourself told us that the matter had been discussed in Cabinet and decided upon. The matter however was refered to General Sherman on his return. He has vetoed it and is about sending

Genl Ruger to that Department, an officer who has never been west of the Missippi River and never seen a hostile Indian. He ranks Genl Miles as a Col and of course would have command. Uncle Cump certainly loses all sight of justice, in his peculiar sensitiveness about doing any thing for a relation. If Genl Miles were a stranger he would do this in a moment and listen to the petitions of the people but he seems to regard this as a favor to be refused because he happens to be connected with his family. An officer should have *some* reward for such faithful and successful work as Genl Miles has done in that country. Genl will not speak to Uncle on the subject he is so indignant and hurt and he does not know that I am appealing to you. Perhaps you might have some influence with him if not the Secretary of War, and the President can easily . . . give him the Department and Command he has so well earned. Uncle will probably say the old Col's would make a fuss about it but none of them have done the work deserving it. I regret having to trouble you on the subject but there is no use appealing to Uncle Cump . . .

On the the back of this letter, John Sherman inked a note which read:

Mr. President:
   Please read this letter, which explains itself.

But Sherman was adamant against creation of another Department and the President accepted the decision of the Commanding General.

The Miles's were in Washington the winter of 1878 and 1879 while Miles served on the Equipment Board. The ill feeling between Sherman and his nephew-in-law threatened to erupt into an open feud. After an interview at the War Department, Sherman suggested to Miles that he put his grievances into writing. Miles complied by a letter from Ebbits House where he was staying. He had, he said, subdued Sitting Bull, Crazy Horse, Lame Deer, the Nez Percés and the Bannocks in movements that had been unauthorized and unwanted by the Department Commander. And what had he received as a reward? Sherman refused to allow him to pursue Sitting Bull. He turned down the pleas of the Montana Legislature and Governor to create a Department of Montana and sent a colonel senior to Miles (Ruger) to Yankton who, in an emergency, would supersede Miles.[11]

To this, Sherman replied the next day that he had repeatedly offered Miles a recruiting detail which he had refused, so that he could not say he had been forced to remain in a job with no future. As to the creation of a Department of Montana, it had been looked into and voted against by the War Department and there the matter should end.[12]

Miles answered the same day that, ". . . after the urgent appeals, the approval of the President and his Cabinet, I cannot but regard your unfavorable decision and action the severest injury that has been done me by any official or friend . . ."[13]

Back came a short note from Sherman wishing Miles all due honor "and warning you against a fatal mistake. I am as ever Sincerely your friend . . ."[14]

Miles spent a sleepless night over this letter of Sherman's and, in the morning, wrote a letter to Sherman which came as near an apology as he ever came and which he would not have written to another man in the country. Despite his differences with Sherman, he respected the General who was dedicated to the Army. The Montana citizens, Miles wrote, not he, had interceded with the President to create a new Department. ". . . I have no rights or claims beyond those of a soldier, who has endeavored to do his duty." He intended to leave Washington that night, Miles told Sherman, "and I remain with great respect your friend . . ."[15]

En route back to Fort Keogh, Miles stopped in Cleveland where he was operated on for a "tumor" that was caused by an injury received in one of the Indian campaigns. While he lay abed, he asked Mary to write and thank Senator Sherman for his interest and to say he — Miles — was perfectly satisfied with the decision of the Secretary of War. But Miles was not thoroughly subdued. Within a short time, he was back in the saddle, and in the summer, when Sitting Bull's camp was reported over the Canadian border, he set out after his old enemy. Mackenzie had crossed the border after the Apaches in 1872. Miles did not see why he could not cross the Canadian border after the Sioux, although Sherman had warned him, ". . . Because as you explained Generals Sheridan and Mackenzie once consented to act unlawfully and violently in defiance of my authority in a certain political contingency, is no reason why I should imitate so bad an example . . ."[16]

Ignoring Sherman, Miles rode north of the Missouri and the Milk to Frenchman's Creek where he encountered the Indians. Seven troops of the Second Cavalry and as many companies of the Fifth Infantry, mounted on the famous captured ponies, charged across the dun-colored prairie with a shrill of bugles. The artillery, galloping into position, unlimbered and fired into the milling mass of Sioux. Terrified by the attack, the Indians ran, leaving their lodges and horse herd to the soldiers. Miles was not satisfied by victory in a single skirmish. The Sioux, he felt, should be routed completely and for all time, so that the frontier could be safe for settlers and he — Miles — could do it if Sherman would not hinder his operations. In a letter to Mary dated the thirteenth of July, he expressed his resentment.

Camp on Rocky Creek

If I had not been active I would have been prevented from driving Sitting Bull over the Canadian border by orders from the General of the Army, who telegraphed me that the object of my movement was to defend our friendly Indians, not to move north of the Milk River and to protect the navigation of the Missouri (a river that has been free for twenty years). I was also informed that if there were more Indians than I had troops the 18th Infantry would be brought down and General Terry would come up, etc., etc. Although Sitting Bull had five warriors to my one, the work was accomplished before any restraining orders were received, without loss of a single soldier and without any assistance.

Sherman, undoubtedly, felt that Terry would be a restraining influence on the impetuous Miles. The papers were beginning to critize the commander on the Yellowstone for rashness. Mary, reading the papers at Fort Keogh, sprang to her beloved husband's defense. In a letter to Senator Sherman, she said the General was ordered to take the field a few days after his return to Keogh.

He was ordered out with a very small command to operate against such a strong and well armed force as Sitting Bull is now almost universally admitted to have. He started north more than a month ago and has had an engagement with them and has driven them over the line. Now dispatches from the East tell us that the President has ordered the withdrawal of the troops, not wanting to provoke hostilities and wishing to avoid any international questions. It is stated also that the President and Secretary of War admit their confidence in Genl Miles fighting abilities but fear he may be rash and . . . provoke a fight. Now any one who knows anything of Genl Miles's character *knows* he never is rash, and as to his being ambitious to get into a fight, there is nothing he so much deprecates, and he had no heart in *this* campaign, frequently telling me he considered it most unfortunate and ill advised at this time, being sure of bringing on an —— questions. The blame and censure for this ill advised campaign should rest where it originated and not upon Genl Miles shoulders where it seems to be laid by men who are trying to break down his reputation with the President and Secretary of War. Would you object to explaining to the President if you have an opportunity. Genl Miles as a subordinate officer would not explain this. He is now hundreds of miles away from me and unconscious of all the criticism he is subjected to, but I cannot allow so palpable an injustice to remain unexplained. Pardon me for troubling you with so unimportant a matter. —— is of such vital importance to my husband's future that I know you will be interested in it . . .[17]

Mary was incorrect when she said Miles did not know how he was being criticized. He was fully aware of it, and he was not as reluctant as Mary thought to take the field — only reluctant to fight under restrictions.

Terry did not "come up" and Miles refused to "come down" until he had accomplished his mission. The Sioux were being supplied with ammunition, food and liquor by a group of mixed French and Indian traders called the Red River breeds. The most effective way to strike at the Sioux was through their supply lines, so Miles rounded up all the Red River breeds south of the Canadian line, together with their carts, horses, tents and other property, and escorted them out of the country. On the 12th of August, he wrote Mary from Fort Peck.

After all the fuss and hubub they have made over my expedition, it has been emminently successful. We drove the whole Sitting Bull following out of the country, so badly frightened that they promise not to come back again. We then turned and scattered from Pacafun Creek almost to

Belknap and captured 829 half breeds with over six hundred carts and finally wound up the campaign by capturing Short Bull's band as they were crossing the Missouri. This band had left the southern agencies, stole some stock about the Black Hills and crossed the Yellowstone below O'Fallon Creek. I had scattered the Fifth Infantry and some Indians along the Missouri to watch for them, and day before yesterday Whistler with four companies of the Fifth captured them. They were over fifty with about one hundred head of stock. I wonder how the troops south, who allowed them to come up from the Department of the Platte, will like this? I intend to send them down the Missouri on the steamer Sherman, when she goes down.

Miles could not resist the crack at Crook who commanded the "troops south." In a second letter from Fort Peck, he took another crack at his rival.

I have very little now to do myself as my command is deployed along the Missouri and at New Beaver Creek. I am ordered to look out for Indians both ways. It seems strange that the troops of the rest of the army have nothing else to do but draw their pay and rations. They allow the Indians to escape and to pass several posts without the least effort being made to capture them, and then I am ordered to try and catch them, besides attending to the great area north of the Missouri.

General Terry has sent the most complimentary dispatches of congratulations.

Miles was not concerned that the line was extremely thin between congratulations and official reprimand.

A number of people, in addition to the members of the Montana Legislature, urged Miles's promotion. Westerners did not agree with Easterners that Miles was rash. Some officers felt

Miles's services should be recognized. Hancock, Miles's old division commander and presently commander of the Division of the Atlantic, recommended Miles for a brigadier general in 1878 and for Chief Signal Officer in 1880.[18] In the fall of the same year, the Governor of Massachusetts recommended Miles for the position.[19] In 1879, Grant remarked in the presence of Mr. Charles Fairchild of Boston that ". . . If called upon to name the five best officers in our army, now living, I should name Sherman and Sheridan, ranking them alike, Schofield, Miles, Mackenzie. The two younger men have not had a chance to show all thats in them and may belong higher than I have put them."[20]

Sherman, in all fairness, could not hold back longer. In 1880 when a vacancy occurred, Miles was appointed a brigadier general, and detailed to command of the Department of the Columbia. If Sherman had his doubts about his strong-minded nephew-in-law, he did not say so. At least, he could no longer strain relations with Canada by threatening to pursue Sitting Bull beyond the border.

PART FIVE

The Apache Campaign

CHAPTER XVII

MILES commanded the Department of the Columbia from 1881 to 1885 in what was, for him, a remarkably routine manner. He sent an exploring expedition to Alaska and settled a threatened disturbance with the Okinagan Indians and, in 1885, finally succeeded in bringing the Nez Percés back to the Northwest. Now and then the spark flared, as when the Finance Officer docked him for approximately a week's pay for being AWOL en route from the East to Vancouver Barracks. Miles told the Finance Officer his child had been ill and he'd had to remain in the East for medical attention and he wanted his money. The discussion went on for some time. Miles was afraid that, eventually, he was going to end up in the poorhouse. Army pay was disgracefully low and expenses were heavy. If he were killed, Mary would not have enough to support herself. The widow of a young officer with two small children received seventeen dollars a month pension. Crook and Sheridan, to augment their pay, invested in a gold mine which did not materialize. Grant, ex-President and commander of all the Union armies, pawned his sword to get funds. Miles invested in a gold mine, too, without success. Miles's concern was for his family. He now had two children. In 1882 Mary bore a son who was named Sherman Miles, his mother's maiden name as well as that of his two prominent great-uncles, the Senator and the General. The boy was blond and slight and, the first years of his life, not unduly strong, which bothered Miles. He had been so extraordinarily robust in his own youth. But he was delighted with the boy and wanted him to have every advantage. In 1884 Miles was forty-five years old. He was heavier than he had been on the Yellowstone and his hair was thinner on his temples. He was still remarkably handsome and he could out-ride any man in his command.

In 1883, Sherman retired from active service to live quietly in St. Louis and, finally, in New York. An attempt to capitalize on his reputation in the presidential election of 1884 was a failure when the General issued his famous ultimatum that if he were nominated, he would not run and that if he were elected, he would not serve. Miles was disappointed. He might not see eye to eye with Sherman but he would have been glad to have his uncle-in-law as President. From experience, he knew Sherman's integrity. Miles was in Washington off and on and took a keen interest in politics, stating his views with his customary forthrightness.

Sherman's successor was Phil Sheridan, a fortunate choice for Miles. Sheridan liked aggressive officers and while he'd had his differences with Miles (as who hadn't?) he knew that if a situation demanded action, he could depend on the ex-commander from the Yellowstone. In the summer of 1885, Sheridan and Miles made a trip together to the Indian Terri-tory where an outbreak was feared among the tribes driven to desperation by starvation and abuse. Miles had been transferred to the command of the Missouri with headquarters at Fort Leavenworth and en route to his new station, he met Sheridan. From Chicago the two generals traveled south.

In seventeen days, Miles and Sheridan traveled three hundred and thirty-five miles in a wagon. Miles did not say why he did not ride. He would have been more comfortable on a horse. Perhaps Sheridan preferred a wagon. Miles complained of the "disagreeable and fatiguing journey." Actually, he was not very tired and he got along well with Sheridan. The trip, Miles wrote Mary, was successful; an outbreak was averted.

Miles had been a brigadier general for five years. Wesley Merritt, still a colonel, was Superintendent at West Point. Ranald Mackenzie, who had been made a brigadier general two years after Miles, had become so irrational that he had to be confined in an asylum in New York. In 1886 General Pope retired for age, and Hancock, Miles's old friend, died at Governors Island. This created two vacancies. Miles felt he was eligible for promotion. Francis Barlow, Miles's friend of the 61st New York Volunteers in the Civil War and still his admirer, wrote a letter recommending Miles for a major generalcy. Howard, Terry and Crook were senior to Miles, Barlow said, but the President did not have to be bound by the rules of seniority. Miles was superior in military ability to the others, especially to Crook who had been made a brigadier general over all the lieutenant colonels and many colonels in 1873[1] by Grant and since then had done nothing to warrant a new promotion. No volunteer officer, as distinguished from a West Pointer, had been made a major general since the war. Miles, Barlow said, was the most outstanding volunteer in the Regular Army. Not only was he successful in war but he was successful in peace. He was respected by the tribes and he understood their management and problems.[2]

Not content with writing this letter, Barlow went to Washington to see the President personally. Letters were also written by the Governor of Oregon, the Mayor of Leavenworth and various other prominent citizens. It was to no avail. The President (who was Cleveland by this time) decided to rely on seniority and made Alfred Terry and Oliver Otis Howard major generals. Perhaps Sherman had something to do with it. Sherman believed in seniority. Sheridan, evidently, did not agree with the President, for in April of 1886 Mary's sister, Miss Elizabeth Sherman who had visited the Mileses at Fort Keogh and who had married Senator Don Cameron, wrote that in an interview with her husband Sheridan had gone over the list of officers with the comment, "In fact, Miles is the only man who amounts to anything, and on whom we can count, and I told the President and Secretary so yesterday."[3]

The letter did not console Miles. He had thought he should, and would, win the promotion. In a somewhat touchy mood, he received a wire from Sheridan directing him to proceed immediately to the Department of Arizona to "prevent the spread of hostilities among the friendly Indians . . . and to carry on the most vigorous operations looking to the destruction or capture of the hostiles."[4]

Miles was to relieve the present Department Commander, General George Crook.

Miles was not pleased. He did not like the Southwest or the Apaches, whom Crook called "human tigers." For years, the Apaches had terrorized the southwestern United States and Mexico. They were "cruel, crafty [and] wary . . ." said Colonel George Forsyth who knew them well.[5] When pursued by troops, the Apaches retreated across the desert to the mountain peaks, where cavalry broke down from the heat and lack of water but where the Apache subsisted easily on field mice and cactus. If pursuit drew too close, the Indians scattered so that the soldiers found themselves trailing a single pair of moccasin tracks which soon disappeared among the lava rocks. By his campaigns of 1871–1875 Crook finally succeeded in placing these Indians on reservations. In 1886 the two main tribes, the Warm Springs and Chiricahuas, were on the Fort Apache and San Carlos reservations. The great chiefs, Cochise, Victorio and Mangus Colorado, were dead and the tribes broken up into small bands. Leader of one of these small bands was Geronimo, a squat, broad-shouldered Indian with lank hair hanging to his shoulders, close-set eyes and a mouth turned down in an ugly line. An officer who served with Apache scouts described him as a "thoroughly vicious, intractable and treacherous man."[6] Geronimo was the main instigator of a new outbreak which, after some months of strenuous campaigning, resulted in a conference between Crook and Geronimo. A number of the hostiles who surrendered to Crook were shipped off to prison in Florida, but Geronimo fled back to the hills. The escape of the chief resulted in Crook's relief by Miles.

At the same time that Miles was ordered to take over the Department of Arizona, Oliver Otis Howard, newly made major general, took over the Division of the Pacific, which included the Arizona Department. Thus, Miles found himself under his old commander who was still smarting from his defeat by the Nez Percés and sensitive about the younger officer who had succeeded where he had failed . . . Whether Miles was aware of how deeply Howard was hurt by adverse newspaper publicity is uncertain. Miles bore Howard no rancor. Indeed, he was careful not to criticize him, and if an officer senior to him had to be promoted in his place, he preferred Howard to Crook.

Crook was still in Arizona when Miles arrived on the eleventh of April and detrained at Bowie Station on the Southern Pacific Railroad. Miles had one man with him, Frank Brown, a clerk and stenographer, whose fare he had paid from Leavenworth. Strung out along the tracks were the tents and picket lines of a battalion of Second Cavalry. The heat beneath the canvas was stifling, and flies swarmed everywhere. In the post's depressingly arid cemetery stood a number of wooden headboards reading "Killed by Apaches." "Tortured and killed by Apaches."

That evening Miles wrote to Mary after his conference with Crook.

> I arrived today after a long, hot and very dusty trip. I think this is the most barren region I have ever seen.
>
> From what I can see and hear of the troops, they are very much discouraged by being kept in the field so long and by the prospect that the campaign must be continued for some time to come. General Crook leaves tomorrow. He appears to feel very much disappointed but does not say much. He tells me that only two of the Apache warriors have been killed since they broke out.
>
> In many respects this is the most difficult task I have ever undertaken, on account of the extensive country, the natural difficulties and the fact that the hostiles are so few in number and so active. Still I can only make the best effort possible.[7]

The situation had to be very bad, indeed, when Miles sounded depressed. He was unfamiliar with the country, the members of the command and the Indians. If he'd had officers whom he knew on his staff, he would have felt more confident. He made no mention of resentment among Crook's officers but he can hardly have failed to see the men did not like the manner in which Crook had been relieved — anyhow, those who had been closely associated with Crook during the last few years. It would have been interesting to know whether Crook, as he talked to Miles, remembered how he had relieved General Stoneman in 1871. Then, Crook had noted that Mrs. Stoneman, while trying to be polite, would have liked to tear him to pieces.

The next day Miles took over the Department of Arizona and with a continued lack of enthusiasm wrote Mary.

Fort Bowie, Arizona
April 12, 1886

Today I assumed command of this Department and have taken up the difficult burden. It will take me some days to get control of affairs, as it is a very extensive country. The troops are scattered over three Territories and well down in Old Mexico.

General Crook seems very much worried and disappointed, and the troops are somewhat disheartened as they had all hoped to go home.

The taciturn, bearded Crook concealed a futile anger and disappointment at the manner of his leaving Arizona. For eight years he had fought the Apaches and when the job was nearly done, he was replaced by Miles. He cannot have been happy. Crook had relied on his Apache scouts. His devotion to them was almost as well known as his devotion to his pack trains. In his wire to Miles on the second of April, Sheridan had said he deemed it advisable to make "active and prominent" use of regular troops. The scouts, Sheridan felt, were unreliable.[8]

On the 17th of April, after Crook had departed to his old command of the Department of the Platte, Miles wrote Mary.

Fort Bowie, Arizona

The latest news of Geronimo was that his band had gone four hundred miles down into Old Mexico, and I shall not object if they keep going. We can spare them and others as well. But Indians are very unreliable, and when we think them the farthest away some times they come back. I will endeavor to arrange the command so that it may be as effective as possible in case they do come back.

I have not yet decided who I shall appoint [to the staff] but probably some officer out here who has done good service. There are many fine officers serving in these regiments.

Miles's spirits improved as he grew more active and his customary confidence returned, although there was little enough to be confident about. A number of citizens of the Territory told him it was useless to try to subjugate the Apaches. The army had been fighting them for years without success. Miles paid no attention. With his strategy firmly in mind, he organized the country into districts, each with a troop commander. Guards were stationed at the water holes. The infantry was ordered to pursue the Indians through the mountains and to guard the passes and supply dumps. The cavalry was to be employed in light scouting parties and in long pursuits. A limited number of Indians were to be used as scouts. Pursuit of the hostiles south of the border was assigned to command of Captain Henry W. Lawton of the Fourth Cavalry, an officer with a distinguished Civil War record and years of experience on the frontier. Lawton was a giant of a man who agreed with Miles that white troops could outdo the Apaches. The doctor with Lawton's select force was Assistant Surgeon Leonard Wood, a young athlete recently graduated from Harvard Medical School.

Last but not least, Miles established heliostat stations on high peaks to flash information of the hostiles.

The heliostat, which was a system of flashing messages by mirrors, was an innovation in the campaign. Stations were situated on high mountains, manned by two or three operators. Reported movements of the Indians were flashed from one station to another; military messages were transmitted. There were even weekly weather reports. The saving in time and manpower were incalculable. The heliograph, Miles felt, played an important part in the control of the Apaches.

But before Lawton's command was organized, the Apaches attacked three places simultaneously in central Sonora south of the border.

THE APACHE CAMPAIGN 233

On the 13th of May, Miles told Mary that he had "received information of quite a serious engagement between the Mexicans and Indians about fifteen miles south of the boundary." He might, he continued, have to go west the next day. Troops were stationed north and east of the Indians but Miles did not expect to carry on a campaign in Old Mexico. All he could do at present was endeavor to keep the Indians out of the United States.

"In all my experience on the frontier," Miles declared, "I have never found so distressed and terror-stricken people, and if I succeed in giving them some security and protection it will afford me much gratification."[9]

Settlers were afraid to travel during the day, and at night slept with their guns beside them. Many ranches and mines were abandoned. The alarm spread as the hostiles moved north to the border, crossed and went through the Santa Cruz valley stealing stock and killing a number of settlers. Among the victims were a mother and child. The Apaches had no use for a child too young to walk. They either dashed its brains out on a rock or impaled it on a cactus. A detachment of the Tenth Cavalry found the Indian trail and followed it for two hundred miles across arid, mesquite plains, down canyons cut deep in solid rock and over deserts of volcanic scoria where the lava cut the horses' feet and the heat shimmered with mirage. In the Pinito Mountains thirty miles south of the border in Sonora, the troop caught up with the Indians, who scattered in their usual manner. The troops, horses and men, too exhausted to follow, gave up the chase to another detachment of the Fourth Cavalry who pursued the hostiles south and west until the trail was again taken up by the Tenth Cavalry, and then by Lawton. Captain Charles A. Hatfield of the Fourth Cavalry intercepted the hostiles east of Santa Cruz, Sonora, and taking them by

surprise captured twenty horses and most of their camp equipment, but the Indians scattered again and got away and, while
Hatfield was passing through a rock-walled gorge, they ambushed him. The Apaches were past masters at ambush. Con-
cealing themselves behind boulders or clumps of mesquite,
they waited for their prey — bodies naked except for breech
cloth and moccasins, long hair hanging to their shoulders,
black eyes glittering, faces smeared with deer blood.

In the first savage attack, one soldier was killed and several
wounded.

Miles, who had moved down to Nogales to be closer to the
scene of action, wrote Mary that he had received the news of
Hatfield's engagement and that at first Hatfield had been
successful.

> He captured the camp and some of the stock of Geronimo.
> He was placed in a good position and where he was wanted.
> But unfortunately in marching back through a deep canyon
> he was attacked and severly injured by the Apaches. His
> skirmishers were too far in advance, which was a mistake. I
> presume he was too confident and too elated with his success.
> The Governor of Sonora came up today to meet me here.
> We have a good understanding and are working together.
> Our troops and the Mexicans have fought the Apaches five
> times in about ten days. There will be no let up of effort.
> The Indians have enough ammunition to last them five
> years, upwards of one hundred thousand rounds.[10]

By the next day Miles was at Fort Huachuca, not far from
Nogales, where he told Mary he had been constantly on the
move.

> The reports of Indians in different places has made it neces-
> sary for me to be on several fronts. Thus far we have suc-
> ceeded in keeping them out of our own country, with one
> exception. They came in west of Nogales and raided some

ten or twelve miles along the border. The troops have been very active and have done good service.

Hatfield's command was not hurt seriously. He captured Geronimo's camp and some twenty head of stock. After that, in a fight, his horses got stampeded and he supposed he had lost them, but he has recovered all but two.[11]

The following day was busy and anxious. "I have heard of another fight," Miles wrote Mary. "Lieutenant Brown got on to them and surprised them, capturing many arms, saddles, camp property and ammunition. From last reports they were much broken down, but the fiends recoup readily and I must give them no rest. I don't get much myself, I must say."[12]

The heat bothered Miles. And the sand that sifted into clothes and eyes and food. The land had a strange and terrible beauty but Miles did not see the saffrons and vermilions of distant mesas or the violet shadows of bottomless canyons or the creamy plumes of the Spanish bayonet; he was concerned only with a vast desert that allied itself with a frustratingly elusive foe.

Lieutenant Robert Brown of the Fourth Cavalry, picking up the trail of the hostiles after Hatfield's fight, followed the Indians east until they separated into two bands. Brown followed one band west, giving over the chase to Lawton when his horses and men grew too fatigued to follow further. Lawton pursued the Indians north and then south into the Patagonia Mountains where they were surprised by a detachment of Fourth Cavalry. In a brief but brisk fight, the Indians' horses and camp equipment were captured but the Indians scattered and by the time the scouts picked up their trail, it was too dark to follow. Lawton, who joined the Fourth Cavalry detachment, sent word to Miles that he thought the Apaches were going south to their old stronghold in the Sierra Madres.

The band which had split off from this group had meanwhile

turned toward central Arizona. The leader was Natchez, the son of Cochise and hereditary chieftain of the Chiricahuas. Natchez was over six feet in height, a skilled warrior and a ladies' man. Natchez got as far north as Fort Apache where he turned south again and, pursued by one detachment after another, succeeded in eluding them all and crossing back into Mexico.

At Nogales, Miles waited impatiently for word from the various commands, often staying at the telegraph station until after midnight sending dispatches. Sheridan watched the campaign closely. Crook and Crook's friends waited to see how Miles would deal with the Apaches. Crook, who had served eight years in Arizona, declared white troops could not compete with the Apaches. Miles had staked his reputation on his faith in the rawboned, blistered and underpaid soldier of the United States Army. Morale was a problem. "The troops," Miles wrote Mary, "have been in the field, many of them a year. Some are discouraged and to some extent demoralized; but I think matters will come out all right in the end. Several men have been killed and many others will undoubtedly be before the end is reached."[13]

Miles wondered how the Indians could stand being hunted so long. They "have had quite a severe time lately," he wrote Mary on the twenty-fifth of May, "and have been constantly harassed. They have not done much damage, but still are in our country and must be destroyed, captured or driven out. They captured a little boy about eight miles west of this place, but he was soon recaptured and the troops and men are closely pursuing the hostiles."[14]

Miles felt Natchez's band had gone north to the vicinity of Fort Apache to get aid and hoped the hostiles would surrender. If they did not and succeeded in returning to Mexico, "the campaign may last much longer," he told Mary. "It is tiresome work and very difficult, but not more so than other undertakings."[15]

The last of May, Miles was in Wilcox, Arizona, "a miserable little collection of mud huts and small buildings about like Hays City or some of those western towns years ago, very hot and very dusty when the wind blows. The people, what few there are, are mostly cowboys and saloon keepers."[16]

Miles spent a lonely Sunday in Wilcox. There were few people in whom he could confide the doubts and fears that threatened to swamp his confidence. He had other troubles than the Apaches. The newspapers were beginning to criticize him as they had Crook.

"If the papers had not so much to say about it, I would like it better. But the trouble is this war has been going on so long — in fact, it has been a chronic condition of war for the last thirty years."[17]

On Miles's return to Calabasas on the border, he wrote Mary again that

the reports of Indians escaping or avoiding the troops and occasionally killing some one have annoyed me very much. Last night I was tossing about restlessly and could not sleep. Finally about one o'clock I heard the sound of horses feet, and was very glad to hear from the couriers who arrived that they were from Lt. Walsh. He had been quite successful in intercepting the Indians and capturing their horses, saddles, supplies, etc., putting them on foot in the mountains. This occurred just before dark and Walsh will continue the pursuit at daybreak. Lieut. Bigelow has been close behind them for several days. In fact, they have been hunted by one detachment of troops after another for 36 days. They have tried every device to throw the troops off the trail but have not succeeded. They have been followed rapidly for about one thousand miles. They are heading now straight for Old Mexico and may go far down into that country. I am glad they have been driven out of our country and hope to keep them out. I am expecting some information tonight or tomorrow. I do not expect to remain at this place more than a day or two, and then shall go along the line.[18]

The next day Miles's optimism had vanished. He wrote Mary that he had been at the telegraph the

whole live-long day and am somewhat annoyed because matters do not work out to suit me. When we think we have the best of the Indians they seem to make some move to slip out. But we will get them in time, in spite of their cunning and activity. Yesterday I felt sure they would be driven into Old Mexico today, as a part of them was; but a part slipped out and have been committing some depredations today. I get very tired some nights, but the fatigue does not cause me to sleep for the responsibility and care keep me awake.[19]

Two days later, Miles told Mary the Indians were well down in Old Mexico and that he was organizing a new command to start after them.

CHAPTER XVIII

ON JUNE 15, Miles wrote Mary from Fort Huachuca that he had a "very difficult undertaking, and everyone says I can not succeed. But it has been said before, and I have never doubted my ability to make this country untenable for Indians. I have received the most cordial and zealous support from the troops . . . "[1]

The young artist Frederic Remington came to see Miles at Fort Bowie. Miles had been hunting turkeys and Remington's first glimpse of him was galloping over the prairie on a blue roan horse. Miles, as Remington saw him, was a lean, sun-tanned man with grizzled hair and mustache. His uniform was faded and dusty, the trousers reinforced by buckskin. Miles invited Remington into his meagerly furnished quarters and questioned the then unknown artist until Remington felt Miles knew more about him than he knew himself. Then, pleased by Remington's ambition to paint the soldiers on duty, he took the artist with him to San Carlos Agency — a ride Remington always remembered, for he and the orderly had all they could do to keep up with Miles who rode cross-country at a gallop Indian fashion.

Miles was occupied, at the time, reorganizing the force whose duty it was to pursue the hostiles into Mexico. Also, suspecting the complicity of the Apaches at the agencies, he determined to investigate, and, if necessary, to take measures.

Accompanied by Mr. Lamar, son of the Secretary of the Interior, he visited the San Carlos and Fort Apache agencies.

I am somewhat annoyed by the newspapers publishing such absurd reports and false statements regarding the Indians [he wrote Mary]. One would suppose by their accounts that the whole country was full of Indians and that there was an Apache behind every cactus bush. I am also annoyed by the statements thrown out by Crook. He made a dead failure of this, as he has of every other campaign.[2]

San Carlos was quite different from Apache. The latter was in the foothills while San Carlos was in the lowlands. Drab adobe buildings housed the agency on a gravelly flat. A few scrawny cottonwoods straggled along the slow-moving, muddy stream. Hot dry winds blew constantly. In the summer the temperature reached 110°. There was no tillable land, nothing to hunt but rats and an occasional rabbit. About the agency buildings hung "naked, frightened and dirty Indian children and sullen, stolid, hopeless Indians."[3]

At Fort Apache, the young men were insolent and restless. Nearly every night they indulged in a tizwin drunk. Among them was Chatto, the scout in whom Crook had placed such confidence and who was to be the center of future contention between Crook and Miles. Chatto and Geronimo were on bad terms and a large number of officers believed that it was Chatto's reluctance to be under Geronimo's leadership and not loyalty to Crook that had made him enlist as a scout.

I have been more than busy since I arrived [Miles wrote Mary], and have had long talks and councils with the Indians. There are about 400 Indians about 70 miles below here at San Carlos. There are about 1500 White Mountain Indians here and about 500 Apaches. The latter, although not on the war path, are to some extent in sympathy with the hostiles and liable to go out at any time. It requires a large force to keep them in check and I am anxious to move them to some other

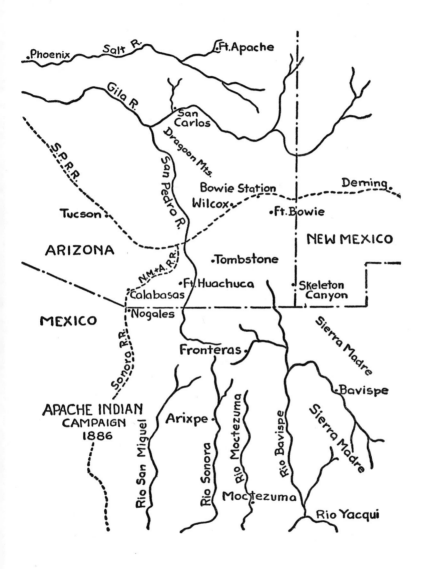

part of the country. I believe this can be done. After much talk I have gotten them to consent to go and look at other lands, and go to Washington to make arrangements about it. I think if I can carry out my plan I can make similar arrangements with these Indians that I have with others.

About a dozen of the prominent Indians have agreed to go. I have requested permission to send them.[4]

Miles believed his solution was sound. The climate of the Indian Territory was similiar to that of the Southwest and there were Apaches already living in the vicinity. Certainly, any place would be better than San Carlos. Co-operation rather than coercion would lead to a peaceful movement of the tribe.

The delegation of ten men, including Chatto, and three women went to Washington to see what terms the government would grant them and to inspect lands in the Indian Territory and Kansas. Opposition from citizens affected by the move of the Indians was immediate. Crook, through Bourke, his ex-aide, did what he could to block Miles's plans.

"When this Indian delegation got to Washington," Miles wrote Mary, "Captain Burke [Bourke] made himself very offensive and went, as you saw, with them to the White House. I think he has furnished the press with very unfavorable reports, has frightened the Indians and in fact has done much mischief. But it was quickly discovered. I telegraphed Dorst and I think Burk's injurious influence has been checked."[5]

Bourke's explanation of his interest in the delegation was that he wanted to be helpful, an excuse that did not pass muster with Miles.

The feeling against these Apaches has been so strong [Miles continued in his letter to Mary], that I fear it will be very difficult to bring about any reasonable settlement. The papers of Arizona and New Mexico are supporting me and howling for their removal out of the Territories. I received a telegram from General Sheridan wanting to know what I thought of sending them to Florida and also one from the delegation in Washington. But that (moving them to Florida) would be bad faith, condemned by all of the eastern press. So it seems a difficult problem to find a foot of U. S. Territory that they can live on in peace and safety. Still I have very strong hopes that I will succeed in placing them where they will do no harm, or under such restrictions as will control them.[5]

Miles wrote a long reply to Sheridan's telegram, hoping it would explain matters. "I do not approve of the suggestion of sending all the Apaches to Florida, especially as a part are now in Washington by authority of the government," he told Mary on the second of August.

"I think they will yet adopt my plan of putting them on some reservation agreeable to them [i.e., the Indian delegation] east of New Mexico and sending all the others there."[6]

But neither President Cleveland nor Sheridan approved of Miles's plans for the removal of the Apaches. The hostiles, when captured, were to be confined at Fort Marion, Florida with the original seventy-seven who had surrendered under Crook.

The orders to that effect reached Miles while Colonel James F. Wade was rounding up the Indians at Fort Apache. Miles, who had hoped for an agency agreeable to the Apaches, was disappointed.

My enemies at Washington have done so much to embarass and oppose my efforts that they are quite likely to spoil the whole thing [he told Mary]. I could have moved them [i.e. the Apaches] without the least trouble if I had not been interfered with, but now they have been ordered to Fort Marion, Florida, and if they find it out many of them will die before they will go there, or break away and go on the warpath. I consider it very bad policy and unjust, particularly to the women and children. One of Geronimo's children has already died since he was sent there.

This campaign is like many others, the annoyances in the rear are greater than those in the front.[7]

Miles had no choice. If he wanted to bring peace to the Department, the Apaches had to go to Florida.

Rounding up the Indians at the agency was a touchy business, for there were many warriors among the Chiricahuas. Miles went to Wilcox where he could be in direct telegraphic communication with the Fort. He did not want to interfere with Colonel Wade, so he asked the operator at Fort Apache, whose window overlooked the area where the Indians were gathered, to report to him.

"Let me know fully what is going on," the operator at Wilcox tapped out to the operator at Apache.

"I will," the operator replied.[8]

Miles paced the floor of the tiny office, pausing eagerly when the key began to clatter. He had ordered additional troops to Apache. The Indians were surrounded and the warriors ordered to a large building under guard while the women were told to gather up their belongings. Everything went according to plan. Greatly relieved, Miles wrote Mary that Wade had succeeded in carrying out his orders. Wade started for Holbrook, the nearest railroad point, one hundred miles distant, with the Indians; and Miles, satisfied that the Colonel would have no more difficulty, turned his attention to Geronimo.

When the Indians at Fort Apache were gone, Miles felt sure the hostiles would surrender, "as they will have no assistance or place to go to."[9]

The last of June, one of Geronimo's warriors who'd had a bellyful of fighting and made his way back to the agency, reported Geronimo was in a bad way. The middle of July, Miles heard that Geronimo had been wounded and that Natchez, his brother-in-law, was in command. A bloody shirt had been found on the Indian trail which was thought to belong to Geronimo, but before it could be identified a hungry mule made his breakfast on it!

Shortly afterward, the papers reported Geronimo wanted to surrender. "There is no truth in the report," Miles told Mary, "and in fact nearly everything you see in these Arizona dispatches are made up out of nothing. The correspondents send anything for a sensation, and seem not to care whether it be true or false."[10]

Before leaving the United States on their latest foray, the Apaches attacked a ranch and tied up the owner, a man named Peck, to witness the torture of his wife until she died, an experience so horrible the rancher went out of his mind. The Pecks' little girl, thirteen years old, was carried into Mexico by the Indians, and later rescued by Lawton.

Lawton's carefully selected command consisted of one company of infantry, thirty-five cavalrymen, twenty scouts, a hundred pack mules and thirty packers. For nearly three months, this small force held grimly to the bloody trail of the Apaches. In one day, Lieutenant Wood reported they picked up the bodies of ten men murdered by the Indians.

The pursuit assumed the proportions of an epic. The trail led south of the Sierra Fronteras and the fortified adobe ranches along the Bavispe River; south of the Sierra Colorado and the dusty town of Moctezuma, deep into the last stronghold of the Apaches on the Yacqui River. The Yacqui was an unknown country of wild horses and lost silver mines. After the first week, the cavalrymen had to abandon their mounts. No grain-fed animals could follow the faint trails into the volcanic wilderness. On foot the men toiled across lava fields and up remote peaks where ancient cliff dwellings clung like swallows nests. The moccasin tracks of the fleeing renegades led through groves of stunted cedar and juniper, over stony ridges and hot, dry sand. Buttes, stratified in saffron and vermilion, shimmered in the heat. From footholds on the mountains, the men caught dizzying glimpses of canyons heaped with pale pink sandstone and purple shadows. At night, the stars glittered cold and near. The sun set crimson and rose to pale green dawns.

Water was scarce, sometimes only a drop in a canteen. Rations grew low and the men ate bacon rind. Their shoes, made in Leavenworth prison and issued by the quartermaster, fell to pieces and had to be replaced by moccasins. Sudden, violent rainstorms drenched clothing and equipment. By this time, Lawton's force bore little resemblance to a military command. The bearded, sun-blistered men wore undershorts and shirts slung about the waist with ammunition belts.

On the Yacqui River, Lawton was reinforced by Lieutenant Charles B. Gatewood. The young West Pointer, a sensitive and conscientious officer, had been selected by Miles to deal with Geronimo because he had served with the Apache scouts under Crook and knew the country and the Indians as well as any white man. Geronimo trusted him and, near the Bavispe River north of the Yacqui, the murdering chief, having had enough of fighting for the present, indicated to Gatewood he might surrender. Geronimo had been on a drunk and had a bad hangover. As he squatted beside Gatewood, he passed his hands over his eyes and, making his hands shake in a pathetic manner, asked Gatewood for a drink. Gatewood told him he had no liquor, which was a great disappointment to the Apache. Geronimo, the wily old devil, thought he could obtain the same lenient terms from Miles that he had obtained from Crook. When Gatewood told him he would have to surrender and be sent to Florida to await the decision of the President as to his final disposition, Geronimo refused to treat with the young officer. He would talk only to Miles himself, no doubt thinking he could argue Miles into granting him better terms. Escorted by Lawton and Gatewood, the Indians moved north to the border for a conference with Miles.

The General did not trust Geronimo. He told Mary that Lawton had sent a dispatch saying the hostile camp was near his and that the runners he had sent out had gone into Geronimo's camp and found the hostiles wanting better terms than he was prepared to offer. "I do not know whether I will go or not," Miles wrote Mary of the conference. "I will not unless I am pretty sure they are sure to surrender. Geronimo and Natchez pretend they want to surrender, but they are very unreliable."[11]

Four days later he had decided to go. Geronimo had sent his brother to Bowie as a hostage of his good intentions. "I go down this morning to see the hostiles under Geronimo," Miles informed his wife. "They have said they wanted to see me. I have very little faith in their sincerity and do not anticipate any good results. But still there is one chance they may come in, and I feel like exhausting every effort to get them in without any more loss of life, if possible."[12]

The place selected for the conference was Skeleton canyon, sixty-five miles south of Bowie. Miles made the journey in two days, accompanied by his aide-de-camp and a suitable escort. The canyon, which was well watered and shaded, had been named because of the human skeletons discovered there, the relics of Apache massacres. Miles felt it was a fitting place in which to conduct negotiations with Geronimo. He reached

Lawton's camp the evening of the third of September and, soon after his arrival, Geronimo came over to pay his respects. The General and the Apache renegade regarded each other with interest. No record exists of what Geronimo thought of Miles but he must have been impressed by the erect, broad-shouldered man with the direct blue eyes and sweeping mustache. Miles was the epitome of the professional military commander.

Geronimo, Miles thought, was one of the "brightest, most resolute and determined looking men"[13] that he had ever encountered and his "sharp, dark" eyes reminded him, interestingly enough, of General Sherman. Miles's description, as usual, was stilted. Geronimo was a mean, ugly-looking Indian.

Right away, Geronimo renewed his demands that he be allowed to return to Fort Apache with his guns, stolen stock and loot.

Impossible, Miles told the Apache. He would have to surrender as Gatewood had told him, as a prisoner of war and be sent to Florida.

"And more than that," Miles instructed the interpreter to tell Geronimo, "it is of no use for you to ask to go back to Fort Apache, for there are no Apaches there now."

The news disconcerted Geronimo. "Where have they gone?"

"I have moved them all out of the country," Miles replied. "You have been at war with the white people for many years, and have been engaged in constant hostilities. I have thought it best that you should be removed from this country to some place where these hostilities cannot be resumed."[14]

Geronimo evidently realized he was dealing with a different sort of officer than he had ever dealt with before. He agreed to Miles's terms but with one stipulation — that the lives of the Indians be spared. To this, Miles replied it was not the custom of the U.S. Army officers to kill prisoners of war.

Geronimo returned to his camp and, next morning, came back to resume the talks. He had left the reservation in the first place, he said, because Chatto and Mickey Free, Crook's two trusted scouts, had threatened to kill him. Negotiations were proceeding favorably with Geronimo but Miles was disturbed because Natchez, hereditary chief of the Chiricahuas, remained in the hills. If he could convince Geronimo of the futility of further resistance, Geronimo might induce Natchez to come in and surrender.

"We can watch your movements and send messages over the tops of these mountains in a small part of one day," Miles told Geronimo, "and over a distance which it would take a man mounted on a swift pony twenty days to travel."[15]

Geronimo's dark face expressed incredulity and Miles, turning to the heliostat operator he had brought with him, requested him to flash a message to Geronimo's brother at Fort Bowie. Within a short time, the message came back that the brother was well and waiting for Geronimo. Miles's ruse succeeded. Geronimo sent word to Natchez that the white men were too powerful to resist, and within a few hours the six-foot handsome Apache chief came into camp and surrendered.

The next day Miles started for Bowie. He had no intention of allowing Geronimo to escape as Crook had done, so he personally escorted Geronimo, Natchez and four other important hostiles north to the military post. They covered most of the distance at a fast trot and a gallop. As they were approaching Bowie, Geronimo looked toward the Chiricahua Mountains and observed affably to Miles, "This is the fourth time I have surrendered."

"And I think it is the last time . . ." Miles told him grimly.[16]

At Bowie, Miles telegraphed Mary that the last of the hostile

Apaches had surrendered the day before at Skeleton Creek. A day later he wrote elatedly:

> We have at last been most successful.
>
> I am making a clean sweep of the hostile Apaches out of this country and it has given a feeling of relief and security to thousands of homes that they have never felt before.
>
> If you had been here you would have seen me riding in over the mountains with Geronimo and Natchez as you saw me ride over the hills and down to the Yellowstone with Chief Joseph.
>
> It is a brilliant ending of a difficult problem.[17]

But it was only the beginning of troubles with Washington.

CHAPTER XIX

SHERIDAN and Endicott, the Secretary of War, telegraphed congratulations to Miles on the "unconditional surrender" of the hostiles.

Unconditional?

Miles wondered at that. He acknowledged the telegrams briefly, giving credit to the troops for Geronimo's capture. At the moment, he was too busy to straighten out misconceptions in the War Department. His full report, which he had sent to Howard, would shortly be in Washington to explain the terms of surrender.

The citizens of the Territory were clamoring to get at the prisoners. Miles had to station a guard around the post until the eighth of September when, escorted by Lawton, the Indians were put on an eastbound train. Even then, a number of citizens talked of wrecking the train to avenge themselves on their hated enemies.

Within a few hours after the train left, Miles was on his way to Albuquerque where, on the fourteenth, the train carrying the Warm Springs band from Fort Apache paused en route to Florida.

Miles's departure from Bowie prevented the receipt of a most important wire: the President wanted Geronimo and the hostiles kept as prisoners at Bowie until they could be tried for their crimes or otherwise disposed of.

When the President's order at last caught up with him, it was a surprise to Miles. "There has never been a line or word in any dispatch sent here about wanting to have them tried or handed over to the civil authorities," Miles wrote Mary on October 19 from Whipple Barracks, "and all such statements, or that I was ordered to accept only unconditional surrender are able-bodied lies."

Miles was at Rincon, New Mexico, when he received the President's message; by this time, the train bearing the hostiles was well on its way into Texas.

Miles wired Washington that he had not kept the hostiles at Bowie because it was "unsafe." How could he explain the hatred seething on the frontier? Few officials in Washington had seen the mutilated bodies of Apache victims.

The wire was not understood by authorities in Washington. They still thought the Apaches had surrendered unconditionally. Miles still thought Howard had forwarded his report.

The situation was further complicated by the fact that the President was vacationing in the mountains and the Secretary of War was in New Hampshire. Messages had to be relayed with endorsements and recommendations. Cleveland got in touch with Sheridan and the Secretary of War. How did it happen that General Miles had sent the hostiles to Florida without waiting for orders? Telegrams flew back and forth. The train bearing the hostiles was stopped in Texas and General Stanley of that Department ordered to confine Geronimo and his band under strong guard until Miles explained his actions.

Cleveland, pressured by congressmen from Arizona and New Mexico, wanted Geronimo and the hostile leaders turned over to the civil authorities for trial. Miles felt prisoners of war were not subject to civil courts and he was ready to fight to keep the Indians from a lynch mob. "They [the Apaches] placed themselves entirely at our mercy," he wrote Mary on

October 14 from Albuquerque, "and we were in honor bound not to give them up to a mob or the mockery of a justice where they could never have received an impartial trial. After one of the most vigorous campaigns they surrendered like brave men to brave men, and placed themselves at the mercy of the government."

By this time, Miles was angry. He had learned that Howard had telegraphed Washington the seventh of September that the Apaches had surrendered unconditionally. "One cause of the trouble," he wrote Mary, "was that General Howard or some one at his headquarters suppressed my full account of the surrender of Geronimo, and sent a short dispatch of his own saying they had surrendered unconditionally."[1]

He asked Howard for leave to go to Washington to explain the situation. The leave was refused. Miles then telegraphed Senator Don Cameron telling him the War Department would not grant him emergency leave and asking him to see the President about it. Cameron called on Cleveland and showed him Miles's telegram. When he had read it, the President looked up and said, "It's a mistake. The War Department did not refuse the leave. It was I that refused it."[2]

So Miles could expect no help from the President. He was out of favor with both the Executive and the War Department — a strange situation for an officer to be in who had just ended the Apache outbreaks.

Presidential displeasure was not enough to discourage Miles. Indeed, he renewed the attack to vindicate himself.

The confusion was lightened somewhat when Howard admitted he had been at fault in wiring Washington that the Apaches had surrendered unconditionally. He defended himself on the grounds that Miles's dispatch had not been clear. Miles had spoken of the Indians as being "wholly submissive" and had failed to list specific terms. Howard had some excuse. Miles was fond of rhetoric, but Howard had been overhasty.

When the President understood the terms under which the hostiles had surrendered, he reluctantly allowed Geronimo and his band to proceed to Florida. Even the Chief Executive could not turn the Indians over to civil trial if they surrendered with the understanding their lives would be spared. But bitterness lingered.[3]

In Omaha, Crook wrote a letter to the Adjutant General defending his use of Apache scouts and, indirectly, impugning Miles's use of regular troops. Crook deeply resented the imprisonment of Chatto and his ex-scouts and in this he was supported by his former officers, John G. Bourke, Britton Davis, and Charles King, all of whom wrote for publication at one time or another on the subject.

At the same time that Miles was engaged in controversy with the War Department, he was cleaning up the remainder of the hostile Apaches. The end of October, Mangus, the last hostile chief left at large, surrendered and was sent to Florida.

The Department of Arizona was enlarged to include a portion of California. Miles's headquarters were moved to Los Angeles.

Rumors were circulating that Terry was thinking of retiring, which meant there would be a vacancy for a major general. Crook was senior but that did not mean Crook would get the promotion. A station as far from Washington as Los Angeles was a disadvantage and Miles requested transfer to the Department of the Missouri. The request was refused.

In July of 1887 Miles visited the San Carlos Agency to investigate the threat of another Apache outbreak.[4] He made the long, hot journey to Fort Grant by rail and wagon. On his arrival June 15, he wrote Mary (after nineteen years of marriage, he still called her "My darling"). He was not overly worried about the Indians because, as yet, they had committed no crimes against white settlers. However;

It seems rather more discouraging this year than it did last year. I did think that if I was successful it would be appreciated and not used to my disadvantage but now I know differently and have no confidence whatever that anything that might be done however important or valuable would be truthfully represented or considered of any value. Still it is well to know this as I will not be disappointed in the future.

The desolation of the agency depressed him.

All Indian agencies are bad enough, but this I think one of the worst . . . I should about as soon expect to have people remain quiet and comfortable in a hot oven . . . a barren waste with no grass and the light, hot sand drifting and blowing about like snow . . . There is much dissatisfaction among these Indians. They do not get enough food . . . about one hundred of their children have died . . . It requires any amount of patience to have anything to do with Indians . . .[5]

By his prompt and tactful handling of the situation, Miles prevented another outbreak. The terror that had paralyzed the Southwest for so many years was gradually relaxing. When the San Carlos trouble subsided, the citizens of Arizona and New Mexico regained their confidence. Mines that had been shut down for years resumed operations. Ranchers grazed stock unmolested. Emigrants, checked by tales of Apache cruelties, once more turned their wagons southwest.

The people of Arizona, feeling they had not done enough to express their gratitude, tended a celebration in honor of Miles at Tucson in December of 1887. Miles was presented a sword by Tiffany with a fifty-six carat sapphire in the hilt and a gold scabbard engraved with scenes from the Apache wars. Following the public festivities was a reception and ball. Mary stood beside her husband in the receiving line wearing a gown of white ottoman silk and greeting the guests with her accustomed graciousness.

In his public speech of the day, Miles gave credit for capturing the hostile Apaches to the Regular Army troops, saying he wished they could be with him to witness the ceremonies. Miles felt the country was too indifferent to the hard-worked, understrength army that guarded their borders and, in his annual report, he recommended better pay and food for the enlisted men and not so much labor and hard service except in line of military duty. Special consideration, he thought, should be given to the older lieutenants and captains who had been high-ranking officers in the Civil War but who, exiled to remote stations in the West and South, had served for twenty years without promotion. For their relief, Miles advocated promotion in one grade if advancement was not forthcoming in twenty years. He also advocated three battalions to an infantry regiment, which would create vacancies for more captains and majors. This change was adopted and existed until after World War II.

To make it possible for the troops to fight Indians without relying on native scouts, Miles instituted field maneuvers, a practice that was not common at that time but that was later to be accepted as a routine part of training.

As is often the case when a military man becomes prominent, he is considered for political office. At a banquet in San Francisco, a move was made to support Miles for the presidential race in 1888. Miles did not say he would not run. He made no public statement one way or another in regard to the nomination, which convinced the eastern politicians and many officials in the War Department that he would accept the nomination if it were offered to him. Miles would have been wise to issue a denial as General Sherman had done four years previous. The attacks began immediately. When the congressional delegations from the Pacific coast recommended Miles for a major-generalcy vice Terry who was retiring, reports were circulated that Miles's promotions had been due to his relationship with the influential Cameron and Sherman families and not to his ability. The *New York World* of March 7, 1888, defending Miles, declared that "the misrepresentations periodically thrown out from Washington regarding Gen. Nelson A. Miles are evidently for a purpose."

In the end Crook got the promotion to major general and command of the Division of the Missouri. Crook was senior but he was, also, supported by ex-President Hayes and a number of other influential people.

As a consolation prize, Miles was given command of the Division of the Pacific, a major general's job without the rank, for there had been a limitation put on the number of senior officers. The headquarters was San Francisco, far enough from Washington to keep Miles out of the public eye. Howard, whom Miles replaced, went to the Division of the Atlantic.

Meanwhile Crook intensified his campaign to have his Apache ex-scouts repatriated to Indian Territory. Ostensibly his interest was in the "loyal" Apaches, and Crook was genuinely concerned over what he considered an injustice in the exile of the Indians who had served with him, but at the same time, the campaign was designed to reflect on Miles. Crook had the support of numerous Indian Rights Societies. The case of the Apache prisoners attracted wide attention.

Crook was devoting much time to this cause when, suddenly, in March 1890, he died of a heart attack.

PART SIX

The Last Sioux Uprising
1890

CHAPTER XX

Miles did not pretend regret at Crook's death. He was no hypocrite. But he experienced a feeling of emptiness. For nearly eighteen years, he had rivaled the bearded, taciturn officer who had twice been promoted over him.

With Crook gone, the quarrel over the Apaches lapsed into the back pages of the newspapers and, eventually, disappeared. The commanding officer at Mount Vernon Barracks the next year reported that a number of the Apaches had enlisted as scouts and others had found work. They were not suffering. In 1894, they were moved to Indian Territory.

Crook had cast the Apache fight like a rock into a pool which spread ripples of bitterness. When the ripples showed signs of dying down, Miles started them up again by casting a few rocks himself. He might not have Crook to fight with but that did not mean he would not continue to be engaged in controversy. He was not the least concerned by the fact that as he gained in rank, his controversies affected a wider and wider public. Right or wrong was clearly defined and be damned to the delicate balance of politics.

Ironically, Crook's death created a vacancy for a major general for which Miles, as the senior brigadier, was eligible. With his customary determination, he set out to gain the promotion. Haste was necessary since a successor to Crook would be appointed within a short time. Crook died the 21st of March. Less than a week later, a group of prominent Pacific coast citizens, including Leland Stanford and George Hearst, wrote a recommendation for Miles to the major-generalcy. Miles himself wired his uncle-in-law, Senator John Sherman, and the first part of April received a disquieting letter in return. It was doubtful if Miles would get the promotion. "The President recognized the merits of your service," Sherman wrote, "but thought you were if not disobedient, at least a troublesome man to get along with; that instead of acting like Thomas and other favorite Generals of his, obeying orders, you made difficulties."[1]

The President, Sherman continued, was particularly annoyed by Miles's objections to moving the Apaches to Fort Sill. "His mind has been poisoned against you. . ."[2] The President had not made up his mind whom he would appoint to the major generalcy but Sherman did not think it would be Miles.

Miles felt the letter called for immediate action. Disregarding Sherman's admonition not to come to Washington, he took the first train for the Capital. He was in the East, anyhow, so it was easy to get to Washington. On the fourth of April, he wrote Mary, enclosing a copy of Sherman's letter "which will explain the influence and intrigue. In this I can see Howard's former work with Drum, McKeever possibly Burr and Bourke." He had, Miles told Mary, wired for an interview with the President which was granted. "My future rests on that interview. And I hope to have an opportunity to talk freely to the President. Other influences have been at work in my favor and very strong deputations and letters have been sent. I have not been idle."[3]

Miles had his interview with the President.

At first I found the mind of the President was prejudiced by some one although he received me cordially. I soon disarmed his prejudice and removed from his mind some irronous [sic] ideas that he had formed. I think in half an hour we were on good terms and at the end of an hour I am satisfied he had made up his mind to appoint me. I did not know this however or the impression I had created but the result of the conversation was that I had formed a good opinion of him.

We went over the whole subject and I thanked him for the interview and withdrew. I had made up my mind to do no more and to leave Washington within a few hours. I was surprised however when in the office of the Secty of War who said, "I suppose you know that your name has been sent on to the Senate." I told him that I did not and was much gratified and thanked him for his kindness in the matter. He has been my friend and recommended me.[4]

Miles wanted to telegraph Mary who was anxiously waiting for news in San Francisco but the Secretary told Miles the nomination would only be announced if the messenger reached the Senate before it adjourned. Mary's mother, Mrs. Charles Sherman, whom Miles called "Gramma," was waiting outside in a carriage and, joining her, Miles said she could be the first to congratulate him. Mrs. Sherman was delighted and as she and Miles drove through the grounds of the Smithsonian Institution, they watched the flag above the Senate building to see if it was still flying ". . . for if it did," Miles wrote Mary, "I was sure my nomination would be announced and I could telegraph to the counterpart of my heart . . ."[5]

Fortunately, for Miles's peace of mind, the nomination was announced that day. Miles sent a wire to Mary and then to twenty-one-year-old Cecelia who had been "much depressed when she learned it seemed to be going against me." He sent wires to his friends, too, and after that, wrote Mary a long letter from the Senate Office Building. He couldn't wait to get back to the hotel.

The top round of the ladder gives me more pleasure I think than any of the others, and I know how delighted you will be

. . . the future looks bright . . . I only need one thing more to make me perfectly happy and that is my own darling in my arms the recipient of all my love caresses and devotion and to share with me my pleasure. With lots of kisses I am entirely and devotedly thine own. . . Nelson A. Miles, Major General U.S.A.[6]

Miles's first thought was always of Mary. With her he shared his triumphs and despairs. That April day it seemed to Miles that he had indeed reached the top of the ladder when he could sign his name Major General U.S.A. No other officer held a higher rank, including Schofield the Commanding General.

It was one of the happiest days of Miles's life and although he attained higher honors in the future, none shone as brightly as the twin stars of his new rank in the spring of 1890. Perhaps it was as well he enjoyed it for the holiday did not last long.

With Miles's promotion came a change of stations from the Division of the Pacific to the Division of the Missouri which Crook had commanded at the time of his death and which included the Departments of Dakota and Platte — the old hunting grounds of the Sioux. Times had changed since Miles had pursued Sitting Bull and Crazy Horse through the snows of Montana. The Indians were herded onto reservations. There had not been an outbreak for years. The Brûlés were at the Rosebud Agency; the Oglalas at Pine Ridge. To the north at the Cheyenne River Agency were the Two Kettle and Blackfoot Sioux, the Minneconjous and Sans Arcs and still further north on the Standing Rock Agency, which was partly in North and partly in South Dakota, were the Upper Yanktonais, some of the Blackfoot Sioux and the Hunkpapas. Sitting Bull, Miles's foe of the seventies, was at Standing Rock. In 1881 he had returned from Canada, where he had outworn his welcome, and surrendered at Fort Buford. The summer of 1885 he had toured in a Wild West show with Buffalo Bill earning a substantial sum selling his autograph. Now he was camped with a small band of his followers forty miles from the agency. Members of the Indian societies in the East were pleased to think the Sioux had, at last, become peaceful and congratulated themselves that they had done well to support the Sioux land commission of 1889. The Christian missionaries and liberals who belonged to the Indian societies believed that if the Sioux were given a few acres of land and tools they would become self-supporting farmers. The old traditions were to be abolished and the chiefs disposed. The chiefs — the humanitarians said — were reactionary and despotic. The sooner the Sioux became civilized, the better and, since the Sioux themselves displayed little enthusiasm for following the white man's way, they were to be forced to do so — all for their own good, of course. The Indian sympathizers were sufficiently powerful politically to get a commission appointed in 1889 to reduce the size of the Sioux reservation in the Black Hills country, the idea being to take away the hunting area so the Indians would turn to farming. In return for giving up nine million acres, the Sioux were to be granted certain lands in severalty, stock and farming implements. Roads and schools were to be built from funds from the sale of the nine million acres. The commission was supported in this worthy project by land hungry settlers who could hardly wait to claim what little country remained to the Sioux in their once sacred stronghold. Crook served on the commission before his death and the same people who advocated the sale of the Sioux reservation aided Crook in his fight with Miles over the Apache prisoners in Florida.

The Sioux voiced immediate protest to signing the treaty requested by members of the commission. Only a few chiefs who felt it was futile to oppose the whites, put their mark on the paper at Crook's request. Old Red Cloud and Sitting Bull were loud in their denunciation of the land commission but their opposition was unheeded. Nearly half the Sioux reservation was opened to settlers and land speculators. Simultaneously the Indian Bureau began the process of civilizing the red men within their charge. Creation of an Indian police force was one move to break down the influence of the chiefs. McGillycuddy, agent at Pine Ridge until 1886, ex-army officer and something of a dandy, made efficient use of the police. So, too, did McLaughlin at Standing Rock. McLaughlin, married to a half-breed woman, relied on his Indian soldiers to support him in his feud with the nonprogressive Sitting Bull. The Indians who had opposed the land commission were called nonprogressives. Those who had signed the treaty were called progressives. The eastern liberals seemed unaware that the elimination of the chiefs helped to make the agent a virtual dictator. At Standing Rock, for instance, no one really knew what was going on. McLaughlin discouraged investigation. The agent had little to fear from his treatment of the Indians. What he had to be concerned about, mainly, was holding his job under different administrations. McGillycuddy, a Republican, was replaced by a Democrat in Cleveland's administration. Often not only the agent but the clerks, schoolteachers and other minor employees lost their jobs with the change of political parties. Experience was not necessary. What mattered was whether an appointee was a Republican or a Democrat. Morgan, the Commissioner of Indian Affairs, was a Republican. The Republicans were the party to which the majority of the Indian humanitarians belonged, so that with Harrison in office, the Indian Rights Association, the Indian Treaty-Keeping and Protective Association and all the other Associations felt free to carry out their experiments with the Sioux. Hardly had the ink dried on the treaty of 1889 when Commissioner Morgan cut the beef ration, explaining that the Indians had been padding the ration rolls with additional names to get more beef than they were entitled to. This was all right with Congress who, as usual, had failed to appropriate the money to feed the Indians. Incredible as it seems, it was agreeable to the humanitarians, too. Free rations, they felt, kept the Sioux from the plow. Few of these Indian Friends visited the reservations to see how their experiments were working, and those few saw only what they wanted to see. Besides being blind, they were deaf, for they did not hear the disturbing rumors of an Indian Messiah and a Ghost Dance that was spreading among the tribes of the plains from the Crows in the north to the Arapahoes in the south and as far west as the Paiutes in Nevada. One of the Ghost Dance songs went as follows;

> My Father have pity on me,
> I have nothing to eat,
> I am dying of thirst.
> Everything is gone![7]

The words did not sound as though the experiments were a success.

Miles was no liberal. In fact, he had little patience with the humanitarians and did not hesitate to say so. Months before he assumed command of the Division of the Missouri he knew that all was not well on the Sioux reservations and encouraged an investigation by the War Department. By the time he arrived at his headquarters in Chicago on the fifteenth of September, he was in possession of some shocking facts. The Sioux had existed for some time in a state of semi-starvation and, in their desperation, had turned to a mysterious half pagan, half Christian cult that, originally one of peace, had become one of hostility. In his report to the Secretary of War, Miles listed ten reasons for the trouble among the Indians. Failure to ensure title to the allotments of land promised by the treaty of 1889. Failure to turn funds for the sale of the reservation over to the Indians. Failure to issue seeds and implements for farming. Failure to pay for ponies and other property taken from the Indians in 1876. Failure to issue sufficient beef ration. Failure. Failure. Broken promises.

Only one failure could not be attributed to the government and that was the crop failure of the last two years. For months in the summer, there had been no rain. The sun glared from a heat-paled sky. The leaves shriveled on the cottonwoods and even the hardy buffalo grass crackled underfoot like straw. Repeated conferences with the land commission had kept the Indians from caring for what few crops they might have saved. At Fort Randall, the commanding officer reported the Yanktonais subsisted on scraps from the military garbage pails. When starvation lessened the Indians' resistance, they became susceptible to influenza, measles and other diseases. Child mortality rates soared. Old Red Cloud, half blind, grieved over babies with the swollen bellies and hollow eyes of malnutrition. Chief Little Wound watched his daughter slowly dying of hunger. She needed medical attention but could not get it from the agency doctor. Starving, ill and in rags, their old traditions destroyed by the whites, the Sioux gave up hope. They might as well die. And indeed there seemed little reason to go on living.

In the moment of their extremity, a tale came from the Shoshoni Reservation in Wyoming of an Indian who preached salvation for the starving people. The buffalo, the elk and the deer were to come back to the plains and the spirits of the dead Indians were to return to earth. Once more, the Indians would be free to roam their old hunting grounds. Hope stirred in the Sioux as it had over a thousand years ago in the people of Judea when they heard of the birth of Christ. Three Sioux sought the Messiah — as three Wise Men sought the Christ Child. The three Indians were Kicking Bear, Short Bull and Porcupine. Kicking Bear, as described by Miles, was a "tall, stalwart savage, a fierce fighting man, a natural leader and ideal warrior." Short Bull was "a small, sharp featured dreamer . . . an exhorter." Porcupine was "a keen, wiry, active Indian, hostile to the white race and devotedly interested in the welfare of the Indians."[8]

By foot, by pony and by rail, they traveled west until they found the Messiah, who was a Paiute Indian called Wovoka, in Nevada. Wovoka told them that the prophecy was true and taught them certain religious ceremonies and a dance called the Ghost Dance. Months later, the Sioux retraced the long, weary journey to the Dakota reservations to tell their kinsmen about the new religion, only in the telling it grew confused. Wovoka advocated peace. Short Bull and his companions predicted that all the whites would be destroyed in a great dust storm. The prediction reawakened life in the despairing Sioux. They began to dance in the camp of Big Road, former Crazy Horse hostile, on Wounded Knee Creek. Then the Minneconjous began to dance. Hump, who had surrendered to Miles in 1877, was chief of the Minneconjous on Cherry Creek, the fiercest and proudest of all the ex-hostiles. Hump alone retained the old soldier societies and the scalp shirt men. Sitting Bull at first ignored the dancing, but after a while he began to think there might be something in it and sent for Kicking Bear to tell him about the Messiah. At Pine Ridge reservation, at Standing Rock and Rosebud the Indians were forming hands in a great circle and revolving quickly to the left, singing the sacred songs of the Messiah. Occasionally, a dancer would fall unconscious and when he — or she — returned to life, he would tell of seeing his dead parents or friends in the spirit world.

A few of the agents became alarmed and ordered the Sioux to stop dancing. Agent Gallagher at Pine Ridge did succeed in stopping the dancing near the agency. McLaughlin at Standing Rock issued no orders, believing the craze would die out. Perhaps it might have if a series of events had not given it impetus. The first was another cut in the beef ration of the already starving Sioux. Commissioner Morgan proved on paper that the Indians were getting more than enough meat by citing the weight of cattle brought to the agencies. There was only one trouble with these figures. A steer weighing twelve hundred pounds at the time of purchase in the fall weighed only six hundred pounds in April after the winter. The steer, however, was issued to the Indians as weighing twelve hundred pounds. Resolutely refusing to admit that the Sioux were starving, Commissioner Morgan went off to tour the southern reservations where he was interested in building new schools.

As though this were not enough, the Senator from South Dakota who had charge of political patronage for the agencies removed nearly all of the old agents, with the exception of McLaughlin, and replaced them with inexperienced appointees of his own party. At Pine Ridge, where there was the most interest in the Ghost Dance, he put D. F. Royer, a man who had no experience with Indians and was in addition a weakling. Within less than a month, Royer was writing the Indian Department that the Ghost Dance craze was getting out of hand and troops were necessary to put down the disturbance.

CHAPTER XXI

THERE IS a story that Royer, fleeing the agency in horse and buggy, galloped his lathered horses down the main street of the town of Rushville shouting that the Sioux were "up." This may or may not have been true. Whatever the case, Royer was scared silly of his charges and let them know it. Nothing could have been worse, psychologically, at this crucial moment, than a timid agent. The Indians needed firmness and justice. What they had, thanks to the worthy Senator, was an agent who aroused their contempt for governmental authority. With grim humor, they nicknamed Royer "Young-Man-Afraid-of-His-Sioux."

Anyhow, if Royer did flee the reservation, he was back the next day when the troops arrived on the 19th of November. Royer had some reason to be afraid by this time. Kicking Bear had been holding Ghost Dances in Sitting Bull's camp on Grand River, and, according to McLaughlin, Sitting Bull had proclaimed himself chief of the new movement. The craze was spreading from one band after another and growing more openly hostile in character. Many of the dancers wore ghost shirts which were supposed to make them immune to bullets. At Chief Red Leaf's camp on Black Pipe creek on the Rosebud reservation, Indian police found Sioux warriors brandishing Winchesters, their naked chests crossed with rifle belts. The police, who had been sent by the agent to halt the dancing, were smart enough to withdraw. Interference would have cost them their lives. At Standing Rock, Cheyenne River, Pine Ridge and

Rosebud, the authority of the agents was openly disputed by the Ghost Dancers. White men were unsafe in the nonprogressive camps. Schools were closed. Early in November, the jittery Royer told the whites and breeds at isolated stations on Pine Ridge reservation to come to the agency for safety. Some of these people were so scared that they kept on going until they were on the far side of the Missouri River. The fear spread among the settlers in the Dakotas and Nebraska, whose imaginations were fed by newspaper stories predicting a Sioux war with burnings and scalpings reminiscent of the Minnesota outbreak and the Custer Massacre. Townspeople in the Black Hills organized militias. Farmers in northwestern Nebraska built fortifications in which they and their families could take refuge.

Royer continued to telegraph the Indian Bureau that troops were needed to put down the disturbance. McLaughlin at Standing Rock and Reynolds at Rosebud, who had more or less ignored the Ghost Dancing, now reported their concern to Washington. Commissioner Morgan was still inspecting schools on the southern reservations. The Assistant Commissioner, twelve days later, advised McLaughlin to tell Sitting Bull that if there was any trouble, he would be held personally responsible. This was tantamount to tapping Sitting Bull's wrist and saying naughty, naughty.

The last of October, Short Bull, who was beginning to have delusions of himself as a Messiah, predicted that the millennium would come in December instead of in the spring. "We must dance the balance of this moon, at the end of which time the earth will shiver very hard . . ." The spirits of the dead Indians would then return to life. Buffalo, deer and elk would once again be plentiful.[1]

The Indians, Short Bull declared, must desert their homes and move to a sacred tree on Pass Creek which grew close to the boundaries of the Pine Ridge and Rosebud reservations.

There they would await the great day which would fall on the 11th of December.

Miles watched these developments with growing concern. In the early fall he stopped at Pine Ridge on his way west on an inspection trip, had talked with some of the Ghost Dancers and told them, sternly, to stop dancing. At the time, Miles had thought the Messiah craze would die down and that military interference would intensify the trouble. Agent McLaughlin agreed. So, too, did American Horse, an intelligent chief and friend of the whites. Miles's mistake was in underestimating governmental ineptitude and indifference.

The middle of November, Royer telegraphed Washington frantically, "Indians dancing in the snow and are wild and crazy . . . Why delay for further investigation? We need protection and we need it now . . ."[2]

Reluctantly, the officials at the Indian Bureau approached the War Department. Miles, as commander of the Division of the Missouri, was put in charge of the operations against the Sioux. Miles did not hesitate to state publicly that the Sioux were starving. The humanitarians threw up their hands in horror. They could not believe their utopian plans for civilizing the Sioux had gone wrong. The decision to call in troops, they felt, had been motivated by ambitious army officers. Senator Henry L. Dawes, who had for years been the spokesman for the humanitarians in Congress, declared that if the Sioux were hungry, it was their own fault. They should have tended to their farms instead of going off on the warpath.

While Dawes defended himself in Washington, the Ninth Cavalry moved into Pine Ridge. Shortly thereafter eight troops of the Seventh Cavalry commanded by James W. Forsyth arrived at the agency. Other troop units occupied strategic positions in the entire area.

There were few men left in the Seventh Cavalry who had

escaped with Reno on the Little Big Horn but the Custer Massacre was a tradition. The Sioux were considered hereditary enemies of the regiment. The ranks had recently been filled by a number of recruits who were laxly disciplined and inexperienced in Indian warfare. Forsyth, who commanded them, had been Sheridan's Chief of Staff from 1864 to 1865, and had much of a cavalryman's swaggering confidence. Confusion of identity often arose between him and George A. Forsyth who had the famous fight with Roman Nose on a branch of the Republican River in 1868.

The Seventh had little use for Miles's policy, which was not to take aggressive action against the Indians but to remove the troublemakers and exert pressure on the Ghost Dancers to return to their homes. The situation demanded patience and diplomacy, qualities Miles sometimes did not display to members of his own race but that he evidenced time and again in his relations with Indians. Miles's first move in the cause of peace was to go to Washington to inform the officials of the War Department and Bureau of Indian Affairs of his plans to suppress the disturbance among the Sioux. Foremost was a request to increase the beef allotment immediately. Second, Miles asked that the agencies be placed under military control.

Miles's greatest worry was that the new religion would spread to all the tribes on the plains. The Gros Ventres, Utes, Snakes, Piegans and Bannocks had all made pilgrimages to the Messiah in Nevada while Sitting Bull, so Miles had been informed, had sent runners to tribes throughout the Northwest to rise against the whites. "It was a threatened uprising of colossal proportions," Miles declared, "extending over a far greater territory than did the confederation, inaugurated by the Prophet and led by Tecumseh, or the conspiracy of Pontiac."

Inevitably, Miles was accused of enlarging on the Sioux

uprising for purposes of personal publicity. The question naturally arises. Did Miles have political aspirations? He probably would have accepted the nomination if it had been offered to him. Why not? He had the examples of Grant, Washington and Jackson — all generals who had been elected to the presidency. He was supremely confident, ambitious and vital.

But military rank was not, to Miles, a means to political ambition. The army meant too much to him to use it callously — something that people who translated his every statement and action into political terms failed to understand. His popularity in the West, his handsome appearance and his military reputation made him a natural for a presidential possibility. Certain elements of the press and politics advanced Miles's candidacy as similar elements had advanced the candidacy of Grant, Sherman and Frémont and as they would, in the future, advance the candidacy of Leonard Wood, Pershing and Eisenhower. It was a pity Miles did not state flatly he had no interest in the nomination. By not doing so he left himself open to political attack, and he was no match for the politicians. He lacked the guile and the shrewdness. But then Miles seldom said or did what was tactful unless he was dealing with Indians.

Miles did not have to exaggerate the seriousness of the Ghost Dance trouble to get publicity. No Indian outbreak was covered as fully and, at times, as inaccurately, as the last Sioux war. Americans standing on the threshold of a new industrial age of telephones, automobiles and electric lights were startled and intrigued by a war with Stone Age savages. At Pine Ridge were gathered representatives of the Associated Press, the Omaha *Bee,* the Chicago *Tribune* and half a dozen other papers. The railroad and telegraph facilitated transportation and communication. The coverage by this swarm of reporters tended to be sensational. Few of them understood the tragedy of the Ghost Dance.

Miles was not perceptive but he sensed the pathos in the uprising. He had served in the West for twenty-one years and had learned to respect the once free Sioux as a soldier respects a soldier. Even he did not guess this was to be the final battle. If possible, he felt, the uprising should be settled without bloodshed. Fortunately, President Harrison agreed, indeed urged, that the Sioux be controlled without resorting to open hostilities.

It would have been easier to wage a shooting war.

There were several thousand hostiles in the Badlands along the White River of South Dakota. Two Strike of the Brûlés had fled to the Ghost Dance camp when the troops arrived. So had Long Mandan and his band of Two Kettle Sioux. These Indians feared all soldiers, especially the Seventh Cavalry. Little Wound with his Kiyuksas had allied himself with the Ghost Dancers, too. The Indians took refuge on a mesa that could be reached only by a narrow causeway. The top of the mesa was flat and grassy and watered by two springs. Here, the bands set up their tepees in a great arc, the Brûlés, the Oglalas, the Minneconjous and the Two Kettles. Scouts were sent out to watch for the approach of troops and women began to dig rifle pits at the edge of the causeway.

The troops could have attacked the hostiles with Hotchkiss and Gatling guns and driven or starved them out of this nearly unimpregnable stronghold. Such a battle would have been decisive, but it would have been bloody and resulted in lasting bitterness. Yet it seemed impossible to persuade the fanatical Ghost Dancers to abandon their hopes and return to the agency. Miles opened the campaign by instructing General John R. Brooke to increase the beef ration to the friendly Indians camped about the agencies. An emissary, Louis Shangraux, a half blood, was sent to the hostile camp to persuade the chiefs to return to their homes. Shangraux was successful in getting Two Strike to take his Brûlés back to the agency. The defection of Two Strike was a severe blow to the Ghost Dancers. There were to be other setbacks, too. American Horse and old Chief Red Cloud were doing their utmost to aid the whites by sending runners to various bands to talk them into submission. Ironically, Red Cloud was one of the chiefs the humanitarians had tried to depose, while in the Ghost Dance camp were several Carlisle graduates whom the brethren had educated to teach civilization to their race. By mid-December Miles's policy of patient diplomacy was beginning to show results. Kicking Bear, who had been a prophet with Short Bull, joined the friendly Indians. So did Little Wound and Big Road of the Oglalas. Almost all of the leading men of the Brûlés and the Oglalas had come into the agencies. Still to be reckoned with were the potentially dangerous and influential chiefs Hump and Sitting Bull.

Miles was well acquainted with Hump, who had served as a scout with the Fifth Infantry in the Lame Deer and Nez Percé campaigns. During that time, Hump had been under the command of Captain E. P. Ewers. Hump respected Ewers, so Miles sent to Texas for the Captain to come to South Dakota to deal with the Minneconjou. The civil authorities, who considered Hump the most formidable of all the ex-hostiles, thought Miles was wasting his time. No army officer could get into the Minneconjou camp alive. Ewers was willing to try. He had a talk with Hump which resulted in the chief telling the army officer, "If General Miles sent for him, he would do whatever was desired."[3] Without protest the Minneconjou chief of whom the agents were so terrified told his people to pack up their camp. Within a few days he was at the agency, and shortly thereafter enlisted as a scout for the army.

This left Sitting Bull. Miles's experience with the Hunkpapa chief had convinced him of his unswerving hostility to the whites, and all reports bore this out. Sitting Bull had not taken an active part in the Ghost Dancing but he had allowed Kicking Bear to hold Ghost Dances in his camp. Despite his inactivity of recent years, he could prove a rallying point for the Sioux in case of open warfare. Again Miles, with his knowledge of Indians, hit on an ingenious plan. He wanted no trouble with Sitting Bull which would alarm his people and ignite the explosive situation at the agencies. A solution presented itself when Miles encountered Buffalo Bill Cody, the famous showman who had scouted for him the summer of 1876 on the Yellowstone. Sitting Bull liked and trusted Cody, who had given him his favorite gray circus horse and a hat he wore only on special occassions. If anyone could persuade Sitting Bull to submit peacefully to temporary confinement, it was Cody. Miles discussed the matter with Cody at a banquet in Chicago and, making one of the quick decisions characteristic of him, authorized Cody to take Sitting Bull into custody. The assignment was exactly the sort of thing that appealed to the showman.

Miles, however, reckoned without Agent McLaughlin.

When Buffalo Bill arrived at Standing Rock, McLaughlin tried to dissuade him from visiting Sitting Bull. McLaughlin was ambitious, vain and petty. He resented Sitting Bull's influence and position among the Sioux and felt the chief's refusal to become a progressive reflected on his administration among the officials of the Indian Bureau. If Sitting Bull was to be dealt with, he wanted to do it himself. When he couldn't talk Cody out of going to Grand River, he enlisted the help of the military at Fort Yates. The officers at Yates felt that Cody was a publicity-hunting fake, and that Miles was reflecting on their abilities by detailing him to arrest Sitting Bull. With McLaughlin, they planned to get Cody drunk, delaying him long enough for McLaughlin to wire Washington to revoke the order to arrest the chief. Cody was invited to the Officers' Club where relays of officers were assigned to drink him under the table, but Cody's capacity was greater than the plotters had counted on. By morning, most of the officers were "hors de combat" while Cody was still going strong. At eleven o'clock, accompanied by eight newsmen and a wagonload of presents, including candy which Sitting Bull liked, Cody started out for Grand River. No one in the party was armed and there was no military escort. A show of force, Cody knew, would defeat his purpose.

But McLaughlin had not given up. When he learned the military had failed, he sent a group of mounted Indians to intercept Cody with directions how to reach Sitting Bull's camp. The directions were misleading and succeeded in delaying Cody until McLaughlin received an order from the President rescinding Cody's authority to take Sitting Bull into custody. Cody's expedition was laughed at as a publicity stunt, which it probably was, to a certain extent, and Miles was criticized for enlisting the services of the showman. Nevertheless, if Cody had been allowed to reach Grand River, he might have averted the tragedy that now became inevitable.

In his official report Miles stated that friends of Sitting Bull had deceived Cody as to the chief's whereabouts. From this it appears Miles did not know the full extent of the plot, for McLaughlin was certainly no friend of Sitting Bull. However, Miles did know that McLaughlin had wired Washington, and he took immediate steps to counteract further interference by the agent by seeing that the President was informed how necessary it was to arrest Sitting Bull. As a result, McLaughlin was told to co-operate with the military. General Thomas H. Ruger, acting on Miles's orders, instructed Lieutenant Colonel William F. Drum at Fort Yates to make it his special duty to secure the person of Sitting Bull. The agent could be called on to co-operate and render such assistance as needed.

Drum lacked initiative, or possibly he continued to be unsympathetic with the aims of his division commander. Instead of arresting Sitting Bull himself, he allowed McLaughlin to talk him into letting the Indian police make the arrest with the support of the troops from Fort Yates.

The police arrived at Sitting Bull's camp before daylight, in advance of the troops. The Hunkpapas had been holding a Ghost Dance the night before and were still asleep. In the wintery gloom, the tepees stood seemingly deserted among the naked branches of the cottonwoods. No smoke showed from the chimney of Sitting Bull's log cabin. Forcing their way in, the police woke the chief and dragged him outside. Nervousness made them rough. Sitting Bull's wife and son created a stir. In a moment, a crowd gathered. Sitting Bull suddenly appeared to resent being pushed around by the police. "I'm not going!" he shouted loudly. Simultaneously, one of Sitting Bull's warriors fired at Bull Head who, mortally wounded, shot Sitting Bull in the back. Red Tomahawk, another policeman, shot the chief at the same time. The killing of Sitting Bull began a savage battle between the Hunkpapas and the police who took refuge in Sitting Bull's cabin and succeeded in holding off the angry Indians until the cavalry arrived. The Hunkpapas, firing from the woods at the police, fled south across the river when the troops appeared, making no attempt to stand up to the cavalry. Their anger was directed to the police of their own race who had killed their chief.

Without ceremony, Sitting Bull's body was loaded in a wagon and hauled to Fort Yates where it was nailed in a wooden coffin and buried in quicklime. McLaughlin was satisfied. He had, at last, rid himself of the reactionary chief.[4]

Miles, who did not know the details of Sitting Bull's death, wrote Mary the 19th of December from Rapid City, South Dakota, where he had located his headquarters.

> I have been so intensely absorbed with the campaign, or in trying to prevent a campaign, that I have not written one word to you.
>
> I was intensely anxious to know whether I would have to encounter my old antagonist, Sitting Bull, or whether he would be arrested. I gave a very positive order to that effect, and directed the commanding officer to make it his special duty to secure his person. It resulted more seriously than I anticipated, but it was well done.

Miles felt a grave danger had been averted when Sitting Bull had been prevented from joining the Ghost Dancers. Later, when he learned more about it, he wrote, as an obituary to his "old antagonist," that "the last real encounter of that great Indian chieftain was tragedy in which he fell by the hands of men of his own race." Sitting Bull was, Miles said, "the strongest type of hostile Indian that this country has produced . . . No other Indian possessed such power to draw and mold the hearts of his people."[5]

Of immediate concern was the effect of the killing of Sitting Bull on the Sioux. The news spread like the wind. Kicking Bear and Two Strike with his Brûlés escaped back to the Ghost Dance camp. Thirty-eight Hunkpapas who sought refuge with Big Foot's people on Cheyenne River panicked their rescuers into breaking away from Lieutenant Colonel Edwin V. Sumner's escorting force of cavalry and fleeing toward the White River in the badlands.

Sumner was still parleying with Big Foot when Miles wrote Mary the twentieth of December from Rapid City.

> So far, no white man has been killed and actual war has not commenced. I have done everything in my power to prevent one, but at times it seems impossible.
>
> The administration and the Republican Party are making a fatal mistake in not at once confirming the treaty their commissioners made with the Sioux.
>
> We have taken away their land and the white people now have it. The Indians have been half fed or half starved. Neither I nor any other official can assure the Indians that they will receive anything different in the future. They say, and very justly, that they are tired of broken promises.
>
> I do not think the government should disregard its promises and get the Indians into such a condition, and then order the military to prevent an Indian War.
>
> Thus far no serious war has been started, but no one can tell when it may start.

Again, on the twenty second of December, Miles expressed his opinion of politics in the administration of the Indians.

> I see they are talking in Congress of disarming the Indians [he wrote Mary]. That has been done two or three times, and the citizens sell them arms again. If they were disarmed there are enough horse and cattle thieves around the reservations to steal the Indians blind in six months. There has been no branch of the government so corrupt and disgraceful to the Republic as that which has had the management of our Indian affairs.[6]

Miles was beginning to feel that twenty-one years was a long time to spend rectifying the mistakes of the Indian Bureau. As he gathered more information about the condition of the Sioux, he had less and less heart for open hostilities. He spent long hours poring over maps, reading intelligence reports and directing the disposition of the troops. Everything seemed to be going well in the strange war where every effort was being made not to fire a shot. The question was, how long could the situation be maintained? Even then, events were building to a climax. Miles, learning that Big Foot's band had escaped Sumner, ordered General Brooke at Pine Ridge to send troops after the Sioux.[7] Brooke ordered out Lieutenant Colonel Guy Henry, who had fought with Crook on the Rosebud, and his four troops of the Ninth Cavalry with three Hotchkiss guns, but although Henry scouted north and northeast of Pine Ridge, he could not find Big Foot. It was bitterly cold, and the wind, howling down from the north, swirled dust and sleet about the troops.

Finally Big Foot's band was discovered by Major S. M. White-side of the Seventh Cavalry on Porcupine Tail Creek. The Indians were moving toward the agency and seemed peaceful. Nevertheless General Brooke felt reinforcements were needed. A battalion of the Seventh Cavalry under Colonel Forsyth rode out of Pine Ridge for the Indian camp on a small stream called Wounded Knee.

CHAPTER XXII

A T PRESENT the prospects are very good," Miles wrote Mary on Christmas day, "and General Brooke reports that the Indians are coming in. He believes all will surrender. We have a perfect cordon of troops around the Bad Lands, and hope to force the Indians to surrender without fighting. That would be a most complete success, without loss of life.

"Since commencing this letter I have received another dispatch which is not quite so favorable. So it goes."[1]

The dispatch that Miles had received concerned the escape of Big Foot's band.

Major Whiteside caught up with Big Foot the 28th of December and Forsyth arrived with his battalion the same night on Wounded Knee Creek. Being the senior officer, Forsyth took over command. His orders were to disarm Big Foot's band, take them to the railroad and thence to the reservation where they belonged.

The morning of the 29th continued cold with a clear sky. The hills about the Indian camp on which the troops were bivouacked were swept bare by an icy wind. The Sibley tents of the soldiers looked down on the Sioux tepees pitched in a bleak and treeless depression. Forsyth, who did not intend to let Big Foot get away, completely surrounded the camp with his troops and trained four Hotchkiss guns on the village. The soldiers far outnumbered the Indians, who counted 106 warriors and approximately 260 old men, women and children. Forsyth had eight troops of cavalry, one company of scouts and four pieces of light artillery, numbering 470 men. The young bucks were sullen and resentful. A number of them wore Ghost Shirts beneath their blankets, but the majority of the band were cold, hungry and anxious to get to the agency. Big Foot had pneumonia and had spent the night in the soldiers' hospital tent, but in the morning he asked to go back to his tepee. When Forsyth, speaking through an interpreter, told the men they must surrender their guns, suspicion increased their fright. They were like a herd of wild animals who scented danger. The first unexplained move would start the stampede. The men were separated from the women and ordered to squat in a semicircle in front of Big Foot's tepee. Twenty men were then told to go into the tepees and bring out their guns while the soldiers stood with their weapons ready in case of treachery. The result of the order was two old muskets. Annoyed, Forsyth directed a detail of cavalry to search the lodges. The black eyes of the young bucks glittered dangerously. Some of the women began to wail. The tension was communicated to the troops, who tightened their grasp on their carbines. Forsyth must have been extremely insensitive not to have realized the pressure building up around him. Yellow Bird, a medicine man, leaped up from the circle of squatting Sioux and began to shuffle in a Ghost Dance circle, bending to pick up handfuls of dust and throwing them in the air. A warrior began his death song.

From beneath his blanket, an Indian drew a pistol. The shot cut across the wailing of the women and the chanting of the warrior, a sharp, hollow crack. An officer's shout was lost in the fusillade that burst from the soldiers' carbines. Many of the warriors squatted in a semicircle before the tepee were killed instantly. From the bluff above the camp, the artillery commander snapped: Fire! The four Hotchkiss guns threw shell after shell into the Indian camp where the old men, women and children were gathered. Tepees exploded in gouts of flame and earth. Others flared like torches. Above the crash of shells and the ripping tear of carbines rang the screaming of women and the crying of babies. In the smoke and dust Indian and soldier fought savagely hand to hand. Big Foot was dead. Yellow Bird was killed in the first volley. Sergeant Tritle of E Troop, blood spurting from a wound in his hip, saw a fellow sergeant killed at his side.

The warriors, overwhelmed, broke through the line of K Troop for the sheltering ravines and gulches of the creek. Women and children, seeking to escape the terrible slaughter, fled across the prairie. After them came the enraged soldiers, hunting down and killing the fugitives. "The women as they were fleeing with their babies on their backs were killed together, shot right through, and the women who were very heavy with child were also killed."[2] An officer shouted at his men not to shoot the women. The scouts protected what mothers and babes they could, but the troopers, lusting for revenge, killed indiscriminately. So excited were some of the troopers that they could not distinguish between the scouts and the hostiles and fired on one of their allies. When the scout made his way back to the bluff with the straggling soldiers, an officer observed, "with much gluttonous thought in his voice, 'Now we have avenged Custer's death.' "[3]

They had done more than that. They had set off the explosion that Miles had tried so hard to prevent. Eighteen miles away at Pine Ridge the Sioux camped about the agency heard the Hotchkiss guns and stood to listen with growing fear. On that winter morning, smoke drifted from nearly a thousand tepees. For days the Indians had been coming into the agency to surrender, having decided to trust the white men. They knew Big Foot had been coming to the agency, too, and that he had been intercepted by the Seventh Cavalry. A mounted runner flagged his lathered pony into the circle of tepees shouting that the soldiers were killing Big Foot's people. In the camp of the Ghost Dancers who had barely settled down at the agency, panic broke out. The women tore down the lodges. Ponies were packed for the flight back to the badlands. Groups of angry warriors attacked the agency. There were no troops and the Indian police held them off while Royer, according to reports, hid in the cellar. A group of Brûlés encountered a troop of the Seventh returning from Wounded Knee and fired on the soldiers, who had to abandon a number of captive women and children. All about the agency and the barren hills to the west and north rose clouds of smoke. By nightfall nearly four thousand Indians, ex-hostiles and friends of the whites, had fled from Pine Ridge. Two Strike and Crow Dog left with the frightened, outraged Indians, and Little Wound and Big Road. Even old, half-blind Red Cloud was carried away with the tide. In the darkness the Seventh Cavalry who had caused all this rode into Pine Ridge with twenty-five dead officers and men and thirty-five injured troopers. Behind them on the frozen ground at Wounded Knee lay a hundred and forty-six members of Big Foot's band, eighteen of whom were children. The bodies lay where they had fallen. Among them were some who stirred and whimpered in the cold: a woman terribly hurt by gunfire; a baby in the arms of its dead mother. Later estimates placed the number of Indians who were killed at Wounded Knee or later died as nearly three hundred.[4]

The night was sleepless, filled with danger and apprehension. In the morning the Sioux attacked the Ninth Cavalry pack train. A detail of the Ninth, which had ridden all night to the relief of the agency, drove them off. Within a few hours, Forsyth booted his weary troopers back into the saddle to ride to the Catholic Mission where a column of smoke was spiraling into the air. The Brûlés under Two Strike had set fire to some log cabins and a school. The fire was a ruse to lure the soldiers into a narrow canyon walled in by bluffs on which the Sioux lay in ambush. Despite his experiences on the frontier, Forsyth nearly fell into the trap. Leading his troops past the Mission, Forsyth dismounted the men just beyond the school. At this point, the valley was over a mile wide with hills on either side. Surmising the Indians were on the hills, Forsyth ordered the men to ascend the slopes. The men, spread out in a skirmish line, began the advance when a cry went up: "We're surrounded!" Along the summits of the ridges rode hundreds of mounted warriors. Others darted and raced among the ravines. For the second time within twenty-four hours, the Seventh engaged the Sioux, only this time the odds were against them. There were no women or children and the warriors out-numbered the cavalry. The Brûlés might have had their revenge for Wounded Knee if, at the critical moment, Colonel Guy Henry in response to Forsyth's plea for reinforcements had not ridden up with the Ninth Cavalry. Henry, with trumpets sounding the charge, swept the Sioux from the hills, permitting Forsyth to make his way out of the valley. The Seventh Cavalry commander felt no guilt for Wounded Knee but he was discomfited by this rescue of his vaunted regiment by colored troopers.

Miles, informed about Wounded Knee, was as angry as he had been at any time in his life. Gone was his hope to end the Ghost Dance trouble without bloodshed. The general uprising he had feared now threatened to erupt. On the thirtieth of December he wrote Mary from Rapid City that he had been intensely anxious for several days.

Two nights ago I thought I had the whole difficulty in my hand, and without the loss of a single life. But all my efforts to prevent a war appear to have been destroyed by the action of Lt. Col. Sumner and Col. Forsyth. That affair of the Seventh Cavalry is yet a mystery. It has placed over 3,000 Indians in a hostile attitude and it may result in a serious campaign. Forsyth's reports have been very indefinite and misleading.

I start tonight for Pine Ridge at eleven o'clock after being up nearly all night last night, and I do not expect to get any sleep tonight or tomorrow.

A week later he wrote again from Pine Ridge.

To overcome the failures caused by others, either through blind stupidity or criminal indifference, I have had much additional work. I think Col. Forsyth's actions about the worst I have ever known.

I doubt if there is a Second Lieutenant who could not have made better disposition of 433 white soldiers and 40 Indian scouts, or who could not have disarmed 118 Indians encumbered with 250 women and children. There must have been nearly 100 women and children killed.[5]

Schofield, in a dispatch to Miles, asked that his thanks be given to the "brave Seventh Cavalry for its splendid conduct." A grim reply came from Miles that the action of the colonel commanding the Seventh was of serious consideration and was to be subject to an investigation. Under the circumstances, did Schofield want to congratulate the Seventh? Schofield replied that it might be better if he waited until after the investigation which Miles proposed. Schofield conferred with the President and the Secretary of War who expressed their concern. If there had been any unsoldierly conduct, the President told Miles, the officer concerned should be relieved. On the 4th of January, Forsyth was suspended from his command of the Seventh Cavalry pending an investigation of Wounded Knee and Major

Whiteside appointed to succeed. The news was broadcast to the nation in headlines: "Forsyth in Disgrace." The public read the story with varying reactions. In the War Department in Washington, the staff officers were dismayed and then outraged. It was against all the rules and regulations to relieve an officer in the face of the enemy!

Miles was too busy to bother about the War Department. The fire was out of control. He had to quench the flames and salvage what he could from the threatened holocaust. Within a matter of hours after his arrival at Pine Ridge, he had a new campaign activated. General Brooke had huddled the troops in the center of camp in defensive positions. Miles threw them out in picket lines on top of the ridge encircling the agency. Rifle pits were dug and board shelters erected over them. A wire to Washington recommended that the agents be replaced by officers who had years of experience in Indian administration. This request was, of course, immediately protested by the Indian Bureau and relayed to the public under such headlines as "Shall The Army Rule?" Reinforcements were ordered from Fort Keogh, from Fort Douglas and as far away as San Francisco. General Brooke, put in command of field forces, started west via Beaver Creek. Brooke was to swing out in a long line forming the western and part of the northern side of a huge hollow square. Colonel Eugene Carr with his command moved in east of Pine Butte in the vicinity of Wounded Knee to form the eastern and part of the northern side of the square. Thus surrounded, the Indians were to be driven slowly to the agency. The troops were not to come in direct contact with the Indians and there was to be no undue pressure. While this was being done, emissaries from Miles were to visit the Indians to tell them their only hope was to surrender and that they could trust the division commander — no easy task, after Wounded Knee.

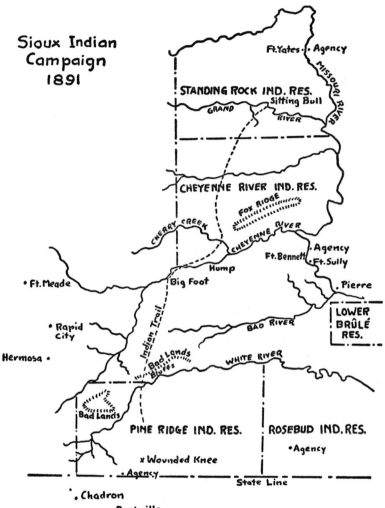

Sioux Indian
Campaign
1891

It was a bold and daring plan. Miles labored under terrific tension. He had to know and direct the disposition of every infantry and cavalry unit and keep informed of the whereabouts of the main Indian bands. Added to the strain of the over-all campaign were the smaller distractions. A rumor spread that a group of Ghost Dancers had sneaked into the friendly Indian camp about the agency and persuaded their kinsmen to help them massacre every white man, woman and child at Pine Ridge. The refugees at the agency were already in a state of nerves. The rumor upset them even more. Armed men escorted frightened women and weeping children into warehouses and other strongholds. All Indians, except the scouts and the police, were barred from the area. The reporters, titillated by the danger, had a field day. Miles, who could not afford to ignore the rumor, stayed up until three o'clock.

All this while, the hollow square was forming about five thousand Indians to begin the slow drive to the agency.

Matters improved somewhat when Young-Man-Afraid-of-His-Horses, an able chief and a friend of the whites, arrived at the agency to confer with Miles and then to proceed to the Sioux camps to persuade the Indians to surrender. About the same time, Jack Red Cloud, son of the old chief, came in and requested help to bring in some of the Indians who had fled the night of Wounded Knee. Among these Indians was Red Cloud who claimed he was a prisoner in the hostile camp. Red Cloud wanted the soldiers to come get him. According to friends, Red Cloud hadn't wanted to leave the agency but when the general exodus began his wife threw the old man's belongings into a wagon declaring she was going on the warpath even if her liege lord was not.

By the 6th of January, small bands of Indians were beginning to straggle into the agency. An army emissary, Captain E. P.

Ewers, was having some success in persuading the northern Cheyennes to return to the agency while reports said Little Wound, Two Strike and Big Road wanted to give up but that Short Bull and Kicking Bear were arguing against it. At this critical moment an Indian called Plenty of Horses fired a shot that nearly blew Miles's careful plans wide open again. Plenty of Horses was a Brûlé from a Ghost Dance camp on White Clay Creek near White River. Lieutenant E. W. Casey, in command of Cheyenne scouts attached to General Brooke, was reconnoitering the camp when the Brûlé shot him in the back of the head. Yankton Charley, an Oglala scout, rode his horse to death through a blizzard to bring the news to Pine Ridge. The murder occasioned great excitement in the hostile camp and among the military. The next day Miles wrote to Mary that he had thought the night before that the Indians were coming in, "but the killing of poor Casey may delay matters somewhat. It was a great shock to every one as he was dearly beloved by all who knew him. It was a case of murder. Casey was too confident. He rode up on a hill and met two Indians. One of them warned him of his danger, saying that the other was mad and desperate. When Casey turned to go away, not thinking of the treachery of the savage, the Indian shot him in the back of the head."[6]

Interestingly enough, Plenty of Horses was one of the Carlisle graduates in whom the humanitarians placed so much faith. Education had made him neither an Indian nor a white, and so, in desperation, he had turned on those responsible for his unhappy plight.

The Indians were quarreling among themselves over whether to surrender or fight. Yet every day they moved camp a little nearer the agency and the troops, held carefully in the background, moved a little closer on their tracks. One hour Miles would receive a dispatch saying the Indians were all coming in; the next, that the fanatics had won out and the Indians were going to fight. In Miles's favor was his acquaintance with Broad Tail, Spotted Eagle and other chiefs who had surrendered to him on the Yellowstone. These Indians knew and trusted the General.

Miles's policy of nonviolence was being severely critized in Washington by some members of the War Department who felt that a single assault with intent to kill would precipitate a battle so full of lasting benefit that the loss of a few men would not be regarded. In other words, these officers felt a dead Indian was worth more to the government than a captured Indian. The "Crook people" claimed loudly that if Crook had been alive, he would have settled the Ghost Dance uprising weeks before. The Forsyth case, too, was causing a greater disturbance than had at first been anticipated.

The attacks increased the tension under which Miles was working. He felt strongly about the matter. "That Forsyth case is very bad," he wrote Mary. "He [Forsyth] showed himself to be utterly incompetent and unfit for any command. I see my enemies have taken up his case and propose to attack me on that score. If they wish to support the most abominable, criminal military blunder and a horrible massacre of women and children I am ready to meet them on that ground."[7]

No compromise for Miles when he felt military justice was involved.

Again he wrote his wife.

The Forsyth action was a useless slaughter of innocent women and children. Every day we hear of poor women, little girls and boys and children found dead and frozen to the ground, or crawling over the prairie, for a distance of one hundred miles north and south.

If Sherman, I mean our boy, could not make a better disposition of his troops I would be disappointed. At the time
the fight commenced only about two troops could fire upon the
warriors, but they could and did fire upon the women and
children.[8]

The general public did not share Miles's indignation. Who
cared about a few dead Indians? Miles's treatment of Forsyth
was considered very harsh, while Secretary of War Proctor and
Schofield agreed unanimously to vindicate the Seventh Cavalry
officer. The Board of Inquiry found there was no evidence that
Forsyth was guilty of carelessness. The killing of women and
children had been unavoidable, so it held, and so far as it could
discover, no troops were killed by the fire of their own side; a
blunder of which Miles had also accused the Seventh Commander. Forsyth was exonerated and restored to command.

Miles felt the honor of the army had been sacrificed. He
never backed down once he had taken a stand, and he wouldn't
back down in the case of Forsyth. His enemies were thus increased in Washington. To the Crook faction was added the
Forsyth faction, and the Seventh Cavalry, with all its tradition,
never forgave him. The President was annoyed because, for the
second time, Miles had placed him in an embarrassing position.
The humanitarians were angry because Miles had announced
that they were partly to blame for the starvation of the Sioux.

The Board of Inquiry was conducting its investigation
during the tense days the Indians were advancing toward the
agency. By the 9th of January, five thousand Indians were
camped within a short distance of Pine Ridge while the troops,
gradually closing around them on three sides, continued to keep
in the background so as not to stampede the hostiles. The
morning of the tenth, two Brûlés in white shirts, one with a
streak of blue paint across his nose, galloped up to Pine Ridge

from the great hostile camp and demanded to see General Miles. The Indian police, after disarming them, allowed them to enter headquarters where they had an interview with Miles who told them to return to their people and tell them to surrender. Miles then, instructed the police to return the Brûlés' weapons. Grimacing derisively at the police, the Brûlés caught up their rifles and galloped off with Miles's message.

Nerves tightened as the Indians drew closer and closer to the agency. A few apprehensive squawmen, certain that armed truce could not prevail and that everyone at the agency would be massacred, fled with their families to the railroad.

Miles himself could not tell what would happen. He was prepared for any eventuality. The larger part of the troops were in the field, leaving only six hundred infantrymen to guard the agency. If the hostiles attacked, Miles would have to depend on his artillery. North of the agency, he had stationed a three-inch gun protected by a breastworks. On the east, Hotchkiss guns and a Gatling covered the ravine along which the Sioux had to approach Pine Ridge. On the west was another Hotchkiss and on the north a three-inch rifle was trained on Red Cloud's house.

The hostile camp was formidable. Scouts reported tepees were strung out for three miles along a ravine and that the fanatics were still wrangling with Two Strike and Little Wound. On the night of the tenth, the Indians moved three miles closer to the agency.

Miles was encouraged when he wrote to Mary the following day.

> I am in very good spirits today as I think the Indians are all coming in to surrender. At least that is what they say, and they are moving in that direction. The troops are moving close behind them, under General Brooke. He has about 1600 troops and Col. Shafter has about 700 here.[9]

If they come in and surrender the military problem will have been solved. But the government of twenty thousand Sioux Indians and their restoration to peace and confidence is not an easy task.

The Sioux were in no hurry to give up their freedom; they were still not sure of the whites, and with good reason — they carried with them wounded women and children from Forsyth's fight. A storm heightened the tension. Wind tore at the canvas of the tepees and rattled the windows of the agency. Sand and snow blinded the sentries. In the shrieking, icy darkness the Indians imagined the advance of soldiers; the whites, starting nervously, heard a war cry in the whirlwind.

Colonel Eugene Carr held close to the flank of the hostiles. Brooke, with the Second Infantry and the Ninth Cavalry, moved every mile the Indians moved. One night he camped at the same place the hostiles had camped the night before. If a soldier were to discharge his rifle by fright or accident, it could precipitate catastrophe.

At Pine Ridge, officers with field glasses watched for the first sign of the Indians. Sentries pacing their beat glanced in the same direction. Squaw men, newspaper correspondents, refugees and all the motley collection of people at the agency aided in the vigil. On the eleventh, the watchers saw Indian police riding down the bare, snow-streaked ridge in front of the agency with a number of Sioux. The police had been out all night scouting in the hills. After them came Indian scouts with rifles slung across their saddles, then more stragglers. The hostile camp was less than two miles from the agency and the watchers jumped to the conclusion that this was the vanguard coming in to surrender, but scouts informed Miles that the hostiles were still quarreling. The young men wanted war and the closer they got to Pine Ridge, the touchier they became.

Buffalo Bill, who had staged a reappearance, and McGillycuddy wanted to go out and parley with the Indians but Miles would not permit them to endanger his careful and precarious plans.

At noon of the same day, a sentry saw hostile scouts surveying the agency from nearby ravines. They disappeared, and, within a short while horsemen rode over the crest of the ridge. More appeared, and then more and more until the white slopes swarmed with Sioux. There were no women or children among the warriors, and for a few moments they sat their war ponies staring sullenly down at the agency before they wheeled and descended the ridge to Red Cloud's house. To the watchers at the agency, the old men seemed to be arguing with the young bucks. Without warning, one of the bucks fired his rifle over the head of an old man. The others fired their rifles into the air and then, astonishingly enough, they began shooting their ponies and dogs in a sort of wild, futile rebellion.

On the 13th of January, Miles telegraphed Mary.

Success. The Indians have surrendered and will soon be under our control. They are now camped between General Brooke's troops and this place under the guns of both commands. I would have closed this affair two weeks ago had it not been for the mistakes of two men but am very much gratified with the results after four weeks of incessant care and anxiety. I hope to go home before many days.[10]

Two days later, Miles wrote:

Every hour of the day is occupied and much of the night with intense anxiety and responsibility. Night before last I was awake every hour. Of course you see the lying reports and false rumors that are sent out from here by irresponsible reporters; but here where they and many more originate, every rumor has to be investigated.

The Indians are now moving past this place to camp down in front of the Agency. The principal leader, Kicking Bear, has just handed in his rifle and the others will follow. They are gathering them up now in camp.

I regard the trouble as over, and the work of finishing up I will soon leave to subordinates.

The relief from the intense responsibility will be very gratifying to me.

I shall go east as soon as I can establish a permanent peace. I have had to encounter many difficulties of which I can not write.[11]

The people at Pine Ridge would never forget the fog that obscured the agency in the morning — opaque, gray and stifling. Toward noon, it evaporated to show the Indians moving through the scattered pines in the ravine. They came around the base of Horse Shoe Butte, into the valley and past Red Cloud's house. The warriors were in the lead driving the ponies while Brûlé scouts advanced on the bluffs above the ravine like skirmishers. Behind the warriors, came the squaws driving wagons loaded with tepee poles, canvas and camp equipment. In all the four mile long procession there was no sound but the tinkling of bells on the ponies.

PART SEVEN

The Spanish-American War

CHAPTER XXIII

In February of 1891, General Sherman died, marking the end of an era. The Sioux had risen for the last time against encroaching civilization. A phase of Miles's career was finished which he would remember with nostalgia although, at the present time, he was still looking ahead.

The Sioux campaign had been tiring. The Forsyth investigation had been difficult. Miles was irritable and tense. He needed a vacation with his family. He was happiest when he was with Mary and the children. In early spring, the Mileses left Chicago in a special car accompanied by Lieutenant Marion Maus as aide-de-camp. A colonel of the Mexican army, detailed by the President, met the party at the border and escorted them to Mexico City where they received an impressive welcome. A regimental band serenaded their hotel every evening. Miles was invited to review the Mexican army and the Military Academy at Chapultepec and the family was entertained by President and Mrs. Díaz at their private residence.

In June, Miles was back in Chicago rested and ready to take up the cudgels again.

The world was entering a new period of progress and development. Industry was burgeoning: railroads, steel, hydroelectric power. Edison patented a kinetoscope using a new celluloid film developed by Eastman. A daring gentleman drove a three-wheeled phaeton powered by a gasoline engine. It was the heyday of the railroad and copper magnates and of political battles for free silver, tariffs and temperance. Miles approved of industrial progress. Indeed, he encouraged it. During the time he commanded the Department of Arizona, he became interested in irrigation and wrote a long article on the advantages of bringing water to the arid regions. The heliostat system he employed against Geronimo foreshadowed the radio network. While he commanded the Division of the Missouri, he experimented with a bicycle corps. He was one of the first to recognize the value of gasoline-powered vehicles for the army. He promoted new equipment for the infantry and improved communications.

Miles could not so easily comprehend the sociological changes that accompanied the growth of industry and science. He was still the rock-bound conservative he had been born and raised in pre–Civil War New England. He was prejudiced in many ways, an old-fashioned idealist in others and opinionated in all his views.

He had no patience with rioters in Chicago who had been harangued to rise against the capitalists by the agitator Eugene Debs. Since Miles's headquarters was in Chicago, he was fully aware that the close of the Exposition in that city and the financial panic of 1894 sweeping the country had left many unemployed. The pot of labor unrest, simmering throughout the nation for some time, threatened to boil over. Violence flared and there was theft and beggary, and shouted threats from mobs in various parts of the country.

Miles did not object to labor reform or to unions but he did object to violence. "Whatever changes are made in the status of labor," he wrote afterward, "must be brought about by moral influence, by fair and honorable discussion, by civic reformation and by the modification of laws governing society, rather than by acts of violence and lawlessness."[1]

Grover Cleveland had been returned to the presidency and

he called Miles to Washington when a strike against the Pullman Company in a suburb of Chicago threatened to get out of control. Miles had been vacationing in New England with Mary and the children and was on his way back to Chicago when he received a wire from the Secretary of War to report to Washington immediately. At the station he was met by his aide-de-camp, Captain Maus, who delivered a note from the Secretary of War, Daniel Lamont, requesting him to come to his house immediately. Miles complied and was taken directly by Lamont to the White House where a consultation was held between the President, the Secretary of State, the Attorney General, the Secretary of War, General Schofield and Miles. "All appeared quite anxious about the situation," Miles wrote Mary later in the day. He did not say so, but there was some coolness between him and the Commanding General. Schofield did not like Miles's insistence that he had been right to relieve Forsyth. But if Miles did not get along with Schofield, he hit it off splendidly with the President. His first impression of Cleveland — whom he encountered for the first time — was of a great, hulking, taciturn man. Miles was not sure whether the President would back up the troops if it came to a showdown and troops had to be called out to quell the riot in Chicago. Miles set himself to "smoke out" the President. At first Cleveland would not commit himself. Miles persisted. What support could he expect?

"If you get too much support," Cleveland replied, "it's my fault, if too little, it's yours."

Encouraged by this, Miles came directly to the point. The Regular Army was small and scattered. Would militia be called into Federal service if necessary and, if so, where would they come from? The President grunted he would call out militia if he had to.

"If you do," Miles said boldly, "may I suggest you call them from the Deep South?"

"I thought you were a New Englander," Cleveland retorted, regarding Miles from beneath his brows.

"I am, sir," Miles replied, "but I understand that the South does not know much about labor troubles and their troops might be less sympathetic to a mob."

The President leaned back with a great bull roar of laughter. "General, if it comes to that, you shall have your Johnny Rebs, and I'll go to Chicago for the fun of seeing a Damn Yankee command them!"[2]

Miles had time for only a brief visit to Senator Sherman, who was having breakfast at his home, before he caught the train to Chicago where, arriving twenty-four hours later, he found a state of anarchy. The Pullman Company, against whom the strike was directed, had pioneered in labor reform but that did not seem to make much difference to the vicious element that had taken over. The union called out the railroad engineers and firemen in sympathy with the Pullman strikers, resulting in a paralysis of freight and passenger traffic in the western half of the United States. The food supply was growing short in the city. Bridges were dynamited. Rails were torn up. Stations were burned. Men were beaten and stoned. Three thousand special deputies were powerless to handle the mob.

Miles acted swiftly. Even before he arrived in Chicago from Washington, troops were on the way from posts in the vicinity of the city and from Kansas and Nebraska. Since the railroad employees were on strike, the troops in some instances took over the trains and operated them to protect the mail and provide transportation to Chicago. The Seventh Cavalry was one of the regiments called into the city. Frederick Remington, the artist and friend of Miles, visited the troops where they were bivouacked on the lake front before the Auditorium Hotel. It was a strange scene for the prairie-bred Seventh Cavalry with the sunlight winking on the blue water and city buildings. Sentries paced between the neat rows of Sibley tents. Horses fidgeted and stamped on the picket lines.

Miles wanted to avoid bloodshed and issued orders accordingly. Feeling ran high between the strikers and the troops. When K Troop appeared and tried to push the rioters back from an assault on the railroad, the mob shouted vile names and threw stones. The troopers, boiling inwardly, kept their eyes straight ahead.

There were other incidents, some of them not so serious. A detail was escorting wagons into the city early in the morning. One of the wagons stalled and the officer in command went back to see what was wrong just as a striker on the sidewalk shouted to a little dismounted trooper, "Hello, Gen'l Miles, I'd like to kick the face off you."

"Hold my horse, some one," the little trooper begged. The officer tactfully disappeared and the 130-pound cavalryman lit into the striker, giving him a licking he was not likely to forget for a long while.[3]

On the 5th and 6th of July, Miles wrote Mary, a mob of one thousand men moved from 51st to 18th Streets destroying property and firing buildings, shouting, "To hell with the government." Miles moved troops to Park Street and "should have attacked the mob had it gone near the U. S. buildings below Adams and Jackson on Clark Street."[4]

Miles had few moments to write to Mary. He was constantly interrupted; he worked far into the night and the heat was stifling. When he could get away, he took a swim in the athletic pool to cool off. But he did send Mary a check for a hundred dollars which he hoped would last as long as possible, and despite the pressing matters that demanded his attention, he found time to be concerned about how Mary liked the resort in New England where she was staying and to hope that Sherman would grow stronger with the opportunity to be out of doors.

By the eighteenth, Miles wrote Mary, "the revolutionists have seen the teeth of war and want none of it." The violence was dying down in other parts of the country, too.[5]

Miles gained nothing by his suppression of violence in Chicago, unless it was the appreciation of Cleveland for his prompt action. Schofield, later, criticized him. Miles did not expect thanks. He hadn't liked riot duty any better than the troops. The only satisfaction he derived was seeing the men perform well under a difficult situation. Miles was proud of his regulars.

In October of 1894, Miles was transferred to the Department of the East at Governors Island. General O. O. Howard, whom Miles relieved, retired to write his autobiography and preach in Sunday school. The names of Civil War veterans were thinning on the active duty roster. Sherman, Mackenzie, Crook, Hancock, Sheridan and Custer were dead. Howard and Gibbon were retired. Only Schofield was senior to Miles. During the Ghost Dance uprising, a correspondent pointed out that if Miles lived long enough, he would succeed Schofield on the latter's retirement in 1895, a fact of which Miles was well aware. He was in the best of health and had every intention of living until 1895 and a good many years thereafter.

The tour at Governors Island was an interlude enhanced by the prospect of becoming, before long, the Commanding General of the Army. Miles enjoyed those few months.

On pleasant afternoons, Cecelia and Master Sherman often joined their father in a bicycle ride. Miles's first love was still horses, but bicycling had a novel appeal. In 1895, Miles's hair and mustache were beginning to turn quite gray and he had put on weight.

During this period, Miles put the finishing touches on his first autobiography, which was entitled *Personal Recollections and Observations of General Nelson A. Miles.* The following year, the book was published but it was a disappointment. Miles's style was stilted and he refrained from personal comment, which made his autobiography less interesting than it might have been.

In September of 1895, Schofield retired and Miles received the following order: "By direction of the President, Major-General Nelson A. Miles is assigned to the command of the Army of the United States."[6]

So the New England farm boy who had raised a company of Massachusetts Infantry thirty-four years ago moved into the position once occupied by Sherman and Sheridan.

Mary went to Washington to find a house. She found a small place on the corner of Twentieth and G Streets, North West, but the district was deteriorating, and the following year the family rented a larger, more modern home on Rhode Island Avenue a half block west of Seventeenth Street. As Commanding General of the Army, Miles felt he should maintain his position socially as well as professionally. Mary was a great help in this respect as, indeed, she had always been. In middle age, she was a fine-looking woman with graying hair, blue eyes and what was termed at the time "an aristocratic carriage." Cecelia was as popular in the Capital as she had been in New York. Master Sherman, who was nearing thirteen, was enrolled in the Friends School. It was generally accepted that Sherman would someday go to West Point and follow in his father's footsteps by becoming a professional army man. Actually, Miles did not try to influence the boy. He felt it was better if he made up his own mind.

Miles's office was in the massive gray War, State and Navy Building, a large room on the east side of the second floor. From the day he assumed command, trouble was inevitable. Under the law, the Commanding General exercised only partial command. The Adjutant General and the Inspector General were partly his responsibility and he was entitled to pass on all army orders issued in the name of the Secretary of War, but the Quartermaster and Subsistence Bureaus were answerable directly to the Secretary. Sherman's quarrel with Stanton, which resulted in the General's move to St. Louis, grew largely out of this division of authority. Nor was the situation helped by the personality of the Secretary whom McKinley (elected in 1896) had appointed to his Cabinet. Russell Alexander Alger was a wealthy Michigan politician with a courteous manner and a neat gray beard, pleasing enough in appearance but weak and evasive in character. His Civil War record was suspect. He had sought votes in the Republican convention in 1896 in the hope of being nominated for the presidency. John Sherman, appointed Secretary of State, had no use for Alger. Why McKinley put him in his Cabinet, was a mystery, unless the appointment was purely political. Alger had been Commander in Chief of the Grand Army of the Republic, the organization of Civil War Veterans which was still powerful, and he had contributed money to McKinley's campaign.

Miles did not respect Alger and saw no reason why he should be a party to what was considered Alger's mismanagement of the War Department. With his customary energy, he immediately began a fight to enlarge the army, which then numbered twenty-five thousand men. He also wanted to quicken the promotion system, which had grandfathers serving as first lieutenants, and modernize the coastal defenses. The United States was emerging as a world power and Miles felt the country might find it necessary to engage in a major conflict for which it was unprepared.

Unfortunately, Miles was not a good lobbyist. His statements were blunt. His conviction sounded like military autocracy. His naturally stilted manner was regarded as pomposity. Congress was not interested, nor were the people.

Miles was still trying to get the money he felt was so sorely needed when, in 1897, he was ordered to Europe to observe the Greco-Turkish War and to be military representative to Queen Victoria's Jubilee. Miles was anxious to make the trip, which he thought would enlarge his military knowledge. Alger did not object. Miles's absence would remove an aggressive irritant from administration circles.

Mary accompanied her husband as far as Paris where she stayed with friends while Miles and his aide, Captain Maus, visited Turkey and Greece. In the former capital, he had an audience with the Sultan and inspected the Turkish army, coming away much impressed by the statement of Osman Pasha, the able Turkish general, that "persistency is the great secret of success in war. If an army is not successful one day, tenacity of purpose and persistency will in the end bring victory."[7]

This was Miles's belief; he had demonstrated it many times during the Civil War and on the plains.

In Greece, he was received by the Crown Prince and taken to the historic Pass of Thermopylae not far from where the Greek and Turkish army picket lines were halted less than four hundred yards apart. Miles was primarily interested in military matters but he was also an interested sightseer. He didn't miss much. The "children" didn't write and he had only two letters from Mary, which bothered him. He didn't stop to think that mail might have a difficult time catching up with him. He wrote to the "children" often, hoping they were in the best of health and happy.

From Greece, Miles returned to France where he picked up Mary and continued to England. In his official capacity, Miles was the guest of the Queen and was given a suite of rooms in the Buckingham Palace Hotel opposite the Palace. Mary wrote the "children" that she wished they could see them moving about in state. "Papa" was given a horse from the Royal Stables complete with an orderly from the Life Guards. In the afternoon, a royal carriage was at their disposal. There were balls at Buckingham Palace; dinners and luncheons at the Duke of Marlborough's; a presentation to the Queen. Mary spent hours practicing her curtsy and did "quite as well as any Englishwoman." Miles bowed profoundly.[8]

There were operas; a review of the troops at Aldershot; a review of the fleet at Portsmouth. Mary was thrilled by the gaiety and the lovely gowns and the jewels and the graciousness of the many people they met, but she missed the "children" and no place in Europe was as attractive as home. The constant round of activity tired her. She had not been feeling well for some time. In fact, Captain Maus wrote Cecelia that her mother was not at all like herself; she was low in spirits and worried.

Captain Maus was worn out, too, by attending to his general and to official correspondence. He tried to catch up on his work at the only desk in the living room of the hotel suite, and if he was interrupted was, Mary said, "crosser than two bears."

Miles did not miss a thing and never seemed to tire. He rode in the Jubilee Parade on a fine, prancing charger which he handled with the skill born of years on the plains. His uniform had a high velvet collar embroidered in gold and, as Mary wrote the "children" afterward ". . . in the glittering throng of Princes, Field Marshals and Generals, he looked better than any of them in spite of their elaborate uniforms."[9]

The English liked Miles. Always fascinated by the American West, they were intrigued by the general who had fought Sitting Bull and Geronimo. The Prince of Wales came forward and shook hands with Miles at Buckingham Palace; the Duke of Connaught invited him to lunch at Aldershot.

The Jubilee celebration was the highlight of the trip. When the festivities were ended, Mary went to Carlsbad to take the cure and Miles went to Russia to observe the Russian army. In Moscow, he was the guest of the Czar in the Imperial Palace. The favors that had been heaped upon him, the hobnobbing with royalty, left him unchanged. He was too much of a New England Yankee to be overwhelmed by titles. A reaction to so many festivities was beginning to set in. For the first time, he felt sightseeing was "tiresome," and took an afternoon off to enjoy ". . . what Napoleon could not, a quiet peaceful rest in the Imperial Palace." He missed Mary and wrote the "children" that after four days of parties and formalities he hoped to "turn my face homeward with joy. Never for a single day," he wrote, did he find "anyplace as agreeable as my own home."[10]

In Berlin, to his relief, he discovered Mary much improved in health and looking much better. The cure at Carlsbad had been rigid and depressing but the result, Miles was sure, would be beneficial.

From Berlin, Miles went to Hamburg to see maneuvers of the German army. He also, before the trip was over, saw the Italian, Austrian and French armies. He thought the French were sloppy in appearance but efficient in action. The German armament and equipment and uniforms were most effective but the cost of maintaining such a strong military force was too great a burden for the country and a temptation to aggression. Seventeen years later, Miles's misgivings were to prove well founded.

The large standing armies of Europe strengthened Miles's conviction that the United States should have an effective fighting force.

Back in Washington, Miles renewed his campaign for an increase in the size of the army, based on a reasonable ratio of national strength. At the time, that would have meant an army of approximately seventy thousand men. But, as it had in previous years, Congress turned a deaf ear to the Commanding General. Military appropriations were not popular with the public, who persisted in the notion the country could spring to arms overnight. Within a few months, this utopian idea was to cost America dearly.

The United States had not been involved in a war for thirty-three years — time for a new generation to grow up who had no experience of the cost and tragedy of conflict. When the Cuban insurgents rose against their Spanish masters and the American battleship *Maine* sent to Havana to protect American property was blown up, the public demanded retribution. Glaring headlines in the yellow press roused indignation and, coincidentally, sent circulation to new heights.

Miles strongly disapproved of the war hysteria. John Sherman, growing senile and shortly to resign as Secretary of State but still capable in many ways, did not think war was necessary, nor did McKinley and the majority of the Cabinet want war. Only one individual in the Cabinet, Miles was to write afterward, favored war.

At the time, Theodore Roosevelt was serving as deputy to

Secretary of the Navy John D. Long. Roosevelt was a rising young politician from a socially prominent family. His toothy smile and eyeglasses had already become familiar to the public. Backed by the influential Senator Henry Cabot Lodge, his career was assured. He was sincere in his patriotism, energetic, ambitious, and had a natural talent for publicity. Roosevelt was a friend of Leonard Wood whom Miles had brought to Washington and who had become White House physician and, by all rights, Roosevelt and Miles should have become friends. Roosevelt loved hunting and the West. He had been a gentleman rancher in Dakota. Perhaps the two men were too strong personalities to be congenial. The antagonism was mutual.

Miles felt the threatened hostilities could be settled by arbitration; that it had been a mistake to send the *Maine* to Havana and that the destruction of the ship was not due to agents of the Spanish government who had reason to discourage rather than encourage United States intervention. His protests were lost in the rising clamor for war. Roosevelt and Lodge were leading advocates of military intervention in Cuba. Senator Proctor of Vermont, who had recently visited Cuba, described the deplorable conditions of the poor Cubans under the cruel Spanish. Letters and telegrams poured into the White House. McKinley, not a man of strong character, yielded to popular demand. On the 21st of April, 1898, war against Spain was formally declared. Fifty million dollars was voted by Congress, to be used at the discretion of the President for national defense. No one seems to have remembered how Miles had begged for less than half that sum in previous years. The Asiatic Fleet sailed from Hong Kong to Manila and on May 1 captured or sank the Spanish fleet in the Bay. It was the first victory of the war and made a hero of Admiral Dewey. An expeditionary force, whose regiments and batteries were designated by Miles, was ordered to the Philippines to fight the Spanish forces then in possession of the Islands. Miles foresaw the need of naval bases in the Orient, but he did not suppose that the Philippines would be taken over against the wish of the Filipinos.

The invasion of Cuba was anticipated and, for this purpose, the regiments of the Regular Army were called from posts in the West, in the South and in the East. The men, Miles testified, were "a body of trained athletes, well disciplined and excellent marksmen."[11] Miles should have known. He had marched and fought with the regulars through Arizona, Montana and the Dakotas. He had the pride of the professional military man in the professional soldier. Call it esprit de corps, or what you will. It is often misinterpreted by the public; it can only be understood by those whose lives have been dedicated to its service. But an army of twenty-five thousand men plus untrained volunteers was a weak force for the United States to employ in a war with Spain. When Miles was directed to take an army of seventy thousand men and capture Havana, he told the President he appreciated the opportunity to command an army to invade a foreign country but that in justice to the men who would be doing the fighting, he thought the expedition would fail. There were, he told McKinley, one hundred and twenty-five thousand Spanish troops with one hundred field guns within a short distance of Havana and one hundred and twenty-five guns in fortified positions. The Americans, on the other hand, thanks to their previous apathy, did not have enough ammunition for seventy thousand men. The storming of heavily fortified positions, like Havana, had become obsolete and Cuba in midsummer was no place for troops unused to the tropics. The men would fall ill of malaria and yellow fever. The war, Miles said, should be fought largely by the Navy until the army could be properly trained and equipped. To his credit, McKinley suspended the order for the army to invade Cuba and an American squadron under Admiral Sampson sailed to the blockade of Havana.

Miles's outspoken opposition to an early attack on Havana and his insistence that the army was not ready for such a campaign antagonized the war enthusiasts who were called jingoists. Already out of favor with the Secretary of War, Miles deepened the rift by his disapproval of politically influenced appointments and suspect contracts in the Quartermaster Department. Alger felt Miles was being autocratic. Miles had reason to be. He saw amateurs taking over the work of professionals, political expediency dominating important decisions. Alger decided to ignore Miles. Popular sentiment supported the Secretary. People shouted, "On to Havana!" Volunteers swamped the recruiting office. Thus the people found themselves with a Secretary of War who, with other officials in Washington, operated through the President as Commander in Chief to conduct the war as they wished. The Commanding General of the Army was not consulted.

There is reason to believe Alger hoped Miles would be forced to retire. The Secretary should have known that Miles never retreated under fire. He had no intention of giving up the fight.

CHAPTER XXIV

BEFORE a campaign could be attempted in Cuba, the United States had to win control of the sea. Reports at the time indicated that the American fleet was superior to the Spanish but only by a slight margin. The United States had a powerful fleet at Key West under the command of Admiral William T. Sampson and a flying squadron at Hampton Roads under Commodore Winfield S. Schley. Sampson's force was to be made even stronger by the addition of the battleship *Oregon* ordered from the Pacific coast. Opposed to this naval strength was a small Spanish fleet off the coast of Spain and a fast squadron commanded by Admiral Cervera at St. Vincent in the Cape Verde Islands. The Spanish squadron in the Pacific was captured or destroyed by Dewey at Manila. The last of April, Washington received word that Cervera's squadron, consisting of four cruisers and three torpedo-boat destroyers, was sailing west.

Popular imagination promptly magnified the power and size of the Spanish fleet. Consternation reigned along the east coast. The Spanish ships were sighted a hundred times. New York expected bombardment at any moment. Congressmen besieged the Navy Department for ships to protect vulnerable harbors. Even old Civil War monitors were hastily commissioned. Not until word was received that Cervera was hundreds of miles south in the Caribbean did the fear abate.

On orders from the Navy Department, Sampson was ordered to the Caribbean to scout for and to intercept the Spanish vessels. Schley was also ordered south for the same purpose.

While the American ships were scouring the tropical waters, the army was training and equipping troops. Roosevelt, resigning as Assistant Secretary of the Navy, raised a volunteer regiment known as the "Rough Riders." Roosevelt was the Lieutenant Colonel and Leonard Wood, who preferred soldiering to doctoring, became the Colonel. Roosevelt, exuberant, bubbling over with patriotism, could hardly wait to get into action. The press soon popularized the Volunteer Colonel and his mounted troops of socialites and cowboys.

Promotions came thick and fast. Frank Baldwin, who had been so long with Miles on the frontier, served as a brigadier general in the Philippines. Guy Henry, who had commanded the Ninth Cavalry at Pine Ridge, was made a brigadier, as was Adna Chaffee, veteran of the Kiowa-Comanche campaign. James F. Wade, who had so capably escorted the Apaches from Fort Apache to the railroad, was promoted to major general. John R. Brooke and James H. Wilson were among others who were made major generals. William R. Shafter, ex-colonel of an infantry regiment at Pine Ridge, was made a major general and so, too, were ex-Confederates Fitzhugh Lee and "Fighting Joe" Wheeler. Fitzhugh Lee, who had served as consul general at Havana, was a rotund, genial gentleman from Virginia, a nephew of Robert E. Lee. Wheeler was an elderly little man with a gray beard. The last time Lee and Wheeler had served in an army had been in the Civil War. Their appointment was an effort on the part of the Administration to enlist southern support.

Shafter was a protégé of Alger, from the Secretary's home state of Michigan. He weighed three hundred pounds, had a tendency to gout and was sixty-three years old. Shafter was the incredible choice of Alger to command an expeditionary force to Cuba.

As Commanding General of the Army, Miles felt he should

outrank the other major generals by more than a few files. He had wanted a promotion to lieutenant general for some time, anyhow. Sherman and Sheridan had both held the rank. The times seemed auspicious, but when he requested the promotion it was refused.

"It is sometimes easy for the thoughtless and inexperienced to involve a country in war," Miles wrote later, "but disastrous when they attempt to direct its military forces."[1]

Miles thought more volunteers had been accepted than could be equipped at the time. He also felt the Cuban insurgents should be encouraged to carry on the fight with Spain during the hot and unhealthy summer, while the army was being trained and equipped and the navy was seeking to destroy the Spanish fleet or blockade it in a Cuban or Puerto Rican port.

Puerto Rico, Miles said, should be the first objective of the army. The war with Spain was, essentially, a naval war, and Puerto Rico lay athwart the sea route from Spain to Cuba and, at San Juan, contained an excellent harbor and coaling station. The capture of Puerto Rico would relieve the American Navy of difficult patrol and blockading tasks and cut the direct Spanish line of communication with Spain.

This plan, however, did not meet with Administration favor. Public pressure for action was growing daily more intense. The Americans, always quick to sympathize with the oppressed, were indignant over the cruelties of Spanish rule — the virtual enslavement of the people, the torture, hard labor and poverty forced on the populations of Cuba, Puerto Rico and the Philippines. Naval action was not dramatic enough for the press, who had correspondents covering every phase of the war. Pulitzer's *World* and Hearst's *Journal* competed for circulation in banner headlines. Richard Harding Davis, Frederic Remington and Howard Chandler Christie drew and wrote glowing accounts of U.S. forces.

Tampa, Florida, was selected as the site for a hasty training and embarkation point of a Cuban expedition and men and material were poured into the southern town in heedless confusion. Tampa was a lethargic little cigar-manufacturing town, the terminus of a single rail line. Ten miles southwest of the town was the port. The troops were camped outside the town, the infantry regiments in the scattered pines, the cavalry among the sand dunes closer to the water. In this force of Shafter's there were only three volunteer organizations. The remainder were regulars. Davis thrilled to see a brigade of regular cavalry galloping through the palmettos, red and white guidons fluttering, sabers flashing. The regulars were showy but they were not as wildly enthusiastic as the volunteers. War was a business and Tampa had its drawbacks. The climate was hot and humid. The uniforms were wool and the men who came from the cool, dry plains of the West suffered intensely. Water and rations were inadequate. One correspondent, more realistic than Davis, reported two regiments were in Tampa for three days without rations of any kind. The greatest confusion existed in the Quartermaster and Subsistence Departments. This was partly due to Alger's appointment of officers for purely political reasons and partly due to the greatly increased demands on Bureaus accustomed to handling small requisitions in a leisurely fashion.

The officers — those who could afford it — fared better than the men. Headquarters was set up in the Tampa Bay Hotel, a huge Victorian building of striped brick with cupolas and porches screened with vines. West Point classmates who had not seen each other for years shouted greetings beneath the gilded minarets. Generals, correspondents, wealthy young men, foreign attachés, visitors and wives thronged the lobby. John Jacob Astor checked in with his valet. Mrs. Clara Barton of Red Cross fame bustled about the veranda. There was Mr. Poultney Bigelow, correspondent and publisher, recently returned from Russia; Count Von Goetzen, German military attaché, arrogant in polished boots and monacle; Lieutenant Colonel Roosevelt; General Oliver O. Howard, who had left his retired home to come down and preach salvation to the soldiers; the handsome British attaché, Captain Lee, in pipe-clayed helmet; General Fitzhugh Lee, laughing and genial, and "Fighting Joe" Wheeler, an old-fashioned Southern gentleman who never failed to assist a woman to her chair.

For weeks the expeditionary force waited at Tampa. The purpose of this force, as orginally determined, was to make a reconnaissance in force in order to gain information and to carry supplies of arms and ammunition to the Cuban insurgents.

At the hotel, the men drank gallons of iced tea and smoked cigars while they argued over the probable date of departure for Cuba. Lines formed eight feet deep before the bulletin board on which telegrams were posted. A rumor circulated that Miles was arriving in a special railroad car.

Miles had heard of the confusion in Tampa and intended to investigate, but before he could leave Washington information was received that changed the entire course of the expedition. Cervera had put into Santiago harbor in eastern Cuba and was blockaded by the American fleet. The harbor was guarded by guns from an old fort, and it was heavily mined and protected by Cervera's ships. Sampson could not risk forcing it. Shafter's force, by arrangement between the War and Navy Departments, was designated to take Santiago and to aid the navy in dislodging or capturing Cervera's squadron. Shafter's Fifth

Corps was chosen because it was the only army group partially ready for combat.

When the order to embark was issued at Tampa, the regiments struck camp and dashed madly for the ships. No assignments had been made, and it was every man for himself. The Sixth Cavalry seized the *Rio Grande,* the Rough Riders grabbed the *Yucatan,* the correspondents and the hospital corps boarded the *Olivette.* Regiments became separated in the melee. Officers lost their companies, and the Second Massachusetts transferred three times from ship to ship. Quartermaster officers in charge of transportation stood about helplessly, or added to the confusion by issuing conflicting orders. Men were detained for hours in the stifling heat of the railroad cars and on the platforms.

The uproar was at its height when Miles arrived in Tampa. A special correspondent of *Harper's Weekly* described the look of amazement that spread over his face. "He was more than angry. He was furious . . . He acted like a man whose breath has been suddenly taken away by a rude shock."[2]

Mary reminded her husband, gently, that the perspiration was running down his face. Miles scarcely heard her remark. He watched the pack mules go aboard the *Gussie.* He saw John Jacob Astor's four horses go aboard the *Seguranca.* He saw the hot, tired soldiers — his regulars — marching through the hot sun to their transports.

Thirty-two transports, four abreast and eight in line, convoyed by sixteen ships of war, sailed out of Tampa for Cuba. Twenty-five miles down the bay, came a cable. The expedition had been suspended. Alger had received a report that a Spanish squadron had been sighted in the Bahama Channel.

Back came the transports. Horses and mules were disembarked. The foreign attachés and correspondents moved back to the hotel. Wives of officers who had said goodbye returned by the next train. Hundreds of the men remained on the transports sweating in the heat.

The Spanish squadron turned out to be imaginary, but the expedition had to remain in Tampa until it was thought safe to proceed. Miles did what he could to remedy the confusion. With a crew of soldiers, he opened boxcars waiting on the siding with no bills of lading to show their contents and with their cargo of food rotting in the heat. He wired to New York for entrenching tools. Shafter, perhaps, would have been happier if his superior had remained in Washington. The heat was particularly hard on the corpulent general who, at the end of nearly a week's waiting to re-embark for Cuba, looked haggard and exhausted. Miles probably added to the strain by telling Shafter that some of the confusion could be attributed to negligence on the part of his staff. Every day Shafter came down the boardwalk on the arm of his acting Assistant Inspector General, Colonel John Jacob Astor. At night the two dined together. Someone asked the millionaire why he had volunteered for the hardships of war. "I'm looking for adventure," Mr. Astor replied. "And I hope I'm setting an example."[3]

Miles saw that Shafter was going to be physically handicapped in the tropics, that the elite of the American army was going into battle under doubtful leadership with inadequate supplies. He wired Alger for permission to assume command of the expedition. The wire was not answered.

On the 14th of June the convoy sailed for Santiago, and the next day Miles received a peremptory wire from Alger: "Important business requires your presence here. Return at once."[4]

Miles had no choice but to obey. He went back to Washington where he was asked if he would command an expedition to Puerto Rico, which he had considered essential in the over-all strategy of the war with Spain. Shafter was considered by the War Department quite capable of directing operations against Santiago.

The first skirmish of Shafter's expeditionary force occurred at Las Guaymas shortly after its arrival. Shafter did not have all his forces ashore when "Fighting Joe" Wheeler with his cavalry brigade, of which the Rough Riders were a part, led a reckless advance into the jungle which, but for the withdrawal of the Spanish forces, might have proved disastrous. By not making a stand, the Spanish commander sacrificed the strongest position open to him between Siboney and Santiago. But Shafter made his mistakes, too. When he finally landed the remainder of his troops and supplies — a somewhat muddled operation — he began a cautious advance on the city of Santiago, resulting in the battles of El Caney and San Juan.

The attack on El Caney with nearly half of the American army was a blunder. The detachment entrenched at El Caney could have been contained by a regiment while the main force concentrated on the main objective of Santiago. Tactically, Lawton, who had served so well with Miles in Arizona and who commanded the Second Division, failed when he was not quick enough to order a charge on the enemy's position. Lawton estimated he could take El Caney in less than two hours; instead, it took him nearly ten. The Spanish were protected by a blockhouse and barbed wire and well supplied with modern Mauser rifles. Lawton's losses were severe.

San Juan was also heavily fortified. Proper reconnaissance was not made of the enemy position; there were no reserves and the attack was made without tactical method. Great courage was exhibited by the soldiers and officers but the loss in dead and wounded would have been less if the attack had been better planned. Losses were particularly heavy in the narrow road hemmed in by the jungle which led to the forward positions.

Shafter had an opportunity to capture Santiago in one bold move. He did not do so. The night of the first of July, the General cabled to Washington that he had carried the outer works of Santiago and was within three quarters of a mile of the city. On the third, after some minor skirmishing, Shafter cabled Alger that he had Santiago well invested but with a very thin line. He was afraid the defenses of the city were too strong to carry by storm and was considering withdrawing five miles to a new position. The road by which supplies were brought to the front was being maintained with difficulty owing to the rains. General Wheeler was seriously ill. General Young was sick and he himself, Shafter said, had been unable to be out during the heat of the day for four days.

Shafter was suffering from malaria and despondent over his losses. The heat, the heavy rains and the jungle discouraged him. The fact that many of the volunteers were equipped with old-fashioned Springfield rifles and black powder that betrayed their whereabouts to the enemy was responsible for a large number of casualties. Breckinridge, Miles's Inspector General who was with the Cuban expeditionary force at the time, informed Miles that "medical supplies were gruesomely inadequate."[5] There were not enough ambulances, bandages, hospital cots or doctors. The wounded had to lie in the rain for hours because they had no shelter. At Las Guaymas, the wounded had to be carried three miles on the backs or in the arms of their comrades. Sanitary precautions could not be maintained. The soldiers did not complain. An Irish sergeant, shot through the head, advised a fellow casualty who groaned to the jolting of the ambulance wagon, "Grit yer teeth; grit yer teeth."

El Caney and San Juan shook the confidence of the Americans. Mutters of criticism began to be heard on all sides. The troops lacked faith in Shafter. When the General in a pith helmet drove slowly along the lines in a buckboard drawn by a mule, there were no cheers.

On receipt of Shafter's cable that he might have to retire, Alger replied in alarm that of course Shafter could judge the situation better than could be done "at this end of the line" but if he could hold his position, particularly San Juan Hill, the effect on the country would be better than falling back. Reinforcements which Shafter had requested could be expected from Miles, who would stop by Cuba with his force destined for Puerto Rico.

Alger was still supporting Shafter but McKinley, dismayed by the situation in Cuba, called Miles in and directed him to go to Santiago and "give such orders as might be required for the welfare and success of the army."[6] It was, however, clearly understood that Miles was not to supersede Shafter in command of the Fifth Corps. Miles immediately cabled Shafter in the patriotic rhetoric of which he was so fond and said, "I expect to be with you within one week with strong reinforcements."[7]

The prospect of Miles arriving in Cuba to turn things upside down and steal the glory woke Shafter to action. He ordered siege guns to be brought up and placed in position before Santiago. Intrenchments were dug and artillery put into line. Previously Shafter had asked Admiral Sampson for help in forcing the harbor of Santiago. Sampson replied he could not force the harbor because it was heavily mined and his ships were too valuable to risk in the operation. Shafter retorted irritably that he was at a loss to see why the navy could not work as well as the army. His losses had been very heavy and he did not want to suffer more casualties in an attempt to capture, as Sampson suggested, the Spanish positions at the harbor entrance by an attack from the flank and rear. The success of such an attack would have securely bottled up the Spanish ships, the true objective of the Americans operations; but the two commanders could not reach an accord by written message, so a meeting was arranged at army headquarters at Siboney. Shafter was too ill to ride the seven miles to the coast and requested Sampson to come to him.

The time set for the meeting could hardly have been more unfortunate for the Admiral. While he was gone, the Spanish fleet under Cervera tried to run past the American ships blockading the harbor. Commodore Schley, second in command, directed the operations that succeeded in the capture or sinking of all the Spanish vessels and the taking of over a thousand prisoners. Admiral Sampson, who returned about the time the battle was over, cabled Washington that the fleet under his command was presenting the nation as a Fourth of July present, the whole of Cervera's fleet. Sampson did not mention Schley. He — Sampson — had mapped out the course of action should the Spanish fleet try to escape. Schley had only followed directions. Inevitably, bitterness arose between the two men as to the credit for the victory.

The destruction of the Spanish fleet encouraged Shafter in his request that Sampson force the entrance of the harbor to bombard the city. Sampson was even less enthusiastic about risking his ships in an operation that, since the defeat of the Spanish squadrons, had lost much, if not all, of its significance. The American ships were doubly important, now. They could be employed as a striking force against Spain itself, or sail through the Suez to the Philippines. Shafter then suggested, and Alger concurred, that volunteers could be called for from the army to man a vessel reinforced by hay bales. The mines could be taken up by grappling hooks. Fortunately it was not found necessary to execute this novel idea. Shafter had requested the Spanish general, José Toral, to surrender on the 3rd of July and the General was showing signs of weakening under shelling from the fleet at long range and by the army by land batteries. On the first day of the bombardment, Miles arrived with reinforcements.

CHAPTER XXV

MILES was glad to leave Washington for active duty. Desk work irritated him and the events of the past few months had strained his patience to the utmost. He left Washington the 7th of July, arriving in Charleston in time to board the steamer *Yale* which, with the cruiser *Columbia,* was loaded with fifteen hundred troops, mostly volunteers since Shafter had the regulars.

On the 11th of July, Miles arrived off Cuba and immediately got in touch with Admiral Sampson. His plans were all made. He would like to land troops on the west side of the harbor of Santiago; enfilade the enemy's line and take their position in reverse. Could Sampson cover the landing? Sampson said he could. In contrast to Shafter, Miles's relations with the navy were, at first, very cordial. Miles then went ashore to see Shafter. The journey to the headquarters of the commander of the Cuban expeditionary force provided Miles with his first glimpse of the tropics. He noted the great rain forests, the tangle of vines, the brilliant, odorless flowers and the raucous-voiced birds. Of even greater interest to his professional eye was the undergrowth that could shelter sharpshooters, the broken terrain and the long stretches of muddy road that should have been (but were not) corduroyed for the passage of troops. He found Shafter comfortably settled in a clearing with a tent fly to shelter visitors from the sweltering sun. Shafter was feeling better although his jowls bore the pallor of fever and his huge body was weakened. In addition to his other troubles, he had suffered from gout and been forced to wrap his swollen foot in gunny sacking. Miles's erect, broad-shouldered figure, his handsome face tanned by the tropical sun, cannot have improved Shafter's morale. Did Shafter, Miles inquired, have enough troops on the east shore of the harbor to maintain his position? Shafter replied that he had. The ailing general resented Miles's aggressive policy, which showed up his own lack of strategy. The war in Cuba was nearly over. Shafter did not want Miles to claim his victory. Miles showed unusual restraint. He was careful not to criticize Shafter, and he would give him credit for capturing Santiago.

However, Miles felt the Spanish commander had taken long enough to save his honor, and that he should agree to the surrender terms that Shafter had offered to him. Haste was imperative. Colonel Greenleaf, Chief Surgeon of the Army, advised Miles that malaria was on the increase among the troops in Cuba and that there were a hundred cases of yellow fever. This was what Miles had warned the administration about at the beginning of the war, and what the jingoists had chosen to ignore. Miles felt the men should be taken out of the trenches and away from the swamps. The men were well aware of his concern. Their commander might not view the Commanding General of the Army with enthusiasm, but there was little doubt about the feeling of the enlisted personnel. A correspondent described how Miles, mounted on a spirited horse, toured the front. All along the line echoed a heartfelt "Praise God."

Miles ordered infected buildings at Siboney destroyed. The Twenty-fourth (colored) Infantry was sent to the hospital to care for the sick. The ill were quarantined. Miles's own troops destined for Puerto Rico were kept away from Shafter's men. As soon as possible, Miles told Shafter, the troops should be shifted to high ground. When transportation was available, they should be sent to the northeastern part of the United States to recuperate.

Shafter's smoldering resentment flared. Sick, overweight, obsessed with the feeling that, despite the appearance of victory, he had failed, Shafter presented a pitiable appearance. He saw glory fading from his grasp. To Miles, who was on board the *Yale,* he wrote that it seemed from Miles's orders that Miles regarded his — Shafter's — force as a part of his command when he had been told by the Secretary of War that Miles was not to supersede him in command.

To this ill-tempered impertinence, Miles replied with commendable restraint that he had no desire to supersede Shafter in command of the Fifth Corps and that he had carefully avoided any appearance of doing so. "Your command is a part of the United States Army," he reminded Shafter coldly, "which I have had the honor to command; having been duly assigned thereto . . . I should regret that any event would cause either yourself or any of your command to cease to be a part of mine."[1]

A meeting was arranged between the lines with Miles, Shafter and General Toral. Liberal terms, including the return of the Spanish troops to their homeland at U.S. expense, were offered to the Spanish commander. Toral, still worried about his honor, hesitated, whereupon Miles informed him that he had until the next day at noon to make up his mind. If he did not agree to the terms, Miles had orders from his government to capture or destroy the Spanish forces. After some delay, the surrender was finally agreed upon and Miles prepared to depart for Puerto Rico, leaving the acceptance of the surrender to Shafter.

By now there was a great deal of dissatisfaction among the

American troops. The correspondents were stirring up people at home with stories of the suffering the men were enduring in the tropics and of the growing number of fever cases. Roosevelt, who had not hesitated to express his view since he joined the army, was openly critical of the scarcity of hospital supplies, of Miles's orders to remedy the situation and of Shafter's ability. Eager to accompany Miles on the new expedition to gather additional laurels, he wrote Alger that he hoped the Secretary would send . . . "most of the Regulars, and at any rate the cavalry division, including the Rough Riders, who are as good as any Regulars, and three times as good as any State troops, to Puerto Rico."[2]

Alger, for once, did not yield to political pressure. His position was precarious. Criticism of the conduct of the war in Cuba was increasing. He could no longer afford to ignore the Commanding General of the Army. Whether Miles had anything to do with his reply to Roosevelt is difficult to say. Miles was not impressed by Roosevelt's military ability. Alger wired Roosevelt that the Regular Army, the Volunteer Army and the Rough Riders had done well but that unless Roosevelt wanted to spoil the effects and glory of the victory, it would be better if he did not make invidious comparisons. The Rough Riders, Alger said, were no better than any other volunteers. They had an advantage in their arms, for which they should be grateful. Permission to go to Puerto Rico was refused.

Within a week Roosevelt declared that the same troops he recommended be sent to Puerto Rico were unfit for service. In a letter he helped to write, and which was signed by almost all the commanders in Cuba, it was asserted that the army was in a weakened condition; one half of the men would die if they were kept on the island, and the only remedy was to ship the men back home immediately to Montauk Point in New York.[3]

The letter was released to the press at a most inappropriate moment. Peace negotiations were being carried on with Spain and the revelation of our weakness could have been disastrous. People grew alarmed for the lives of their husbands and sons. Roosevelt, as well as the other commanders, deserved a reprimand. Instead Roosevelt became in the eyes of the people, the champion of the boys in Cuba.

By July 27 Shafter was cabling the War Department that there were 3750 sick. Of these, 2924 were fever cases.

Miles, who sailed for Puerto Rico on the 21st of July, had one hundred sick in his command. These men had been isolated from the others, and every precaution was taken to insure the continued health of the expeditionary force. As a result Miles's troops were not handicapped by tropical fevers.

Miles was anxious to get to Puerto Rico. He could have sailed a week before the twenty-first but was delayed by the War Department for various petty reasons and by a misunderstanding with the navy about the assistance to be rendered his expedition. If he did not sail shortly, Miles was afraid the war would be over. Peace negotiations were being conducted with officials of the Spanish government. Miles's impatience was not entirely personal, although he was anxious to show the country a well-planned campaign in contrast to the debacle in Cuba. For political as well as military reasons, the occupancy of Puerto Rico would tend to convince Spain that she could no longer hold the Antilles.

Miles's force consisted of 3415 infantry and artillery, together with two companies of Engineers and one company of Signal Corps. The latter detachment was commanded by Lieutenant Colonel Samuel Reber, the handsome and capable young officer who was later to marry Cecelia Miles.

Reinforcements under General James H. Wilson were en

route from Charleston while Brigadier General Theodore
Schwan was about to sail from Tampa with 2897 officers and
men and General John Brooke was waiting to embark with
4000 more men. Both Brooke and Wilson were capable commanders. Wilson, a West Pointer, had served with Custer in
Sheridan's cavalry during the Civil War. Brooke, who had
commanded the Department of the Platte and served at Pine
Ridge, had been a brigade commander in Barlow's division in
the Rebellion.

According to Miles's intelligence reports, there were eight
thousand Spanish regulars on Puerto Rico and approximately
nine thousand volunteers. The troops were similar to those in
Cuba; ill fed and underpaid but when strongly entrenched,
were stubborn fighters. Miles was well informed on the island.
In June he had sent Captain H. H. Whitney to obtain facts
relative to the invasion. Disguised as a German correspondent,
Whitney had traveled about the island and later reported to
Miles with maps and notes which formed the basis of Miles's
strategy.

To facilitate a landing, Miles had requested tugs, launches
and lighters to be sent from the States but these had not arrived
when he left Cuba and were still not in evidence when the
expedition sighted the long blue line of the islands rising out of
the tropical sea.

While he was off the coast, Miles made one of his lightning
swift command decisions that altered the campaign. Cape
Fajardo or San Juan had been designated as landing places; but
Miles had received word there had been a leak in security, the
enemy knew the plans and was reinforcing Fajardo and San
Juan. A direct landing assault against fortified positions there
might well result in severe casualties and a temporary loss of
prestige which, after Cuba, might delay the Spanish negotia-

tions for peace. In a message to Captain Francis J. Higginson, commanding the naval contingent, Miles wrote, "As it is always advisable not to do what your enemy expects you to do . . ."[4] he had decided to sail around the northwest corner of Puerto Rico to Guánica, land there and move on to Ponce, a large city on the south coast. There was deep water at Guánica and a number of lighters and sailing vessels which could be captured to land the troops in place of the absent tugs. Naval ships could be placed near the route to Cape Fajardo in order to redirect the transports from the States toward Ponce.

Captain Higginson was amenable to the change in plan although it dislocated naval as well as army logistics and reinforcements. Miles could not notify the War Department he was landing at Guánica until the move had been made. There was no radio in those days. The decision had to be his alone, even though it presented difficulties and delays. Guánica was on the opposite side of the island from San Juan and considerably farther away than Fajardo. with a mountain range intervening. If the troops were landed at several points, a quick-witted Spanish commander might unite to destroy an American detachment before it could be reinforced. All this Miles accepted, unhesitatingly, in order to land his troops without casualties and to avoid an initial military check.

Guánica had a pretty little harbor protected by high cliffs. The one main street of the village, running inland from the sea, was shaded by crimson trees and bordered by gaily colored houses. A naval contingent, which was first ashore, captured lighters in which to land the troops. A brief fight drove the Spanish out of town and established American possession. The Puerto Ricans welcomed the Americans enthusiastically, crying and laughing and shouting "Viva!" Within a few hours after the skirmish that defeated the Spanish garrison, the natives were selling horses to the officers for three times what they were worth and the soldiers were dandling naked brown babies on their knees. Unlike the Cuban expedition which was accompanied by nearly a hundred correspondents, there were, for the first few days, only two newspapermen on the island. Later more arrived but there were never more than ten at the most.

The first night ashore the volunteer troops were nervous and the pickets kept firing at dark shapes that turned out to be horses or mules. Some of the bullets hit the transport on which Miles was sleeping, resulting in a stern comment on triggerhappy soldiers.

The landing had been accomplished without loss of life. Now Miles's strategy was to be tested further. A mountain range intersected the island from east to west, the high peaks, at this time of year, usually smothered in mist. From the main range ridges ran down to the sea, broken by steep ravines tangled with vegetation. Near the coast the ridges opened into fertile valleys of palms, orange trees and fields of sugar cane, rice and corn. On the entire island there was less than two hundred miles of narrow gauge, poorly equipped railway which connected a few towns on the coast. The roads were little better than trails. Only one decent highway connected the capital of San Juan and the city of Ponce and this highway illustrated the difficulties of traversing the mountains, for although it was forty-seven miles from Ponce to San Juan in a straight line, it was seventy miles by the highway. Spanish troops were stationed in the main villages and in the mountains. Miles's strategy was to dislodge these troops and drive them back into San Juan where, hemmed in by the American army and the navy, they would be forced to surrender.

Richard Harding Davis, who had learned a great deal since he had left Tampa, could not resist comparing the Puerto

Rican and the Cuban campaigns. In Cuba, Davis wrote, the Spanish bull had gored our men; in Puerto Rico the bull failed to touch them. The difference was that Miles was an expert matador and Shafter was not. Every move in Puerto Rico was carefully considered and followed to its conclusion.

The morning following the landing, Brigadier General G. A. Garretson with six companies of the Sixth Massachusetts Volunteer Infantry and one company of Sixth Illinois Volunteer Infantry attacked the Spanish near the village of Yauco, inland from Guánica. The Spanish were defeated and the vital railroad and highway opened from the village to Ponce. Two days later Ponce itself was occupied by Brigadier General Oswald H. Earnst under the command of Major General James Wilson. Ponce surrendered without resistance. The people were delighted to see the Americans. Miles came ashore in a launch with a soldier waving an American flag in the bow. Later in the day Miles and Wilson appeared on the balcony of the Alcalde's Palace to receive the homage of the people. Miles was an impressive figure in dress uniform with his curling white mustache, his bold nose and blue eyes. His natural stiffness of manner made him formal, almost cold. Davis, like Remington and other correspondents, regarded him with something approaching awe. The Generals, Davis observed, played conqueror with tact and like gentlemen.

Miles considered the political relations with the impoverished peasants of Puerto Rico as important as the military maneuvers. After the skirmish at Yauco, he was sitting his horse near the village when he noticed an intelligent-looking native studying him intently. Miles asked him what he wanted. In English, the man inquired, "Is this General Miles?" When Miles told him it was, the Puerto Rican took a letter from his ragged shirt and handed it to the General. The letter, written in Spanish, was from an insurgent leader promising the support of the Puerto Ricans to the Americans.[5]

Miles encouraged this support by respecting the persons and property of the local population. Puerto Ricans were hired as stevedores and oxcarts were rented from the farmers. Churches and schoolhouses were protected. The native constabulary was preserved. Currency, taxes and tariffs were taken care of so that the economy would not collapse.

While this was being done, General Roy Stone of the Engineer Corps was constructing a road through the center of the territory over what was considered nearly impassable country to connect the towns of Adjuntas and Utuardo. This road was to facilitate the movement of General Guy Henry's troops to intercept the Spanish who were retreating before Brigadier General Schwan. Schwan had landed on the 31st of July and marched inland with his regulars. The same day General Brooke disembarked at Arroyo. With his complete force on the island Miles was prepared to advance on several fronts, threatening always to outflank the Spaniards and force them back to San Juan. At the same time Miles protested to Alger about what he understood to be a navy plan to appear before San Juan and demand the surrender of the capital under penalty of bombardment. This, Miles said, should not be tolerated. It would be a violation of civilized warfare to bombard a city containing innocent women and children and it was highly important that Puerto Rico be captured with the least resultant bitterness among its people.[6]

General Wilson advanced up the center of the island. General Brooke, with Brigadier General Peter C. Haines's brigade, swung around to take the town of Guayama and to strike the military road back of Cayey and Aibonita as Wilson closed in from the south. In the north, Henry took Arecibo. On the extreme left, Schwan with his regulars and a roving commission to fight anything he encountered, beat up to join Guy Henry. Every day the four different columns drove the Spanish back mile by mile toward San Juan. Most of the fights were skirmishes; they were not allowed to be anything else. The enemy was surrounded, attacked and defeated with the scientific exactitude of a chess game.

Wilson, as he traversed the steep trails across the mountains, encountered the Spanish strongly entrenched above the gorges of Coamo which guarded two vital roads. Knowing that he would suffer severe losses if he launched a frontal assault on the Spanish blockhouse, Wilson directed Colonel Willis J. Hulings with the Sixteenth Pennsylvania to flank the Spanish positions. At night Hulings and his men, guided by his Engineer officer, Lieutenant Colonel John Biddle, climbed a narrow mountain trail to the hills at the rear of the town. In the morning cavalry, infantry and artillery launched an attack which drove the Spanish back into the waiting arms of the Pennsylvanians happily perched above the only road of retreat to San Juan.

General Haines, meanwhile, captured four hundred prisoners at Guayama with the loss of only one officer and four men wounded of the Fourth Ohio Volunteers. Schwan and his regulars captured Mayagüez, a city of thirty thousand, with the loss of only two dead and fifteen wounded. At Aibonita, Wilson was temporarily halted when he came up against Spanish artillery dug in on the hills above the road by which the Americans had to approach the town. Below the artillery batteries the infantry had dug entrenchments, so that the entire road was swept by fire for a distance of several miles. Wilson decided this opposition could be flanked, too, and ordered an artillery reconnaissance as a diversion to the flanking force. A light battery of the Third Artillery brought four guns into position and, at a range of 2150 yards, opened fire on the Spanish who returned the bombardment with interest. In the ensuing gun duel, a shrapnel struck the road within ten feet of Captain Paget, the British Naval Attaché. Five Wisconsin Volunteers were knocked flat by the concussion and the Captain disappeared in the dust and smoke. Onlookers were certain Paget had been killed. Within a minute, the Captain emerged from the haze to remark with true British aplomb, "There was a shell in the Soudan once did exactly that same thing to me."[7]

Aibonita was one of the last engagements of the war. The next day Miles received orders to cease hostilities. Peace had been signed.

Some of the men tossed their hats in the air and cheered. Others groaned and swore. Miles felt his responsibilities lighten but, in a way, he was disappointed too. After thirty-seven years, he still welcomed the challenge of battle. He felt he had done well. Nineteen days of campaigning had resulted in the capture of Puerto Rico with the loss of only three men killed and forty wounded. Now, back to Washington. Miles had reason to believe he would be gratefully received.

CHAPTER XXVI

THE NEW YORK Volunteer regiment had paraded down Broadway when the men returned from Cuba. No such welcome had been arranged for Miles, but if his return was not celebrated officially, it was enthusiastically hailed by the people who appreciated the fact the Puerto Rican campaign had been nearly bloodless and that the transports were not returning full of wounded and feverish men. In the gray light of a foggy morning, the squatty old ship chugged into the harbor. From the foretruck the Stars and Stripes flew over a Spanish flag. To the bow and stern were lashed Puerto Rican palms signalizing complete and unqualified victory. The railings and decks were jammed by three battalions of blue-coated Wisconsin Volunteers waiting to catch their first sight of the city. Sherman was on board with his father, and Mary and Cecelia who had gone down to Puerto Rico in order to return with the General. The ladies had worked long hours during the war at the hospital at Fortress Monroe and needed a rest. Such rides on military vessels were, at the time, approved by the War Department.

As the transport appeared in sight, whistles screeched; ferry boats hooted; crowds along the docks and on board other ships shouted and waved handkerchiefs. On the warships, the sailors lined the rail to cheer again and again while the band of the *Prairie* played "Hail to the Chief."

From the tugboat came a shout: "Miles, old man, you took care of your boys and you don't have to square yourself with the widows and orphans."[1]

A correspondent from the *World* dashed out in a tug to call to the troops on the transport.

"Are you glad to get home?"

"You bet your life!"

"Have you any sick aboard?"

"Only the homesick."

"How is General Miles?"

"He is the best man on the job."

Another soldier shouted an inquiry about the baseball teams and, when he was told, called back, "The New Yorks . . . ought to have Miles for a captain."[2]

At that moment, Miles appeared on deck. He was wearing trousers and an undershirt and his face and arms were deeply tanned.

"How are you, General?" cried an old friend on the tug.

"Never finer," Miles shouted back.

"You look it."

"Yes, and I feel it!"

When Miles disappeared to put on his uniform, Cecelia came to the rail and immediately became the focus of all masculine eyes with her gold-brown hair blowing in the breeze. Mary joined her, shading her eyes from the sun that had dispelled the fog, to ask the reporters on the tug about old friends.

Mary's smiles concealed apprehension. For some weeks, Miles had been talking about an investigation of Alger's conduct of the war, and in August had publicly criticized the Secretary in an interview with the Puerto Rican correspondent on the *Kansas City Star*. The homecoming was another cause of contention. Miles had decorated the old transport in expectation of a triumphal march up Broadway at the head of his troops. He loved military display and looked forward to it as eagerly as a boy. Now, he was disappointed.

After the transport was inspected at Quarantine, it was allowed to proceed up the North River to Weehawken, where the Wisconsin troops were transferred to the West Shore Railroad to be taken home. In the confusion of unloading the men, Miles bade goodbye to the officers and left the transport almost unobserved with his family. Boarding the *Meigs,* one of the army's new ships, he went back down the river, disembarked at East Twenty-second Street and was driven to the Waldorf. Few people recognized him as he entered the hotel in his fatigue uniform.

The Waldorf was the scene of a dinner which was given by the city to Miles, but even the dinner was a disappointment. Roosevelt, soon to be Governor of New York, shared the honors with Miles. The occasion was impressive. Flags were hung about the great banquet hall. A portrait of Miles decorated the menu cards, while at each place was a souvenir rosette of red, white and blue surmounted by a white dove bearing an olive branch. The guests were of both political parties and many varied interests were represented. Outwardly, the best of feelings prevailed. Miles proposed a toast to Shafter. McKinley was cheered and so was Captain Paget, the British Naval attaché. Miles made one of his stilted, formal speeches which was well received; the real enthusiasm of the evening was reserved for Roosevelt's talk, fiery, human touched with a warmth that Miles could never achieve.

People were waiting to see what Miles would do in his controversy with Alger. Hoping for a statement, a reporter interviewed Miles in his hotel suite to ask him about the article in the *Kansas City Star.*

"This is no time for argument," Miles declared, "but for action. There is too much scattering of the dust in the rear."

This was hardly an answer to the reporter's question. The newsman repeated his query. Was the article correct in which

Miles was quoted as saying that Alger had interfered with Shafter in the Cuban campaign?

"I read the interview," Miles said. "There were, of course, a few errors in it."

"In the main is it correct?"

"I had such an interview," Miles admitted.[3]

Miles could hardly commit himself. He was on dangerous ground, for when he accused Alger of interfering in Cuba, he was also accusing the President. McKinley, acting through Alger, had directed many of the military moves in Cuba.

Stubbornly Miles rushed on to further indiscretion. He could not forgive the bungling that had cost his regulars so dearly in dead and wounded. What had been a highly trained, elite force had been decimated by death and disease. Part of the responsibility for this, Miles felt, was due to the Medical Department and to the Quartermaster Bureau, his old cause-of-all-evil on the plains. The whole thing had been a mess: the confusion at Tampa, the wounded who had lain in the sun for hours waiting to be treated, the lack of ambulances, the old-fashioned Springfield rifles with which the volunteers had been furnished, the ships that had arrived in Puerto Rico without bills of lading. Miles was disgusted with the manner in which the Administration had handled the war and with Alger's interference in military moves. Above all, he was incensed by information furnished him by Volunteer Dr. Daly on his staff, of the beef that formed army rations.

Miles was encouraged in his criticism by politicians hostile to the Administration who saw in the Commanding General an opportunity to avenge themselves on the party in power. Miles was too naïve to sense the reason behind the support of the politicians. He was only aware that the people were clamoring for an investigation and that Alger had become the most unpopular man in the country. The Secretary was compared to Belknap in Grant's Cabinet, and the President's advisers told him he should get rid of Alger, whose incompetence was reflecting on the Administration.

Miles also remembered Belknap, and Sherman's battle with Grant's Secretary of War. Sherman had been, and still was, one of Miles's heroes. Was not his fight with Alger as justified as Sherman's fight with the corrupt Belknap?

With the cheers of the people of New York ringing in his ears, Miles was certain the public would support him. A presidential election was to be held before long. It is likely that Miles saw himself as St. George slaying the dragon of incompetence and corruption.

Mary, more of a realist, saw that her husband was about to engage in another political controversy that would end as all his political controversies ended — in disaster. She distrusted the flashy Dr. Daly and his influence on Miles, and begged her husband to act with moderation. But Miles would not listen to reason.

Miles's criticism of the War Department was largely responsible for McKinley's calling a commission to investigate the conduct of the war. If McKinley had not taken action, Congress would have called for an investigation on its own, which would have been to the disadvantage of the Administration. Chairman of the nine-man commission was General Grenville M. Dodge, the famous Civil War veteran and railroad builder. Dodge had been a friend of Sherman and, as a conservative in his old age, favored the War Department, but his integrity was unquestioned. The Board held hearings in Washington, New York and Cincinnati. Various witnesses were called, among them were Shafter, Leonard Wood, Oliver O. Howard and Alger and Miles. The Secretary of War presented a respectable

picture in his dark suit and neat, gray beard when he gave his
testimony.

At the start of the inquiry, a board member asked courte-
ously, "Would you object if I called you 'General' instead of
'Mr. Secretary'?"

"I would prefer it, sir," Alger replied.[4]

The title, which was honorary, gave Alger an advantage. He
told the Board he knew of no complaints of fraudulent prac-
tices; no complaints of food or medical supplies. If there had
been, they had been promptly remedied. Had he, a Board
member asked, had any conversation with General Miles about
camp inspection? Yes, Alger said, he had issued an order in
May about inspecting the camps at Tampa, Chickamauga and
Mobile. Miles had brought the order back to the War Department and informed the Secretary he was in the habit of
issuing such orders himself. To the best of his knowledge,
Alger said, Miles had never inspected a camp but had spent all
his time at Tampa. This information might have appeared
damaging to the public, but hardly to a military man who knew
the Commanding General was not supposed to spend his time
inspecting camps with the mess of Tampa on his hands.

Miles did not appear before the Board until shortly before
Christmas. He had been asked to testify twice before, but had
refused. A third request sent through the Adjutant General
by General Dodge finally brought results. Miles's reason for
not answering the first summons was that he considered it his
duty to investigate any wrong existing in the army and that he
was doing it in the regular military manner.

He arrived in Cincinnati the morning of the 23rd of December and went immediately to the home of Mary's cousin,
Mrs. Frank Wiborg, in Clifton. At lunch he was a guest at an
informal gathering at the Queen City Club. In the afternoon,

a reception was held at the Wiborg mansion to which five hundred prominent society people were invited. Miles was riding the crest. He had never been more sure of himself. He was cheered by the people, supported by the press and lionized at receptions, dinners and rallies. The adulation encouraged him to rashness.

When he appeared before the Board, he refused to be sworn in, declaring he could make his statements without being sworn, and that he was responsible for what he said, an attitude that did not win the sympathy of the nine committee members. Miles repeated the charges he had previously made against the War Department and added criticism of the canned beef that had been supplied as army ration. The beef had been, according to the affidavits of various officers, a "slimy-looking mess of beef scraps"; "so repulsive in appearance that the men had turned from it in disgust." "It's use produced diarrhea and dysentery." Even graver was Miles's charge against the refrigerated beef, "what you might call," Miles said, "embalmed beef."[5]

The press, that had begun to lose interest in the investigation, headlined Miles's testimony. The lead in the *New York Journal* read: "Miles Makes Grave Charges Against the Administration. Poisons used in Beef Made the Soldiers Ill. Tons of Bad Meat Sent to Troops in Puerto Rico. These Charges, He Declares, Contain Only a Few of the Facts which He has Gathered."[6]

Dr. Daly, called before the Board, produced pieces of beef he testified were part of the army ration and which, when tested, showed traces of preservatives. Demands for Alger's resignation were renewed, but Alger did not resign and the President did not order his dismissal. Another man assumed the blame. General Charles P. Eagan, Commissary General of Subsistence, agitated by the charges, asked to appear before the Commission. Eagan, nervous and wrought up, called Miles a liar and reviled him in such vituperative terms that the War Department was forced to prefer charges of conduct unbecoming an officer. Eagan was court-martialed and sentenced to suspension from duty for six years.

The Board, after listening to testimony that filled eight volumes, exonerated Alger and his associates. At the same time, an effort was made to rule out Miles's testimony because he had refused to be sworn in. The public felt the board had "whitewashed" Alger. The President felt Miles had failed to prove his charges. A second investigating body was convened by the President and by Alger to conduct further hearings. The court of inquiry, which consisted of three officers, heard the witnesses again, employed chemists to examine the beef and visited the packing houses. The report of the court declared the charge that the fresh beef had been doctored with chemicals to keep it from spoiling was untrue, but that the canned beef had been unfit for use of the army in the tropics. Miles was censured for not notifying the War Department of the condition of the beef when he was in Puerto Rico.

The public still felt the facts had been suppressed, but the investigation quieted indignation and, after a few weeks, interest in "embalmed beef" declined.

Undoubtedly some facts had been kept from the people. National pure food laws were non-existent. Refrigeration was inadequate and canned meat was a new product. The war had caught the commissary department unprepared to handle great quantities of supplies. If hostilities had lasted longer, the situation might have been remedied, but the war had lasted only a few months; not long enough to straighten out the confusion that invariably results in the first weeks of conflict. But the great fault lay in the old system of authority divided between the Commanding General and the Secretary of War. There had been no general staff to work out responsibilities between the various branches of the service.

Miles had been incredibly reckless in challenging the Administration and the great meat-packing industry. For a while McKinley considered removing him from command. Wisely, he did not. Miles was very popular with the enlisted men and with the public. His removal would have caused a furore the Administration could ill afford. Unwisely, McKinley retained Alger too, for despite his exoneration, Alger remained, in the eyes of the people, responsible for much of the mismanagement of the war. Eventually, Alger handed in his resignation with the excuse of running for the Senate from his home state of Michigan.

In Alger's place, McKinley appointed Elihu Root, a prominent New York corporation lawyer. Root was later retained by Theodore Roosevelt when McKinley was assassinated in 1901 and Roosevelt, the Vice-president, became President. Miles was to find Roosevelt as a President far tougher to deal with than McKinley. Root, too, was an entirely different man from his predecessor. Root had a cold, decisive mind. He administered the War Department with efficiency and the minimum of politics. Root might be said to represent the new era of expansionism and compromise while Miles supported the old principals of Jeffersonian republicanism.

I N HIS last years of active service, Miles was embroiled in one quarrel after another, which, without exception, he brought on himself. He was an old fighting soldier in a staff job who insisted on using a saber instead of a pen.

Mary's loyalty never faltered. She stood by her husband in every instance, although each new quarrel with its attendant snubs and humiliations taxed her strength. She missed the "children," too. In 1901 Sherman entered West Point and Cecelia married Samuel Reber. Samuel Reber was stationed in Washington, Cecelia's parents saw her often, but it was not the same. The house seemed empty. Miles, especially, missed the "children," and depended on Mary more than ever.

The few occasions Mary felt at ease was when she accompanied Miles west on an inspection trip and Miles took time off to hunt or to gallop at his customary headlong pace across the plains. These trips were made in style with a private car, troop escorts at the stations and dress parades at isolated posts. The baggage car usually held three or four setter dogs. Since the days at Fort Hays when Miles had hunted buffalo with George Armstrong Custer, he had carried his hunting dogs with him. Next to a good horse, Miles loved a good dog.

Miles was regarded highly in the West where men were little interested in the conflicts splitting the War Department or the niceties of eastern politics. Indeed, Miles would always be best remembered in the Sioux country. Army forts would be named after Shafter and Leonard Wood. Miles City, Montana, would be the reminder of the indefatigable Colonel of the Fifth Infantry.

On one of his trips west Miles rode with a detail of the Third Cavalry from Fort Assiniboine, Montana, to the Bear Paw Mountains to disinter and bring back for burial the bodies of the men who fell in the fight with the Nez Percés. Sergeant C. P. Reynolds who rode as a trooper with the detail related long afterward how Miles stopped the detachment and said, "Dig there."

> How he done it God knows. Anyhow we dug up 21 bodies 2nd Cav and 5th Inf. The Cav, we shook their bones out of their jack boots and there was a C on their buttons. There was one pair of low Blucher shoes. Miles said He was a Scout. Anyhow we took the Bones back to Assiniboine and gave them a military funeral. . . General sir [Reynolds wrote fifty-five years later], I'd like to see the Director of the Budget tell Miles how to run the Army. He would spit in His eye.[1]

Miles took care of his regulars and of the scouts who had served him on the plains. When an economy-minded quartermaster general discharged the aging and, with few exceptions, impecunious scouts, Miles, aided by Hugh Scott, got the scouts restored to duty.

On another trip west Miles went down to Indian Territory to hunt with Scott on Cobb Creek. Scott, who was the army's expert on the Indian sign language, was one of Miles's loyal friends when many men felt advised, for reasons of self-interest, to avoid the Commanding General in disfavor with the Administration. In his party Miles had, in addition to Mary, his old scout Ben Clark who had served him so well in the Kiowa-Comanche campaign, Horace Jones, Comanche interpreter with the long-dead Ranald Mackenzie, Jack Stillwell, who rode for the reinforcements that saved Forsyth on the Republican, and Pony Bob, express rider who carried the news of Lincoln's election from St. Joe, Missouri, to San Francisco in seven days. Every night for two weeks Indians from different tribes gathered with Scott and Miles and the scouts in a big central tent to refight old campaigns. With the stars winking above the prairie, the scent of woodsmoke and buckskin and the stamp of horses' feet on the picket line, the Sioux rode once again. The present merged with the past. The "great War" seemed only yesterday. Miles found it difficult to believe a generation had come to power who thought of Chancellorsville as an incident in a history book.

The Administration policy of expansionism, especially in the Philippines, seemed to Miles a violation of the principles of the founding fathers. The United States had annexed Hawaii. We had occupied Puerto Rico, Guam, and Wake Island, and were fighting the Filipinos for control of their homeland. Our forces were even involved in China in the so-called Boxer Rebellion. Miles wanted to go to China, which was a different matter from the Philippines for, in China, fanatics had attacked Europeans. Miles advocated withdrawing fifteen thousand men from the Philippines to be sent to China under his command which would make the United States the supreme military power among the allies and himself commander of all allied forces. How he would have loved the Genghis-Khan type of warfare in North China! But McKinley, who was still President, refused to let him go.

At last, in 1901, Miles succeeded in becoming a lieutenant general. He had his picture taken with his handsome old head thrown back and his hand on his sword. Roosevelt called him a "brave peacock." Perhaps he was. Miles felt that, when the occasion demanded, a soldier should look like a soldier.

Within a few months of the promotion, Miles was at odds with the Administration again. The difficulty this time was the Sampson-Schley affair. The bitterness between the two admirals finally resulted in a Naval Court of Inquiry. The findings of the Court were no business of Miles's. Nevertheless, because he felt strongly on the subject, he came out for Schley, who had fought the battle, as against the verdict of the Naval Court. Roosevelt, who was President, was furious and the report reached Miles that he was considering an official reprimand. Miles requested an interview with Roosevelt. When he got to the White House, Roosevelt, in a burst of temper, publicly upbraided Miles for commenting to the papers on a Naval Court of Inquiry. According to the story, Miles left the White House a "broken man."

Miles was humiliated and angry. He felt his office entitled him to more respect than Roosevelt had shown; but he was not a broken man. On the contrary, the old fighter promptly counterattacked. Roosevelt, as Miles well knew, favored U.S. occupation of the Philippines. Miles felt this was wrong and that the fighting should be stopped. There had been 120,000 American troops at various times in the Islands; 40,000 were still on duty in 1902. The financial cost to the government was enormous. The drain on the Regular Army was heavy. To bring about a cease-fire, Miles requested duty in the Philippines to put into effect a plan based on a principle employed in the past with Indians. Miles would take a delegation of Cubans and Puerto Ricans with him to tell the Filipinos how they had benefited from American aid. Confidence would be restored in the U.S. and a Filipino delegation could visit Washington to discuss peace terms.[2]

Elihu Root's reaction to the plan was immediate and violent. Negotiations, Root said, were already pending between the Americans and the Filipinos. Governor William Howard

Taft and his associates on the Philippine Commission were doing a good job; so was General Adna Chaffee. There was no reason to supersede them. Miles's plan was unwarranted interference. Root forwarded this report to the President who endorsed it: "Conclusions of the Secretary of War are hereby approved. Theodore Roosevelt."

Miles was having no more to say about the campaign in the Philippines than he had to say about the expedition to Cuba. Perhaps less. But he was not an easy man to ignore. In August of 1902 he asked to visit the Philippines again. This time the request was approved. Root had his reasons for wanting Miles away from Washington. He was engaged in a reorganization of the War Department which would eliminate the office of Commanding General in favor of a General Staff. The reform was much needed and approved by nearly everyone except Miles, who felt the change was another violation of American tradition and smacked of European militarism. His opposition was outspoken and adamant.

To prevent certain dissension, the Secretary suggested that Miles might like to take an extended trip. The visit to the Philippines would be purely an inspection trip. Miles was not to interfere in the operation of the military or civil government. From the Philippines, Miles was to go to Japan and China where he was to inspect the Legation Guard in Peking and see if the quarters were suitable! He was then to take the Trans-Siberian Railroad to Russia and Europe, making a confidential report on the military capacity of the Trans-Siberian and military conditions in Manchuria.

Root was sure this would keep Miles occupied until early in 1903, a few months before he was due to retire for age. The Secretary made the same mistake others had made before him of underestimating Miles's tenacity.

Everything went well until Miles reached Guam, which was

the second stop on the trip. Mary accompanied her husband and enjoyed the first stop at Hawaii. Guam was very hot and disagreeable and had no docking facilities for large ships. Miles went ashore on the island thickly tangled with jungle and coconut palms, where he discovered the former Secretary of State for the Philippine Republic, Apolinario Mabine, in close confinement by the Americans. The Filipino was carried out of his prison in a man's arms and put in a chair for the interview with Miles. Emaciated, crippled and paralyzed below the waist, Mabine still retained his spirit. He did not know, he told Miles, why he was kept a prisoner on a remote island like Guam; he could do the United States no harm. Miles, indignant at the treatment of a man he felt to be a true patriot, urged Mabine's immediate release. The request was refused. The U.S. was at war, legally declared or not, with the Philippine Republic.

Elihu Root must have had a few misgivings by this time about the wisdom of Miles's trip. He was to have more when Miles reached the Islands and heard complaints of unauthorized and unwarranted acts of the military toward prisoners in their hands in order to obtain information on the insurgent forces. Miles had always had strong views about the treatment of prisoners. Torture, he felt, was injurious to the good name of the army and to military justice and morale. Without waiting to notify Washington, he issued strict orders prohibiting coercion of prisoners. Army commanders on the Island reacted furiously to the implied slur on their abilities to handle their troops. Major General George Davis, commander of the Philippine Department, who, incidentally, had served on the Beef Investigation Board, cabled the War Department, with the result that the Adjutant General, Corbin, cabled Davis that by direction of the Secretary of War (and Roosevelt) Miles's order was not to be promulgated. In other words, it was to be ignored.

In the future Miles was to seek the permission of the Secretary before issuing orders. The Commanding General of the Philippine Division and not the Commanding General of the Army would take appropriate action![3]

Miles's order implied criticism of the Administration's policy of expansion. The press got hold of the story. Congress demanded papers and correspondence on the subject. Root, losing all patience with Miles, countered by saying Miles's charges were unfounded; that he had jumped to conclusions. Miles insisted he was justified and, eventually, in January 1903, General Davis forwarded the report of an investigating Board that found certain officers guilty of torture by the "water cure," and another of whipping two Filipino prisoners to death.[4]

By spring, Miles was home again. He was becoming quite a trial to the Administration, but in a few months his utterances would no longer be official. There was not much Miles could do about retirement at the compulsory age of sixty-four, although he tried to fight even that, or at any rate Roosevelt's restrictions on retirement.

Roosevelt, who believed there were too many Civil War veterans on active duty, issued an order that all officers should prove their physical fitness by a cross-country ride of ninety miles in three days. If unable to make the ride, they would be eligible for retirement. Miles could hardly let such an order pass unchallenged. At five o'clock on a July morning Miles, accompanied by several officers, an N.C.O. and a packer cantered out of Fort Sill, Oklahoma, for Fort Reno. Miles wore leggings and shoes, a summer helmet and a light blue shirt without insignia of rank. Relay points with fresh mounts had been set up at ten-mile intervals. Miles made the first thirty-four miles out of Sill in two and a half hours. By eight o'clock it was nearly ninety in the shade; by noon, it was a blistering one hundred. As the erect old horseman pounded across the plain, an Indian lifted his hand in greeting, calling, "Nocolsia — Bear Coat." A newspaper reporter timed Miles's ride in nine and a half hours, which seems nearly incredible. Whatever the exact time, it was an equestrian feat. Gray with dust, Miles drew rein at Fort Reno. Only one officer, a thirty-four-year-old cavalryman, was able to stay the entire distance with Miles, and he showed signs of stiffness while the General, nearly as fresh as when he started, changed to a plain blue uniform. He then reviewed the troops on the unshaded parade ground and greeted his old scout, Ben Clark, and the enlisted men who had served with him in the Indian-fighting days. After a quick lunch, Miles rode another four miles to catch a four o'clock train for Fort Riley, Kansas. Such was Miles's answer to Roosevelt's ninety-mile ride order.

But the fact remained that on August 8, 1903, Miles reached the legal retirement age of sixty-four.

To Roosevelt's everlasting discredit, he allowed Miles to retire without the customary honors paid a commanding general. Miles had tried his patience; indeed had been almost insubordinate, but the President would have been a bigger man if he had forgotten personal differences in the record of a soldier who wore the Medal of Honor and the campaign ribbons of three wars. That Roosevelt failed to send a congratulatory message to the retirement ceremonies, and that the Secretary was not present, reflected on the Administration and not on Miles. The Administration was the victor in its long battle with the Commanding General, and could well have been more generous. Within a week, the office of Commanding General would be abolished and Major General Samuel B. M. Young would be the new Chief of Staff, aided by Major Generals Henry C. Corbin and Tasker Bliss — all friends of the Administration and of Elihu Root. It was a great day in the War Department. So anxious were the authorities to launch the new regime that Young was sworn in to his new rank of Lieutenant General before Miles retired. For two hours there were two lieutenant generals in the army, a breach of existing military law that Miles was quick to observe.

Miles did not give his enemies an inch. Promptly at nine o'clock in the morning he arrived at his office with his aides, Lieutenant Colonel Maus and Lieutenant Colonel Samuel Reber. Miles's shoulders were squared; his head was high. Clerks, messengers and old soldiers crowded around to shake his hand. The twenty-five clerks of the army headquarters presented a silver loving cup. The women clerks gave a bouquet of red roses. At ten-thirty the officers of the new General Staff and nearly a hundred others filed in to pay their respects. In the lead was General Young with the three premature stars blazing on his shoulder straps. Miles noted the stars but shook hands cordially with his successor. It was observed with relief that he also shook hands with General Corbin who followed Young. Relations between Miles and Corbin had long been strained. Then came the Second Cavalry from Fort Myer, which drew up before the steps of the War Department and whose officers, led by Colonel Edgerly, came in to say goodbye to the Commanding General. At the close of the reception, General Young, accompanied by Corbin, said, "I wish you a long and happy retired life."

Miles couldn't resist one final barb. "Thank you, General; it won't be so very long before both of you will be in the same box."[5]

At twelve o'clock Miles left the War Department for the last time in uniform. As he left the building, an old man wearing a messenger's badge asked if he might shake the General's hand. "Sir, I was in your command at Fort Monroe at the close of the Civil War," the old fellow told Miles, "and was assigned by you as one of the personal guards of Jeff Davis."

Miles's face lit up with pleasure. He told the messenger he recognized him; he was a member of the old Fifth Artillery. He shook hands and then went on down the steps.

A professional soldier faces a difficult adjustment when he retires. Not only does he lose his job, he loses his way of life. The adjustment was doubly difficult for a man of Miles's great energy. While he was struggling with the task of becoming a civilian for the first time in forty-three years, he received another blow. A year after Miles retired, Mary died very suddenly at West Point, where she had gone to spend the summer near Sherman. Cecelia and Samuel Reber were at her bedside, but Miles was en route from Washington when he heard the news.

Miles never quite recovered from Mary's death. The rest of his life was always lonely. In an attempt to keep busy, he became Inspector General of the Massachusetts Militia, with Sherman and a West Point classmate as volunteer instructors for the summer maneuvers. But directing the Massachusetts Militia was not the same as directing the United States Army. In the winter of 1907 Miles went abroad. He later made several trips to Europe, once with Colgate Hoyt, his brother-in-law and once with Anson Mills who had served with Crook on the Rosebud and led the advance at Slim Buttes. Investments which Miles had made in Texas had turned out well, so that he was financially independent.

In 1906 he sold his big house and moved to a smaller one nearby. Later he had an apartment in the Rochambeau close to his favorite club, the Metropolitan, where he played chess with Truxton Beale and other cronies. He had taken up golf well before his retirement and continued to play it. But his favorite recreation remained with his horses. Many years after he retired he kept his horses in a stable nearby and frequently rode them. A fall from one of his spirited mounts resulted in a note of sympathy from the Chief of Staff, General Bell, quoting the Bible: "The horse is a vain thing for safety." Miles was not amused. He deeply resented having fallen off his horse. When riding became too much of an effort, he drove fancy trotters, but Washington traffic was increasing and Miles paid little attention to the new rules of the road, which resulted in many near-accidents. On Sherman and Cecelia's suggestion, he bought an electric auto, but he never liked the thing and went back to his horses with a colored boy to drive.

He was happiest when he was with Sherman or Cecelia or his grandchildren. Sherman's wedding to a Washington girl gave him a great deal of pleasure. He wanted to do something for the newlyweds and so prepared a surprise. When Sherman and his bride returned from their honeymoon, they found their new quarters at Fort Myer decorated with Indian trophies which Miles had carefully carried out himself and put up on the walls.

One of Miles's favorite occupations was taking his grandchildren to the zoo or for a ride in the park or to see a monument. He wanted his grandchildren to know that the brooding figure in marble and the General on the bronze horse were not just statues. One was the man who had signed their grandfather's commission as a brigadier general; the other was William Tecumseh Sherman. How well Miles could remember the inspection trip that Sherman had made to Fort Keogh! Now Sherman was on a pedestal, and he stood in the sunlight holding the hand of his grandchild and reading the inscription: "War's legitimate object is a more perfect peace."

Old rivalries faded with the years. There were new Presidents, new faces in Congress, new names in the War Department. Miles became less a figure of controversy and more a figure of tradition.

He was seventy-seven years old when the United States entered World War I.

"In view of the impending serious war with the Central Powers of Europe," Miles wrote the Secretary of War, "I have the honor to tender my services under Section 24, National Defense Act approved June 3, 1916."[6]

Some days later came a reply. The Secretary was not clear about what ways Miles's services could be utilized in view of his rank but "it is possible," the Secretary said tactfully, "in time of emergency our government may need to take advantage of your great experience. Please accept appreciation of your most patriotic offer."[7]

Miles refused to be mollified. He wanted to go to Siberia at the head of American troops.

He watched the war closely, following the battles on maps and the names of officers in the newspapers. Pershing had served at Wounded Knee, where Miles had been impressed by him and had later made him an aide. Hugh Scott, Miles's old hunting companion, was made a major general. But there were not many old soldiers of Miles's day left in 1918.

When the war was over, Miles insisted on participating in a parade. He wouldn't ride with his contemporaries, but marched with the Medal of Honor men. The route was a long one from the White House to the Capitol. Cecelia, fearing her father would suffer from the cold and knowing he would not wear an overcoat, bought a light paper garment which she fitted on the old man beneath his uniform which, with the years, had grown tight. The day turned out warmer than expected, and when Miles's group arrived at Capitol Hill, he was not with it. Cecelia and Sherman, after much worry and searching, finally found their father in a Red Cross station, relieved of his paper garment and his uniform coat, and as mad as a hornet — mad at Cecelia for making him wear "that damned corset" and mad at the Red Cross for refusing to let him start out alone after he had collapsed at the foot of Capitol Hill.

Miles's carriage remained erect, his eyes clear and his memory excellent. He continued to walk and golf. In the early twenties, a young boy about to enter West Point was told by his father who was then on duty in the War Department, "Do you see that handsome old man walking down the street ahead of us? I want you to meet him, so that, someday, you can say you shook hands with Nelson A. Miles."[8]

In May 1925, when Miles was eighty-five, the Ringling Brothers Circus came to town. Miles had always loved circuses and he invited Sherman's mother-in-law and his grandchildren to go with him. When the band played "The Star-Spangled Banner," the audience rose to its feet. Miles stood erect to salute the flag. His heart still thrilled to the red, white and blue folds. His pulse still stirred to the roll of drums and the shrill of bugles. He could see long gray lines advancing across the field with the rebel yell, hear the rifles of the Fifth Infantry as the men fired at the painted savages in the smoke of Cedar Creek. Sherman and Custer; Sitting Bull and Geronimo, they were all there.

Few people noticed the stir in the third-row seats as the old man who had collapsed during the national anthem was carried out of the tent.

Newspapers across the country headlined the death of Nelson Miles, the last general officer of the line of the Civil War, one of the remaining veterans of the Civil, Indian and Spanish-

American wars. The funeral was everything Miles could have wished. President Coolidge attended the service at St. John's. Twenty-four hundred men of the Regular Army, navy and marine corps formed the funeral cortège. Miles's body in a lieutenant general's uniform lay in a steel-gray coffin drawn on an artillery caisson by six black horses. At the right flank rode a standard bearer carrying the flag and stars of a lieutenant general. As the column turned into Arlington a battery of French seventy-fives boomed a fifteen-gun salute. About the simple tomb where Mary had been buried twenty years before, gathered groups of Miles's old command, high government officials and representatives of military and patriotic societies. As the casket was put into the tomb, riflemen fired three volleys. Then came the sad, sweet notes of taps, and Miles rested, at last, beside his Mary.

No epitaph is carved on the marble. If there were one, it could well read, "Here lies a fighting soldier."

Notes

NOTES

CHAPTER I

1. *Washington Evening Star,* May 16, 1925.
2. Oliver Otis Howard, *Autobiography.*

CHAPTER II

1. Francis Barlow. No record of to whom addressed. Boston, Mass., January 1863. Miles Collection.
2. Major General Darius Couch, "The Chancellorsville Campaign." *Battles and Leaders of the Civil War,* Vol. 3.
3. John Bigelow, quoted in Matthew Forney Steele, *American Campaigns.*
4. The threatened invasion of Pennsylvania by rebel forces was in June 1863. Gettysburg was fought July 1–3, 1863.
5. Major General Orlando B. Wilcox, "Actions on the Weldon Railroad." *Battles and Leaders of the Civil War,* Vol. 4.
6. Nelson A. Miles, *Serving the Republic.*

CHAPTER III

1. "A Statement of the Facts Concerning the Imprisonment of Jefferson Davis."
2. Charles Sumner to Charles Sherman, Boston, Aug. 16, 1867. Miles Collection.
3. Nelson A. Miles to Charles Sherman, Raleigh, North Carolina, Sept. 6, 1867.
4. Alfred Terry to Miles, St. Paul, Minnesota, March 29, 1868. Miles Collection.

CHAPTER IV

1. Miles to Sherman, Nov. 19, 1870. William T. Sherman Papers.
2. Elizabeth B. Custer, *Following the Guidon.*

3. *Ibid.*
4. Nelson A. Miles, *Serving the Republic.*
5. Elizabeth Custer speaks of entertaining distinguished eastern journalists in *Following the Guidon.* Generals Schofield and Sheridan were among the distinguished military guests at Big Creek.
6. Elizabeth Custer identified the three chiefs as Big Head, Fat Bear and Dull Knife. George Bird Grinnell identified them as Slim Face, Curly Hair and Island, or possibly Younger Bear and Chief-Comes-in-Sight. There seems to have been some confusion about the names of the captives.
7. Elizabeth B. Custer, *op. cit.*
8. Nelson A. Miles, *op. cit.*

CHAPTER V

1. Colonel Richard Irving Dodge, *Thirty Three Years Among Our Wild Indians.*
2. Miles to Mary, Fort Dodge, Kansas (August. 7, 1894).
3. Miles to Mary, Camp South of the Washita (Aug. 25, 1874).
4. Bat Masterson was later the famous gunman and U.S. Marshal.
5. Miles to Mary, Camp on Bluff Creek (Aug. 14, 1874).
6. Miles to Mary, Wolf Creek near Camp Supply (Aug. 18, 1874).
7. Major G. W. Baird, "General Miles' Indian Campaigns." *Century Magazine,* Vol. XX.
8. This did not mean they drank their blood; they moistened their lips.
9. Miles to Mary (Sept. 24, 1874).
10. Miles to Mary (Sept. 18, 1874).
11. Homer W. Wheeler, *Buffalo Days.*
12. Miles to Mary, from Washita (Sept. 18, 1874).
13. Lieutenant Colonel J. W. Davidson, Tenth Cavalry from Fort Sill, operating with a separate command against the hostiles.
14. Miles to Mary, Headquarters on the Canadian River (Sept. 27, 1874).
15. Miles to Mary, Camp on the Washita (Oct. 13, 1874).

CHAPTER VI

1. Homer W. Wheeler, *Buffalo Days.*
2. *Ibid.*
3. George Bird Grinnell says there was no battle at McClellan's Creek and that the children were left on a buffalo robe on a hillside and

were rescued when the Indians fled. All authorities agree the Indians put up little resistance. Stories vary on where the children were found.

4. Miles to Mary, Headquarters Indian Territory Expedition (Nov. 16, 1874).
5. Miles to Mary, Camp on Washita (Dec. 2, 1874).
6. Miles to Mary, Camp on Washita (Nov. 12, 1874).
7. Miles to Mary, Headquarters Indian Territory Expedition (Nov. 16, 1874).
8. General Neil. The General was a brevet rank. Lieutenant Colonel Thomas H. Neil, Sixth Cavalry, operating near the Agency at Darlington.
9. Miles to Mary, Headquarters Indian Territory Expedition (Nov. 16, 1874).
10. Pope to Sheridan. Secretary of War, *Annual Report,* 1875–76.
11. Miles to Mary, Camp at the Head of White Deer Creek, South of Adobe Walls (Dec. 17, 1874).
12. Miles to Mary, Camp on Elm Fork (Jan. 11, 1875).
13. Miles to Mary, Mouth of the Tule (Jan. 5, 1875).
14. Nelson A. Miles, *Personal Recollections.*
15. Pope to Sheridan. Secretary of War, *Annual Report,* 1875–76.

CHAPTER VII

1. Miles to Mary, Cimarron, New Mexico (Dec. 16, 1875).
2. Report of the Indian Commissioner. Not all these Indians were under Sitting Bull. Many were Cheyennes, and many Sioux were under different leaders.
3. John W. Finerty, *War Path and Bivouac.*
4. Crook to Sheridan. Secretary of War, *Annual Report,* 1876.
5. Colonel J. J. Reynolds was found guilty and suspended from rank and command for one year.
6. W. T. Sherman. Secretary of War, *Annual Report,* 1876.
7. J. M. Hansen, *Conquest of the Missouri.*
8. *Ibid.* Companies C., E., F., I. and L. were with Custer and all men killed. The remaining companies with Major Reno and Captain Benteen, while suffering casualties, survived.
9. Miles to Sherman, June 15, 1876. William T. Sherman Papers.
10. Miles refers to W. W. Belknap, Secretary of War, who was tried for fraud and dishonest dealing with the post trader at Fort Sill, Oklahoma.

11. Miles means the other four companies of his regiment, the Fifth Infantry.

12. Nelson A. Miles, *Serving the Republic.*

CHAPTER VIII

1. Lieutenant James Bradley, "Journal."

2. Terry ordered Captain O. H. Moore, Sixth Infantry, to go aboard Grant Marsh's *Far West* to the mouth of the Powder, where a supply depot had been established before the Custer fight, to recover some sacks of grain. The skirmish that Miles mentions took place Aug. 2, 1876.

3. Lieutenant James Bradley, *op. cit.*

4. Charles King, *Campaigning with Crook.*

5. John G. Bourke, *On the Border With Crook.*

6. Crook. Secretary of War, *Annual Report,* 1876.

7. J. M. Hansen, *Conquest of the Missouri.*

8. Fort Buford was located near confluence of the Missouri and Yellowstone.

9. Wendell Phillips was a well-known abolitionist. After the Custer fight, he made violent attacks on the army for mistreating the Indians.

10. E. M. Hansen, *op. cit.*

11. *Ibid.*

CHAPTER IX

1. George E. Pond, "Major General Nelson A. Miles." *McClure's Magazine* (Nov. 1895).

2. Miles to Sherman, Oct. 16, 1876. William T. Sherman papers.

3. *Ibid.*

4. Luther Kelly, *Yellowstone Kelly.*

5. Lt. Col. Otis. Secretary of War, *Annual Report,* 1876.

6. Trumpeter Brown's Diary.

7. Letter to Mary, near the Camp Fire on the Yellowstone 20 miles above Glendive (Oct. 25, 1876).

8. Miles refers to General E. R. S. Canby who was killed by Modocs in April 1873.

9. Red Shirt or Bear Stop, Minneconjou who went on steamboat after the surrender on the Yellowstone. Bald Eagle could be Black Eagle, a Sans Arc, who, also, went on the boat to the agency after the surrender.

10. Letter to Mary, Cantonment on the Yellowstone (Dec. 15, 1876).
11. Nelson A. Miles, *Personal Recollections.*
12. Letter to Mary, Near the Camp Fire on the Yellowstone (Oct. 25, 1876).
13. Trumpeter Brown, *op. cit.*
14. Nelson A. Miles, *Personal Recollections.*
15. Trumpeter Brown, *op. cit.*
16. Letter to Mary, Near the Camp Fire on the Yellowstone (Oct. 25, 1876).
17. *Ibid.*
18. Miles to Sherman, Nov. 18, 1876. William T. Sherman Papers.
19. Commissioner Manypenny was ex-commissioner of Indian Affairs.
20. Miles to Terry, Camp Opposite Cabin Creek, Oct. 27, 1876. Secretary of War. *Annual Report,* 1876–77.
21. Miles to Terry, Camp on Bad Route Creek, Oct. 28, 1876. Secretary of War, *Annual Report,* 1876–77.

CHAPTER X

1. John Bourke, *On the Border with Crook.*
2. Letter to Mary, Cantonment on the Yellowstone, Montana Territory (Nov. 6, 1876).
3. Miles to Sherman, Opposite Fort Peck, Montana, Nov. 18, 1876. William T. Sherman Papers.
4. Nelson A. Miles, *Personal Recollections.*
5. Joe Culbertson was the half breed son of Culbertson, the famous fur trader. Young Joe was called the "Boy Scout."
6. Stanley Vestal in *New Sources of Indian History* says the Indians who were killed by the Crows — according to the modern Sioux version — were young men who were returning some stolen horses to the military, and were not chiefs. Mari Sandoz in *Hostile and Friendlies* says the Indians were peace emissaries and that one of them was Sitting Bull the Good.

CHAPTER XI

1. Miles to Sherman, Cantonment on the Yellowstone, Dec. 25, 1876. William T. Sherman Papers.
2. Miles to Mary, Cantonment on the Yellowstone (Dec. 27, 1876).
3. Mrs. Nelson A. Miles, *Harper's Bazar,* date unknown. Mrs. Miles's Scrapbook.

4. Miles to Mary, Headquarters Yellowstone Command (March 15, 1877).
5. *Ibid.*
6. Miles to Mary, Headquarters Yellowstone Command, Tongue River, Montana Territory (Jan. 26, 1877).
7. Betley was the soldier who was killed and buried on the trail up the Tongue Valley.
8. George Bird Grinnell in *The Fighting Cheyennes* says there were two women and four children in the party. The women were Wool Woman and the widow of Walking White Man.
9. Mr. Lou Grill in the *Miles City Daily Star,* June 18, 1926, quotes John Standing Elk as saying the medicine man was Big Crow. Kelly identified him merely as Medicine Man. Miles says he was Big Crow. There are many different versions of Medicine Chief's Dance.
10. Miles to Mary, Cantonment on Yellowstone, Montana (Jan. 19, 1877).
11. Miles to Mary, Cantonment on Yellowstone, Montana (Jan. 21, 1877).
12. Miles to Mary, Headquarters Yellowstone Command (March 15, 1877).

CHAPTER XII

1. Miles to Sherman, Cantonment on the Yellowstone, Jan. 20, 1877. William T. Sherman Papers.
2. *Ibid.*
3. Miles refers to Crook's report to Secretary of War, *Annual Report,* 1876–77.
4. Wool Woman.
5. Big Crow.

CHAPTER XIII

1. Grinnel reports that White Bull, his Cheyenne informant, said there were thirty-eight lodges. Colonel David Brainard in Grinnell's *Fighting Cheyennes* says he thinks there were sixty-three lodges. Fifty-one is the number estimated by Miles.
2. Lieutenant Lovell H. Jerome, later involved in the Bear Paw battle.
3. This is Miles's report. White Bull, in Grinnell's *Fighting Cheyennes* said five Sioux men were killed, one woman, two soldiers and one citizen packer. Grinnell reported three soldiers and six Sioux killed. Miles's official report of military casualties is considered correct.
4. Nelson A. Miles, *Personal Recollections.*
5. George Bird Grinnell gives a slightly different version in *The Fight-*

ing Cheyennes. His informant, White Bull, who had surrendered after Wolf Mountain and served as a scout on the Lame Deer campaign, said Lame Deer's son was largely responsible for starting the fight.

6. A. F. Mulford, *Fighting Indians in the Seventh United States Cavalry.* Doubt has been cast on many of Mulford's statements, but a number of them are authentic.

7. *Ibid.*

8. *Ibid.*

9. Sherman to McCrary, Secretary of War, July 17, 1877. Quoted in Miles's *Personal Recollections.*

10. Major Brisbin. Secretary of War, *Annual Report,* 1878.

CHAPTER XIV

1. Major General Irvin McDowell, associated with the first Battle of Bull Run in the Civil War.

2. S. G. Fisher, "Journal of S. G. Fisher."

3. O. O. Howard, *Chief Joseph, His Pursuit and Capture.*

4. Nelson A. Miles, *Personal Recollections.*

5. A. F. Mulford, *Fighting Indians in the Seventh United States Cavalry.*

6. *Ibid.*

7. Nelson A. Miles, *op. cit.*

8. Howard to Miles, Sept. 12, 1877. Secretary of War, *Annual Report,* 1877.

9. Miles to Howard, Sept. 17, 1877.

CHAPTER XV

1. It was customary during this period for wives to speak of their husbands by their formal titles. Uncle Cump was General Sherman.

2. Fort Brown was Camp Brown on the Shoshoni Indian Reservation, Wind River Valley, Wyoming. Originally founded in 1869 as Camp Augur.

3. Nelson A. Miles, *Personal Recollections.*

4. Captain Henry Romeyn, "The Capture of Chief Joseph and the Nez Percé Indians."

5. Nelson A. Titus, "Last Stand of the Nez Percé." *Washington Historical Quarterly* (July 1915), Vol. VI., No. 3.

6. Miles to Sturgis. Sept. 30, 1877. Secretary of War, *Annual Report,* 1877.

7. Chief Joseph, "An Indian's View of Indian Affairs." *North American Review,* April, 1879. Many reasons have been given for Miles's detention of Joseph.

8. L. V. McWhorter, *Yellow Wolf; His Own Story.*

9. Joseph, *loc. cit.*

10. C. E. S. Wood, "Chief Joseph, the Nez Percé."

11. A. F. Mulford, *op. cit.*

CHAPTER XVI

1. W. T. Sherman. Secretary of War, *Annual Report,* 1877–78.

2. O. O. Howard, *ibid,* 1878–79.

3. W. T. Sherman, *op. cit.*

4. Crazy Horse was killed resisting arrest at Camp Robinson, which was in the Department of the Platte commanded by General Crook. The date was September 5, 1877, a few months after Crazy Horse surrendered. As he lay dying beneath a red blanket in the adjutant's office the chief murmured, "My father, I am bad hurt. Tell the people it is no use to depend on me any more now."

5. Sheridan. Secretary of War, *Annual Report,* 1878–79.

6. *Ibid.*

7. John Gibbon. Secretary of War, *Annual Report,* 1878–79.

8. Governor Potts to Sherman, Helena, Montana, Sept. 12, 1878. Military Records of Nelson A. Miles.

9. Miles Report. Secretary of War, *Annual Report,* 1878–79.

10. Sherman to Miles, H.Q. Army of the U.S., Feb. 9, 1878. William T. Sherman Papers.

11. Miles to Sherman. March 9, 1879. William T. Sherman Papers.

12. Sherman to Miles. March 10, 1879. William T. Sherman Papers.

13. Miles to Sherman. March 10, 1879. William T. Sherman Papers.

14. Sherman to Miles. March 10, 1879. William T. Sherman Papers.

15. Miles to Sherman. March 11, 1879. William T. Sherman Papers.

16. Sherman to Miles, March 10, 1879. Mackenzie, in 1873, crossed the Rio Grande, made a forced night march and attacked and destroyed an Indian camp. The resulting situation had to be settled by diplomatic exchange between Mexico and the U.S.

17. Mary Miles to Senator John Sherman, 1879. From Fort Keogh.

18. Hancock to Adjutant General, Aug. 30, 1880. Military Records of Nelson A. Miles.

19. Governor of Massachusetts to Adjutant General, Nov. 5, 1880. Military Records of Nelson A. Miles.

20. Charles Fairchild to Secretary of War, Feb. 21, 1886. Military Records of Nelson A. Miles.

CHAPTER XVII

1. Crook was assigned to the Department of Arizona with his brevet rank. He received his regular brigadier-generalcy Oct. 29, 1873.
2. Barlow to Charles Codman, Brookline, Mass., Feb. 1886. Letter to be forwarded to President.
3. Elizabeth Cameron to Mary Miles, Washington D.C., April 1886.
4. Miles Report. Secretary of War, *Annual Report,* 1887.
5. G. W. Forsyth, "Apache Raid." *Harper's Weekly* (Jan. 14, 1899).
6. Britton Davis, *The Truth About Geronimo.*
7. Miles to Mary, Fort Bowie, Arizona (April 11, 1886).
8. Miles Report, *op. cit.*
9. Miles to Mary, Fort Bowie, Arizona (May 13, 1886). On July 29, 1882, an agreement was made between the United States and Mexico allowing U.S. troops to cross into Mexico. The agreement lapsed after two years, and many of the arrangements had to be made by local officials. There was seldom difficulty. The Mexicans were as anxious for the Apaches to be subdued as were the Americans.
10. Miles to Mary, Nogales, Arizona (May 16, 1886).
11. Miles to Mary, Fort Huachuca, Arizona (May 17, 1886).
12. Miles to Mary, Fort Huachuca, Arizona (May 18, 1886). Lieutenant Brown was Lieutenant Robt. A. Brown, Fourth Cavalry.
13. Miles to Mary, Wilcox, Arizona (May 30, 1886).
14. Miles to Mary, Wilcox, Arizona (May 25, 1886).
15. *Ibid.*
16. Miles to Mary, Wilcox, Arizona (May 30, 1886).
17. Miles to Mary, Wilcox, Arizona (May 25, 1886).
18. Miles to Mary, Calabasas, Arizona Ter. (June 7, 1886). Walsh was Lieutenant R. S. Walsh, Fourth Cavalry.
19. Miles to Mary, Calabasas, Arizona Territory (June 8, 1886).

CHAPTER XVIII

1. Miles to Mary, Fort Huachuca, Arizona (June 15, 1886).
2. Miles to Mary, Deming, New Mexico (June 24, 1886).
3. Britton Davis, *The Truth About Geronimo.*
4. Miles to Mary, Fort Apache, Arizona (July 5, 1886).
5. Miles to Mary, Wilcox, Arizona (July 31, 1886).

6. Miles to Mary, Wilcox, Arizona (Aug. 2, 1886).
7. Miles to Mary, Wilcox, Arizona (Aug. 27, 1886).
8. Nelson A. Miles, *Personal Recollections*.
9. Miles to Mary, Wilcox, Arizona (Aug. 29, 1886).
10. Miles to Mary, Fort Bowie, Arizona (June 23, 1886).
11. Miles to Mary, Fort Bowie, Arizona (Aug. 29, 1886).
12. Miles to Mary, Fort Bowie, Arizona (Sept. 2, 1886).
13. Nelson A. Miles, *op. cit.*
14. *Ibid.*
15. *Ibid.*
16. *Ibid.*
17. Miles to Mary, Fort Bowie, Arizona (Sept. 7, 1886).

CHAPTER XIX

1. Miles to Mary, Albuquerque, New Mexico (Oct. 4, 1886).
2. Newspaper clipping, unidentified, no date. Mrs. Miles's Scrapbook.
3. The Case of the Apache prisoners ended in a Congressional investigation. Official correspondence on the subject was called for. Captain Dorst and Bourke testified among many others. Records of the investigation may be found in Senate Executive Document 117, 49th Congress and Sen. Exec. Doc. 85, 51st Cong. Also, Sen. Exec. Doc. 35, 51st Cong., contains testimony on the continuing fight between Crook and Miles over the Apache prisoners. Lawton, Britton Davis, Crawford and Gatewood were among the officers who had served with either Crook or Miles who expressed their opinion publicly. Clum, agent of the Apaches, joined the fray too, as did many others.
4. The outbreak was threatened by five enlisted Apache scouts going AWOL after a tizwin drunk and the murder of several Indians. Malcontents joined the scouts.
5. Miles to Mary, San Carlos, New Mexico (June 19, 1887).

CHAPTER XX

1. Senator John Sherman to Miles, Washington, D.C. (April 3, 1890). Miles Collection.
2. *Ibid.*
3. Miles to Mary, Hotel New Brunswick (April 4, 1890).
4. Miles to Mary, Washington, D.C. (April 5, 1890).
5. Miles to Mary, Senate Building, Washington, D.C. (April 6, 1890).
6. *Ibid.*

7. James Mooney, *Ghost Dance.* 17th edition, *Bureau of American Ethnology.*

8. Nelson A. Miles, *Serving the Republic.*

CHAPTER XXI

1. Miles Report. Secretary of War, *Annual Report,* 1890–91.
2. Report of Commissioner of Indian Affairs, 1891.
3. Miles Report, *op. cit.*
4. There are many versions of the death of Sitting Bull. McLaughlin's, Captain Fechet's and the eyewitness story of Conrad Disstler, trooper in the Eighth Cavalry, found in E. S. Ellis, *The Indian Wars of the United States,* are among three of the references employed here.
5. Nelson A. Miles, *Serving the Republic.*
6. Miles to Mary, Rapid City, South Dakota (Dec. 22, 1890).
7. Brigadier General John R. Brooke, commanding the Department of the Platte, had the troops at Pine Ridge. Brigadier General T. H. Ruger, commanding the Department of the Dakota, had the troops in the northern agency of Standing Rock. The two field commanders were directly responsible to Miles. Lieutenant Colonel E. V. Sumner had two companies of the Third Infantry and three troops of the Eighth Cavalry on the Cheyenne River when Big Foot escaped. Colonel W. B. Shafter had seven Companies of the First Infantry guarding the country south and west of the Rosebud Agency. Colonel E. A. Carr guarded the railroad between Hermosa and Rapid City with six troops of the Sixth Cavalry. Major Guy Henry's battalion of the Ninth Cavalry was at Pine Ridge. Colonel A. N. Wheaton with one company of the Eighth Infantry and eight companies of the Second Infantry was at Pine Ridge. Colonel H. C. Merriam with seven companies of the Seventh Infantry was strung out along the Cheyenne River.

CHAPTER XXII

1. Miles to Mary, Rapid City, South Dakota (Dec. 25, 1890).
2. E. S. Ellis, *The Indian Wars of the United States.* Testimony of American Horse before officers of the Department of the Interior, Feb. 7, 1891.
3. E. S. Ellis, *The Indian Wars of the United States.* Testimony of Spotted Horse before officers of the Department of the Interior, Feb. 7, 1891.

4. George E. Hyde in *A Sioux Chronicle* says various reports of the casualties at Wounded Knee were given. In 1891 a count showed 84 men and boys of fighting age and 44 women and 18 children killed. At least 33 were wounded.

5. Miles to Mary, Pine Ridge, South Dakota (Jan. 6, 1891).

6. Miles to Mary, Pine Ridge, South Dakota (Jan 8, 1891). Lt. E. W. Casey, 22nd Infantry, had been with Miles at Lame Deer.

7. Miles to Mary, Pine Ridge, South Dakota (Jan. 15, 1891).

8. Miles to Mary, Pine Ridge, South Dakota (Jan 20, 1891).

9. Miles to Mary, Pine Ridge, South Dakota (Jan 11, 1891). The Shafter referred to, was Colonel W. R. Shafter who commanded the Cuban Expeditionary Force in 1898.

10. Miles to Mary, Pine Ridge via Rushville (Jan. 13, 1891).

11. Miles to Mary, Pine Ridge, South Dakota (Jan. 15, 1891).

CHAPTER XXIII

1. Nelson A. Miles, *Serving the Republic.*

2. The interview with Cleveland is related in a letter to the author from Major General Sherman Miles, Jan. 2, 1959. The incident was told to his son by General Nelson A. Miles.

3. Frederic Remington, "The Chicago Mob." *Harper's Weekly,* undated. Mrs. Miles's Scrapbook.

4. Miles to Mary, H.Q. Dept of the Missouri, Chicago, Ill. (July 7, 1894).

5. Miles to Mary, H.Q. Dept of the Missouri, Chicago, Ill. (July 18, 1894). This was the period of Coxey's march on Washington with his "army" of unemployed. Debs spent six months in prison after the riots. Some years later he ran for President on the Socialist ticket but did not get many votes.

6. Nelson A. Miles, *Serving the Republic.*

7. Nelson A. Miles, *Military Europe.*

8. Mary to the children, July 8, 1897. London, Reber Collection.

9. Mary to the children, July 16, 1897. London, Reber Collection.

10. Miles to the children, Imperial Palace, Moscow, Russia (Aug. 22, 1897). Miles Collection.

11. Nelson A. Miles, *Serving the Republic.*

CHAPTER XXIV

1. Nelson A. Miles, *Serving the Republic.*

2. Gilson Willets, "General Miles Dismayed." *Harper's Weekly,* undated. Mrs. Miles's Scrapbook.

3. Newspaper clipping, undated, unidentified. Mrs. Miles's Scrapbook.

4. Alger to Miles, Washington, D.C., June 15, 1898. Quoted in Nelson A. Miles, *Serving the Republic.*

5. Breckinridge to Miles, Playa del Este, July 4, 1898. *Army-Navy Journal* (July 1898).

6. Nelson A. Miles, *Serving the Republic.*

7. Miles to Shafter, H.Q. of the Army, July 3, 1898. Quoted in Nelson A. Miles, *Serving the Republic.*

CHAPTER XXV

1. Miles to Shafter, Playa del Este, July 18, 1898. Copy of official communication. Mrs. Miles's Scrapbook.

2. Roosevelt to Alger, (July 23, 1898). *Army-Navy Journal* (Aug. 6, 1898).

3. Signers of the so called "round robin" letter were division and brigade commanders, among them Wheeler, Sumner, Roosevelt, Wood, Ludlow, Ames, Chaffee, Kent, Lawton. Shafter endorsed the letter and forwarded it to Washington.

4. Nelson A. Miles, *Serving the Republic.*

5. *Ibid.*

6. Miles to Secretary of War, Ponce via Bermuda (Aug. 10, 1898). Message marked personal and confidential. Copy of official communication, Mrs. Miles's Scrapbook.

7. Richard Harding Davis, "Puerto Rican Campaign." *Scribner's Magazine.* (Nov. 1898).

CHAPTER XXVI

1. "Enthusiastic Welcome to General Miles by Voices of Men and Steamers," *New York World,* undated. Mrs. Miles's Scrapbook.

2. *Ibid.*

3. "General Miles Story," from a New York paper undated and unidentified. Mrs. Miles's Scrapbook.

4. *Report of the Commission Appointed by the President to Investigate the Conduct of the War Dept. in the War with Spain,* Exec. Doc. 221, 56th Cong., Vol. VII.

5. *Ibid.*

6. *Ibid.*

CHAPTER XXVII

1. Sergeant C. P. Reynolds to author's husband. Leavenworth, Kansas (Nov. 15, 1958).

2. Miles to Secretary of War, Feb. 17, 1902. Roosevelt's endorsement was dated March 27, 1902. Military Records of Nelson A. Miles.

3. Corbin to Davis, Nov. 28, 1902. Military Records of Nelson A. Miles.

4. Davis to Adjutant General Corbin, Jan. 22, 1903. Military Records of Nelson A. Miles.

5. Editorial on retirement of General Miles, *Boston Herald* (Aug. 9, 1903).

6. Miles to Secretary of War, March 17, 1917. Military Records of Nelson A. Miles.

7. Secretary of War to Miles, March 17, 1917. Military Records of Nelson A. Miles.

8. Colonel W. H. Johnson to his son, Cadet-to-be Walter M. Johnson. Story related to the author by her husband, W. M. Johnson, Brigadier General, U.S.A., Retired.

Bibliography

BIBLIOGRAPHY

THIS bibliography is not meant to be all-inclusive. It merely lists some of the more important source material used in the preparation of the biography of General Nelson A. Miles.

UNPUBLISHED MATERIAL

Letters from General Nelson A. Miles to Mrs. Miles. These include letters written during the Kiowa-Apache campaign of 1874–75; the Sioux-Cheyenne campaign of 1876–77; the Nez Percé, Bannock, Sioux and Cheyenne campaign, 1877–78; the Apache campaign of 1886, and the last Sioux campaign of 1890–91. In addition, letters and family documents covering a period from 1867 to 1903. These are in the Miles Collection loaned to the author by Major General Sherman Miles, USA Retired.

Letters of Mrs. Miles. These include a period from 1877 to 1902 and were loaned to the author by General Sherman Miles and by Mr. Samuel Reber.

Mrs. Miles's Scrapbook. This was loaned to the author by Mr. Samuel Reber and includes copies of official orders, newspaper clippings and family documents from 1886 to 1902.

First Lieutenant Frank D. Baldwin, Fifth US Infantry, Diary, November 6–December 21, 1876. Manuscript in the Montana Historical Library, Helena, Montana.

Trumpeter Brown's Diary, manuscript in the Montana Historical Library, Helena, Montana.

Donald Campbell, "Indian Campaigns of General Nelson A. Miles in Eastern Montana and the Political Organizations and Settlement of that Region." Unpublished thesis, Montana State University, 1928.

Military Record of Nelson A. Miles, 1870–1917. Washington, D.C. Bureau of Archives.

William T. Sherman Papers. Letters from Miles to Sherman and Sherman to Miles in Vols. 25, 44, 45, 46, and 50.

PAMPHLETS

A Statement of the Facts Concerning the Imprisonment and Treatment of Jefferson Davis While a Military Prisoner at Fort Monroe, Va. 1865–1866. No author mentioned. Privately printed. No date or publisher. Miles Collection.

FEDERAL DOCUMENTS AND PUBLICATIONS

U.S. Department of the Interior, *Annual Report* of the Secretary, 1874–1891.

U.S. Department of War, *Annual Report* of the Secretary, 1874–1898.

U.S. Department of War. *Official Records of the Union and Confederate Armies,* Ser. I, Vol. XXV; Vol. XXXVI.

U.S. Congress, Senate Executive Document 117, 49th Congress; Sen. Exec. Doc. 85, 51st Congress. "Reports Relative to the Treatment of Certain Apache Indians."

U.S. Congress, "Report of the Commission Appointed by the President to Investigate the Conduct of the War Dept. in the War with Spain." Sen. Exec. Doc. 221, 56th Cong.

Heitman, Francis, *Historical Register of U.S. Army,* 1889–1903.

U.S. Military Academy, *Register of Graduates,* West Point, 1802–1950.

Smithsonian Institution, Bureau of American Ethnology, *14th Annual Report.* "Calendar History of the Kiowa Indians. Kiowa Campaign."

Smithsonian Institution, Bureau of American Ethnology, *17th Annual Report,* "The Ghost Dance Religion."

U.S. Department of War, *Report on Barracks and Hospitals,* 1870.

NEWSPAPERS

Army-Navy Journal, Washington, D.C.
Evening Star, Washington, D.C.
Weekly Herald, Helena, Montana
Daily Star, Miles City, Montana
Tribune Herald, Hardin, Montana
The Tribune, Roundup, Montana
Boston Herald, Boston, Mass.
Daily Missoulian, Missoula, Montana
Kalispell Times, Kalispell, Montana

ARTICLES

Bradley, James, "Journal." *Contributions* to Montana Historical Society, Vol. II.

Carrol, Matthew, "Diary." *Contributions* to Montana Historical Society, Vol. II.

Davis, Richard Harding, "The Campaign in Puerto Rico." *Scribner's Magazine* (Nov. 1898).

Forsyth, G. A., "Apache Raid." *Harper's Weekly* (Jan. 14, 1890).

Joseph, Chief, "An Indian's Views of Indian Affairs." *North American Review* (April 1879).

Miles, Nelson A., "The Indian Problem," *North American Review* (March 1879).

Nickerson, A. H., "Apache Indian Raid," *Harper's Weekly* (July 1897).

Pond, George E., "Major General Nelson A. Miles." *McClure's Magazine* (Nov. 1895).

Remington, Frederic, "The Chicago Mob" *Harper's Weekly* (July 1894).

Romeyn, Captain Henry, "The Capture of Chief Joseph and the Nez Percé Indians." *Contributions* to Montana Historical Society, Vol. II.

Titus, Nelson C., "Last Stand of the Nez Percé." *Washington Historical Quarterly* (July 1915), Vol. VI.

Willets, Gilson, "General Miles Dismayed." *Harper's Weekly* (June 1898).

Wood, Lieutenant C. E. S., "Chief Joseph, the Nez Percé." *Century Magazine* (May 1884).

BOOKS

Adams, James Truslow, *America's Tragedy*. New York: Scribner's, 1934.

Ahearn, Robert T., *William Tecumseh Sherman and the Settlement of the West*. Norman, Okla.: University of Oklahoma Press, 1956.

Baldwin, Frank., *Memoirs*. Los Angeles: Wetzel Publishing Co., 1929.

Barthe, Joe De, *Life and Adventures of Frank Grouard*. Norman, Okla.: University of Oklahoma Press, 1958.

Battles and Leaders of the Civil War. No author or editor given. New York: Century Co., 1887.

Bourke, John, *On the Border with Crook*. New York: Scribner's, 1891.

Boyd, James, *Recent Indian Wars*. No place of publication given. Publishers Union, 1891.

Brady, Cyrus Townsend, *Northwestern Fights and Fighters.* New York: McClure Co., 1907.

Brininstool, E. A., *Indian Fighting Warriors.* Harrisburg, Pa.: Stackpole Co., 1953.

Clum, Woodworth, *Apache Agent,* Boston: Houghton Mifflin, 1936.

Cody, Louis Frederici, *Memories of Buffalo Bill.* New York: Appleton Co., 1919.

Crawford, Louis F., *Rekindling Camp Fires,* Bismarck, N. Dakota: Capitol Book Co., 1926.

Custer, Elizabeth B., *Following the Guidon.* New York: Harper, 1890.

———, *Tenting on the Plains.* New York: Harper, 1895.

Davis, Britton, *The Truth About Geronimo.* New Haven: Yale University Press, 1929.

Dodge, Richard Irving, *Thirty Three Years Among Our Wild Indians.* Hartford, Conn.: Worthington and Co., 1886.

Ellis S., *The Indian Wars of the United States.* New York: Cassell Publishing Co., 1892.

Finnerty, John, *War Path and Bivouac.* Chicago: Donohue and Heineberg, 1890.

Forsyth, General George, *Thrilling Days of Army Life.* New York: Harper, 1902.

Grinnell, George Bird, *The Fighting Cheyennes.* New York: Scribner, 1915.

———, *The Story of the Indian.* London: Chapman and Hall, 1896.

Hansen, J. M., *Conquest of the Missouri.* Chicago: A. C. McClurg Co., 1916.

Hebard, Grace, and Brininstool, E. A., *Bozeman Trail.* Cleveland: Arthur Clark, 1922.

Howard, Oliver Otis, *Autobiography.* New York: Baker and Taylor, 1907.

———, *Chief Joseph, His Pursuit and Capture.* New York: Lee and Shepard, 1881.

Hyde, George E., *Red Cloud's Folk.* Norman, Okla.: University of Oklahoma Press, 1957.

———, *A Sioux Chronicle.* Norman, Okla.: University of Oklahoma Press, 1956.

Johnson, Fletcher, *Life of Sitting Bull.* No place of publication given. Edgewood Publishing Co., 1891.

Kelly, Luther, *Yellowstone Kelly.* New Haven: Yale University Press, 1926.

King, Charles, *Campaigning with Crook.* New York: Harper.

Leech, Margaret, *In the Days of McKinley.* New York: Harper, 1959.

Lossing, Benson, *History of the Civil War.* New York: War Memorial Association, 1912.

Longstreet, General James, *From Manassas to Appomattox.* Philadelphia: Lippincott and Co., 1903.

Manypenny, George W., *Our Indian Wards.* Cincinnati: Robert Clark Co., 1880.

McWhorter, L. V., *Yellow Wolf; His Own Story.* Caldwell, Idaho: Caxton Press, 1940.

Miles, Nelson A., *Serving the Republic.* New York: Harper, 1911.

————, *Personal Recollections.* Chicago: Werner and Co., 1896.

————, *Military Europe.* Privately printed. No press listed. 1898.

Mills, Anson, *My Story.* Washington, D.C.: Byron S. Adams, 1918.

Post, Charles Johnson, *The Little War of Private Post.* Boston: Little, Brown and Co., 1960.

Roe, Frances, *Army Letters from an Officer's Wife,* 1871–1888. New York: Appleton and Co., 1909.

Ropes, John Codman, *The Army Under Pope.* New York: Scribner, 1881.

Rodenbough, General Theo F., *The Army of the United States.* New York: Maynard, Jerrill, 1896.

Sandoz, Mari, *Crazy Horse.* New York: Alfred Knopf, 1942.

————, *Hostiles and Friendlies.* Lincoln, Neb.: University of Nebraska Press, 1960.

Schmitt, Martin, *General George Crook, His Autobiography.* Norman, Okla.: University of Oklahoma Press, 1946.

Scott, Maj. Gen. Hugh L., *Some Memories of a Soldier.* New York: Century Co., 1928.

Sherman, John, *John Sherman's Recollections of Forty Years in the House, Senate and Cabinet.* Chicago: Werner Co., 1895.

Sherman, W. T., *Memories of Gen. W. T. Sherman.* New York: Webster and Co., 1891.

Steele, Matthew Forney, *American Campaigns.* Washington, D.C.: Byron S. Adams, 1909.

Vaughn, J. W., *With Crook at the Rosebud.* Harrisburg, Pa.: Stackpole Co., 1956.

Vestal, Stanley, *Sitting Bull.* Norman, Okla.: University of Oklahoma Press, 1957.

Wheeler, Homer W., *Buffalo Days.* Indianapolis: Bobbs Merrill, 1925.

————, *Frontier Trail.* Los Angeles; Time Mirror Press, 1923.

Wissler, Clark, *The American Indian.* New York: Oxford University Press, 1922.

Index

INDEX